A STEEP TURN

TO THE STARS

a history of aviation in the Moray Firth

by

Jim Hughes

God made all flying things
Eagle and Albatross
With tapered body and spread
of outstretched wings
To hang against the sunset like a cross

Alfred Barrett

A STEEP TURN TO THE STARS

First published 1991
by Benevenagh Books.
Revised and reprinted 1999
by GMS Enterprises
67 Pyhill, Bretton, Peterborough,
England PE3 8QQ

Tel and Fax (01733) 265123
email: gmsimons@BTconnect.com

Vist our website at
www.gmsenterprises.net

ISBN: 1 870384 71 7

Printed and bound by GMS Enterprises.

Foreword

by Group Captain J P Dacre RAF (Ret'd)

The Moray Firth is rich in history of all kinds, but one area which has tended to be overlooked is that of flight. That is until Jim Hughes came along and with characteristic zeal uncovered some of the stories behind the sites of aviation interest in the area. How many people know that the German battleship *'Tirpitz'* was finally sunk by Lancasters from Lossiemouth and Kinloss; that the ill-fated raid on the German heavy water plant at Vermork was mounted from Skitten; and that the Duke of Kent was killed when his Sunderland crashed into a hillside near Berriedale whilst en-route from Invergordon to Iceland.

Jim Hughes has brought these stories and many others under one cover in his latest version of '*A Steep Turn to the Stars*', a history of aviation in the Moray Firth. Jim has been meticulous in his research to produce his very readable book. Eventually he hopes to produce a brochure detailing an 'aviation trail' around the Moray area. This book I am sure will whet the appetite of those aviation enthusiasts who will wish to follow the trail and will give background and depth to those places of aviation intrest which they visit.

Front cover:
Some 85 years seperate these two pictures - in July 1914 Norwegian explorer Tryggve Gran became the first person to fly from Norway to Scotland. In January 1999 – A Lockheed TriStar returning from the Arabian Gulf with crews of 12 Squadron who have just taken part on Operation Desert Fox. As the TriStar is escorted into Lossiemouth by Tornados of 617 Squadron, they pass over the deserted airfield of Banff. 54 years ago this airfield was a hive of activity with three squadrons of the Banff Strike Wing constantly taking off to attack German shipping in Norwegian waters. *[Sgt Jack Pritchard, RAF Public Relations]*

Rear cover: Kinloss Abbey, and the many RAF graves. *[Author]*

Contents

Acknowledgements

Sources of information for my researches were many, and varied from the official Operations Record Books, newspaper reports, magazine articles and books,to the recollections of the many airmen who served in the area over the past eighty years. Memories can be dimmed over the passage of time and there have been instances where I have had conflicting reports of the same incident. In such cases I have used my own judgement as to which account was correct, hopefully offending no one in the process.

Once again I would like to thank the Moray people, both local and farther afield, who have supplied me with so many aviation memories which I have endeavoured to bring together in one volume. With the picture of 12 Squadron crews returning from Operation Desert Fox in Jan 1999, the history of aviation in the Moray Firth is brought completely up to date.

In exploring what is a very large subject I have acquired much material, not all of which unfortunately I have been able to use. For their information and generous help I am indebted to the following :

M.O.D. Air Historical Branch, F.A.A, Museum, Public Record Office, Press and Journal, Northern Scot, Ross-shire Journal, Elgin Library, Peterhead Museum, Tain Museum, Royal Air Force Kinloss, Royal Air Force Lossiemouth, Moray Firth Radio.

Chris Ashworth, Ian Angus, Chas Bowyer, Chris Birks, Harry Bourne, Keith Briers, Don Bruce, George Creamer, John Clarke, Rodney Dick, James Ferguson, Malcolm Frazer, W Forsyth, J Gibbons, K Greene, A Grant, Mrs Griffen, Spike Holly, F Herd, Brian Hansley, D V Harland, Nick Knillans, I Kaye, Ian Keillar, P Kingston, Ron Lyon, F Lawton, James Malcolm, Mick Muttitt, Mr Mitchell, Mr Menzies, David Morgan, I McLean, N T Nicholls, James Park, Jim Ritchie, Doug Sim, Ian Shaw, Frank Simpson, David Smith, R Sturtivant, Mrs Speir, G Short, Bill Tice, C Taylor, Peter Ward, C Wood, E Wylie, Special thanks to Graham Simons and staff of GMS Enterprises for decyphering my hieroglyphics and turning them into a readable book.

Hopefully I have listed all those who have helped me ,but if by chance a name has been omitted I apologise. Although the facts in this book have been set down as accuratelY as my limited experience and repeated checking would allow,I myself must of course assume responsibility for any errors that may surface in the following pages.

Introduction

It is now seven years since I published the first edition of 'A *Steep Turn to the Stars'*. During that period the Royal Air Force has been subjected to probably the most radical changes ever experienced in its comparatively short life span. The end of the 'Cold War' saw a rapid reduction in our Armed Forces but fortunately for Moray, the two bases of Kinloss and Lossiemouth have not only remained intact ,but have actually increased in size. With all the RAF maritime Nimrods based at Kinloss,the station is now basically the equivalent bf the old Coastal Command. The Buccaneers at Lossiemouth have been replaced by two operational squadrons and a weapons conversion unit of Tornados. More Tornados were added to this unit when the Cottesmore Tri-national Tornado Training Establishment closed and the British contingent moved northwards in April '99. When another squadron returns from Germany at the beginning of the next century, Lossiemouth will be the largest Tornado base in the UK.

Largely because of the search and rescue capabilities of the Nimrod, the mountain rescue team at Kinloss and the rescue helicopters at Lossiemouth,the UK Search and Rescue HQ has now re-located from Plymouth and Pitreavie to Kinloss. All this has meant a considerable amount of re-building on both bases and the influx of more men and their families will contribute greatly to the economy of the area.

Apart from the upgrading of the present RAF bases, it was inevitable that more information about old camps would surface after the first edition of my book was published. This extra information has been incorporated in the second edition, and the mistakes which unfortunately escaped the proof readers have hopefully all been corrected.

A history of this type is obviously enhanced by photos and illustrations. Since 1992 a lot more photos have been obtained and as many of these as possible have been included in the second edition. This has meant that a few pictures of dodgy origin have been replaced by better illustrations. I have endeavoured to credit the pictures accurately but a few are still of doubtful origin.

Flying is now taken for granted ,but I would like to think that this book will help us appreciate the efforts of those who made it possible in the Moray Firth.

After much discussion between the publishers and myself it was decided that the lay out of this second edition should be tourist friendly. With this in mind each chapter leads off with an up to date map and a summary of a tour round the area.Tourism is a thriving industry in the North east of Scotland and I would like to think that 'A *Steep Turn to the Stars*' will become a very useful guide book for the many men and women who were stationd in the Moray Firth over the last few decades as well as those interested in our aviation heritage.

Jim Hughes
Elgin
1st June 1999

Chapter One

THE EARLY YEARS

"I see no reason to suppose that these machines will ever force themselves into general use".

The Duke of Wellington on steam locomotives.

DESPITE its northerly latitude, the Moray Firth has often been called the Scottish Riviera. The warm waters of the Gulf Stream swinging into the Firth, combine with the mountain ranges to the south and west to form a meteorological enclave of low rainfall, high sunshine totals, and less winter snow than the surrounding regions.

The good climate and level coastal plain have long been utilised by agriculture, and, in the present century the many sandy beaches have attracted those in search of a peaceful holiday. In the 1990's this peace may prove rather elusive, as the small county of Moray now has on its coast RAF Lossiemouth and RAF Kinloss - the third and fourth largest RAF bases in the UK.

Kinloss, as the only RAF Nimrod base has four squadrons of 'The Mighty Hunter' which day and night depart and return from their training missions in northern waters or, as often happens, take part in rescue missions far out to sea. Lossiemouth, with its more varied aircraft has a lot more local activity. Tornado's and Jaguars are constantly on the move, and always in the background are the yellow Rescue Sea Kings of 202 Squadron on the alert for both military and civil accidents. As well as the home based aircraft, both stations receive a stream of visitors from NATO countries on exercise or in transit. This constant air activity causes considerable noise and air pollution around the Moray coast, but, after 50 years, local people have accepted this inconvenience - knowing that Kinloss and Lossiemouth have become a very important part of the local community and economy.

Although in a military sense the Moray area is now one of the most important parts of the UK, it was comparatively quiet over the last few centuries. The district does contain two former battlefields, that of Auldearn in 1646 and Culloden in 1746. During these conflicts the local people seem to have kept their heads well down, and not being enthralled in the clan system of the Highlands, the Moravians were comparatively unaffected by the aftermath of the Jacobite rebellions. Moray was however a much more violent place a thousand years ago when the Kings of Moravia ruled a huge area around the Firth and there were constant battles between local rulers and invading Danes and Vikings. Few of these conflicts have been expertly chronicled and would probably have vanished from history were it not for Shakespeare's rather inaccurate account of Macbeth, set in

the Forres and Cawdor area. The conflicts of those Dark Ages have left one outstanding monument: Sueno's Stone outside Forres is a large stone obelisk covered with hieroglyphics which experts have failed to decipher but presume to be an account of a local battle.

The quiet sedentary life of Moray was not to be disturbed by aviation until the present century although surprisingly enough the first aerial activity was reported in the Aberdeen *Press and Journal* as early as 1784. In March of that year a Professor Copland of Aberdeen University launched a balloon from Marischal College observatory. This was only nine months after the Montgolfier flights, and, though unmanned, the flight created quite a stir in the local community. Shortly afterwards the *Aberdeen Journal* published a letter from Elgin telling how a '...*young man of uncommon talents...*' launched a balloon from Ladyhill in Elgin. The balloon vanished over Pluscarden to the west and the next news was that it had fallen down the chimney of a building where the unsuspecting householder was happily manufacturing whisky. The bursting of the balloon spoiled the whisky and scorched the legs of a girl warming herself at the fire. The tale ends with the man visiting a lawyer in search of compensation, whether for the whisky or the girl's injuries is not stated. He failed because he could not prove evil intent. We will never know how much truth there is in this story, for the newspapers of the time, like their present day successors, were often more intent on sensationalism than authenticity!

The north east of Scotland did produce an aeronautical pioneer who is now almost completely forgotten. George Louis Outram Davidson was born at Inchmarle near Banchory in 1859. Educated at Greenwich, Davidson subsequently turned his attention to the study of aeronautics. Making his headquarters at Inchmarle Cottage in 1897 Davidson started experimenting with gliders and flying machines. The first aeroplane ever seen in the area was constructed by Davidson but only managed to fly a few yards before crashing. In 1898 Davidson read a paper to the Royal Aeronautical Society - of which he was a founder member - wherein he predicted that flying would be the future means of transport and such would be the speed of flying machines that one day it would be possible to have afternoon tea in London and dinner in Manchester.

Eventually Davidson went to Colerado where in 1907

First aircraft to be built in the North East, George Morrice, John Scott, George Dean and friends show off their machine outside their workshop at Rathen, Fraserborough, 1911. *[J. Park]*

he formed a company for the production of a 'gyrocopter' an unusual type of aircraft completed in 1911. With the Great War approaching Davidson predicted that flying machines would be used for dropping loads of dynamite on enemy countries, though the prophesy was considered far-fetched at the time. Davidson seems to have faded into obscurity after this and his contribution to aviation is now virtually unknown.

In 1911 the *Daily Mail* offered a prize of £1,000 for the first flight between Glasgow and Edinburgh in a Scottish-built aircraft. The offer came to the notice of two ex-Buchan men, George Morrice and John Scott, who were then residing in America. Teaming up with an Englishman George Dean, they returned to Scotland and set up an engineering works at Rathen near Fraserburgh. They then set out on the ambitious plan for building an aircraft which was described as a racing biplane 20ft by 22ft, BHP 60, speed 68mph and revs 870. Morrice and Scott concentrated on the airframe side while Dean worked on an engine. He was very keen to win the £1,000 as he had ambitions to build a plane capable of flying the Atlantic. As none of the three could fly, they found a pilot from Nelson, Lancashire, with the unfortunate name of Bert Nutter.

Disaster now struck from an unusual source. George Dean had got himself involved in rather intricate marital problems and overnight vanished never to be seen again. As

he was the brains behind it the project collapsed, and as there appeared to be no other entries for the race The *Daily Mail* withdrew its £1,000 prize. Two propellers and a few other bits, were, until recently in the hands of the Fraserburgh ATC but seem to now have disappeared. Why two propellers were required is intriguing and if this project had got off the ground could it have been the start of an aircraft engineering industry in the North East!

The first recorded sighting of an aeroplane in the Moray Firth area occurred on 24 August 1912. The occasion was the Highland Gathering at Strathpeffer, and, although the local *Ross-shire Journal* gives a graphic account of the event it does not say where the plane came from or on whose invitation. The plane was a Bleriot named the Firefly sponsored by the *Daily Mail*. It was piloted by B C Hucks, a well-known aviator who later co-invented the Hucks mechanical starter for aero engines. Hucks is also believed to be the first pilot to loop an aeroplane. The local newspaper, 'The *Ross-shire Journal*' gives the following account:-

'The machine was housed in a large tent. Its shape was that of a large dragonfly with extended wings. The 70hp Gnome dynamo was located in the head of the machine. In front was the wood propeller which in motion made 1200 revolutions per minute.

The monoplane, which could carry a passenger in addition to the aviator, weighed 900 lbs. It had in front two

Two photographs take at Strathpeffer on August 24th 1912.

Above: B. C. Hucks about to depart in his Bleriot Monoplane named 'The Firefly'. *[Tain Museum]*.

Below: Local dignitaries, B.C. Hucks (in overalls and flying helmet, standing in front of the propeller) and his mechanics pose for photographs in front of 'The Firefly.' The name of Hucks' sponsors, the 'Daily Mail' can be seen painted on the underside of the Bleriot's wings. *[Tain Museum]*.

The intepid aviator!
B.C. Hucks 'checks the wind' at the Strathpeffer Games on August 12th 1912. *[Tain Museum]*

wheels with pneumatic tyres, somewhat smaller than those of a bicycle." The Firefly made two flights that afternoon, circling the local area until finally - *"...it made a fine graceful descent and the cheers given by the many onlookers expressed their enthusiasm".* The language used to describe the exhibition may seem rather naive to modern readers but it has to be remembered that this was the first flying machine ever witnessed in the Highlands. Many other people must have seen the Bleriot on its way to and from Strathpeffer little realising that this frail machine was the forerunner of the thousands of aircraft which would pass through the Moray Firth skies in the next fifty years.

The history of aviation in an area cannot be confined to accounts of airfields used or dis-used. While airfields are very important, facets of aviation archaeology can be uncovered in almost any part of the country With the abandonment of airfields at the cease of hostilities in World War One and World War Two many of the hangars and more portable of the buildings were sold and transported throughout the country to be used by their new owners as stores or factories. The more permanent buildings were used by local farmers as sheds and sometimes even adapted as dwelling houses. Many others were of course completely demolished to make way for new industries or housing developments. Often the only remnants left are the runways and perimeter track. These are sometimes incorporated into roads, but are often abandoned as being too costly to remove.

The buildings of north east Scotland are predominantly made of stone with sometimes a harled finish. It seems strange therefore that so many military buildings are of a red brick construction. Not only must this have increased the cost as the bricks were not produced locally, but it must have caused a camouflage problem with the red brick buildings standing out prominently against the local grey background. If, while travelling through this area one comes across an isolated red brick building it is almost certainly to have been of military origin.

Apart from exploring the remains of airfields and landing grounds, aviation information can be obtained from a variety of sources. All RAF stations had Operation Record Books which were basically diaries of day to day events at the particular unit. These ORBs are held in the Public Record Office at Kew, and some make fascinating reading depending on who compiled the diary. Some writers recorded just about every aspect of station life while others confined their efforts to basic facts of the flying operations.

A basic history of a RAF unit can therefore be built up from the ORBs, but for more personal details one has to rely on the memories of the men and women who directly served on the stations. Local newspapers often give accounts of aircraft accidents, but these were much curtailed by censorship during the war years. Some of the flying bases in the Moray Firth were operated by the Navy and unfortunately they did not have an ORB system like the RAF. Consequently information about Naval flying is sometimes rather sketchy.

The Moray Firth is rather an indeterminate area. Geographically it is probably the inlet separating Moray and Nairn on the south from the Black Isle and Easter Ross in the north. It is usual however to describe the whole sea area between the northern and eastern coasts of Scotland as the Moray Firth and it is the aviation history of this area which this book endeavours to describe.

Taking Kirkton as the farthest point north it will attempt to uncover all traces of aviation while travelling south and then east as far as Peterhead. The choice of areas may be arguable but as a lot of the flying units were interconnected in many ways, it is hoped that as many aspects of aviation as possible can be covered by this travelogue method.

Chapter Two

FARTHEST NORTH

"And God stands winding his lonely horn
And time and the world are ever in flight".
W.B.Yeats.

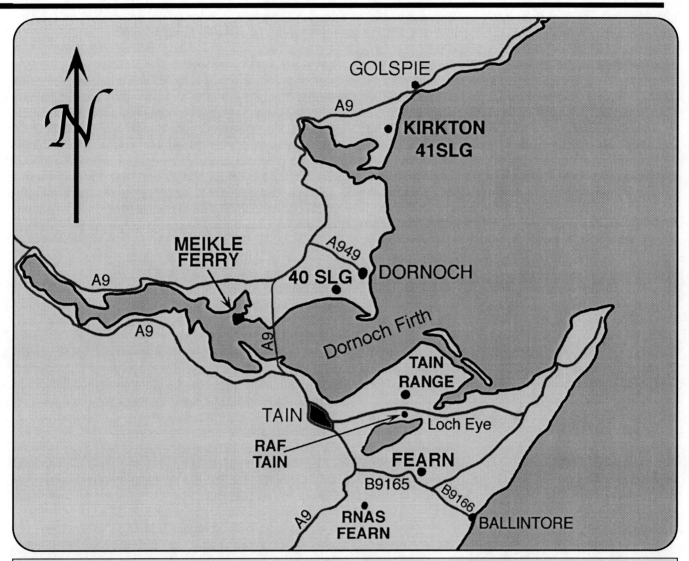

A journey through this area is best started from the little town of Golspie north of the Dornoch Firth.

Two miles on the A9, a farm lane on the left hand side, is the entrance to the former SLG of Kirkton where a few partly demolished huts are the only RAF relics remaining. Eight miles further south on a A9, a left turn onto the A949 takes us through the town of Dornoch to the golf course which was a wartime SLG. The landing strip can still be identified beside the present golf course. The Witch's Stone, sometimes used for picketing aircraft is now in a front garden.

A further six miles down the A9 is the new Dornoch Bridge. The wartime Meikle Ferry Marine Craft unit was sited to the west of this bridge.

The town of Tain is a further 3 miles down the A9 and another 3 miles east along a side road is RAF Tain bombing range. This is closed to the public but aircraft can be seen using the range most weekdays. A lot of old RAF buildings, including the Control Tower and Operations Block, are still scattered around this area.

Travelling along the north side of Loch Eye, a left turn on to the B9165 and B9166 brings us up to the disused RNAS Fearn where quite a few buildings including the control tower are still intact. Returning to the A9, another three miles south completes the area covered in this chapter.

Royal Air Force Kirkton

Travelling south from Golspie on the A9 the first aviation relic to be seen is the old airfield at Kirkton which is not easy to spot unless one is specifically looking for it. About 3½ miles from Golspie, the long level stretch of land between the road and the sea was earmarked for a Satellite Landing Ground in the early days of the war. One wonders why this site was selected as it was a considerable distance from its parent unit at Kinloss and though open to the sea on one side there were high hills quite close inland. However, the decision having been made, hedges and ditches were levelled and various buildings erected. 41 SLG, as Kirkton was officially named was designed as a dispersal airfield for aircraft from 45 M U at RAF Kinloss. An officer from that unit, Squadron Leader Grey, inspected the airfield in May 1941 and obviously found it satisfactory as it was officially opened on 24 August 1941 when Sgt Carle and 14 airmen took up residence.

The first aircraft to use Kirkton were Whitleys and Spitfires flown in for storage by 45 MU. Wellingtons came later and these were followed by Havocs in June 1942. Considering the airfield limitations, accidents were infrequent and the only fatality recorded was the drogue operator of a Battle target tug from Evanton which crash-landed there on 16 September, 1941. The planes for storage were flown in and out by members of the Ferry Pool from Kinloss. These pilots were transported in Oxfords and Ansons, and one Anson, R3399, overshot and crashed on landing on 5 July 1942.

Although not an operational unit the defence of Kirkton was considered important enough for a detachment of RAF Regiment to be stationed there. Regiment personnel were billeted in huts on the seaward side of the airfield while most of the RAF groundcrew stayed in Kirkton House.

A large scale defence exercise was held in July 1942 when 250 Norwegian troops tried to capture the airfield but were repulsed by a mixture of Cameron Highlanders, RAF Regiment and Home Guards. Kirkton had an official capacity of 50 aircraft but by March 1943 it was reported to have 70 on charge. Still in use at the end of 1944, it was

closed when 45 MU took over Brackla for storage and 7 May 1945 saw it de-requisitioned.

Although hardly visible from the main road today, a closer look will reveal some remains. The Watch Office is still intact and used as a farm store. Buildings such as these were usually built of brick and consequently were rather noticeable in an area where stone buildings were the norm. Chimney stacks and concrete floors remain in the local woods and as the hedges were not replaced the line of the grass runway is quite noticable. Kirkton was an unusual site for an airfield but set in a peaceful country area it was probably a pleasant posting for airmen used to the more hectic stations further south.

Royal Air Force Dornoch

Almost directly south of Kirkton and six miles as the crow flies is the small town of Dornoch. Famous for its cathedral in ancient days it is now a quiet little town noted only for its excellent golf course.

The flat sandy plain south of the town, ideal for golf, also had potential as an airstrip. About the same time as Kirkton was being developed, the Dornoch golf course was cleared and prepared for aircraft at the comparatively small cost of £38,000. Squadron Leader Grey inspected the site on 16 May 1941 and the Commanding Officer of 45 MU, Wg Cdr Collins, visited on 3 June 1941. On 10 August 1941 Dornoch was officially opened as 40 SLG by Fg Off. Smith and 12 men who were billeted in the Royal Golf Hotel.

45 MU Kinloss was to use Dornoch for storage of Spitfires, Havocs and Whitleys but Wellingtons may also have been stored there as 45 MU ORB records the overshoot and damage of Wellington 1C, X9930 on 13 September 1941. The airfield was in use for only a short period when it was put on C&M on 30 September 1942. This was largely due to the inability of camouflaging the aircraft on the large open golf course, thus rendering them vulnerable to enemy attacks.

There now followed a period of re-organisation by 41 Group Maintenance Command. 46 MU SLG at Leanach was handed over to Flying Training Command and Dornoch was taken over by 46 MU Lossiemouth. The advance party (ex Leanach) arrived on 24 September 1943 with the main party coming on 11 October 1943. 46 MU used Dornoch mainly for storing Beaufighters, 90 being held in May 1944 and 108 in July. In March 1944 a Super Robin hangar was removed from Field No 13 at Lossiemouth and transferred to Dornoch. The airfield was at its max capacity in April 1945 but the planes were now being prepared for service rather than storage. The last plane took off on 27 September 1945 with the final load of scrap departing before the closing date of 30 September 1945. Although there is no mention of it in 46 MU's ORB, Lancasters were evidently stored for a time at Dornoch. Ex fitter Archie Campbell of Loch Rannoch recalls working on them and getting a dressing down for using a local Witch's Stone as an anchor while towing a Lancaster out of soft ground. An airstrip was re-established in 1967 with Loganair Services operating to Wick and Inverness until

The Watch Office at Kirkton, still intact and used for storage in the 1990's *[Author]*

Above: 40 SLG Dornoch as seen from the Cathedral in 1945. Lancasters and Beaufighters predominate, but is that a B-17 Flying Fortress in the top right-hand corner? [D.A. Goskirk]
Below: Some of the buildings at Dornoch, as used for the current airstrip in 1996. *[Author]*

1972 when the service proved uneconomic. Light aircraft still land occasionally, although the new strip is in a different direction to the days of the RAF. The only sign of wartime occupation is an old tin hut near the caravan site.

Meikle Ferry

About four miles west of Dornoch there is a small stone jetty pointing south across the Dornoch Firth. A ferry used to operate from here and Meikle Ferry was the site of a rather unusual RAF unit during WW II.

The area around Ferrytown had been considered as a seaplane base before World War One and Lt Cdr Longmore (the Commanding Officer of Cromarty seaplane base) noted in his log for 1 October 1913 that he had flown up and landed at Ferrytown but had considered the area too remote for a base. By 1941 the considerable marine craft presence in the Cromarty Firth required a

secluded deep water base for major servicing and repairs and Meikle Ferry seemed to fit the criteria.

On 3 February 1942 Flg Off Dudgeon, 3 SNCOs and 20 airmen arrived to set up 88 MU (Marine Craft) at Meikle Ferry. Work started almost immediately on a whaler and inboard dinghy. Living accommodation was primitive - consisting mainly of tents. In August, two Hurricane packing cases arrived from Henlow and these were ready for occupation in September just after the tents had been blown over in a gale. Despite the primitive conditions, and a visit from ENSA, the ORB for September '42 states that morale on the unit was high.

The MU was basically tasked with repairing marine craft from the Moray Firth region but if necessary they were able to take part in Air Search & Rescue. On 13 October 1942 when a Lysander crashed in Cambuscurrie

Meikle ferry pier in the 1990's. *[Author]*

Bay three quarters of a mile away, a seaplane tender from the MU was able to rescue the pilot though the crewman was killed in the crash.

The spring of 1943 saw a Sgt's Mess and unit canteen occupied. Five Handcraft huts (Nissen huts with asbestos roofs) were occupied on 4 October 1943. On 8 May 1943 a Mk F boat from the base rescued the crew of a Swordfish which had crashed near Dornoch.

By 1944 the MU was in full production, dealing with HSLs, pinnaces, marine tenders, seaplane tenders, airborne lifeboats, wireless tenders and flare path dinghies. To help with the servicing a docking barge had been installed by the end of 1944. By this time 88 MU had a strength of four officers, 75 NCOs and 101 airmen. The severe weather of January 1945 caused a pinnace to be damaged by ice floes. On 14 January 1945 a marine tender picked up the crew of Sunderland W6009 which had crashed nearby.

With the end of the war in Europe the MU's task was running down and with more leisure time a sailing club was organised. Despite the run down a new main store was opened in July 1945. This building lost its roof in the autumn gales of '45 which also sank the sailing club's yacht. Most of the camp buildings were flooded by heavy seas and these were followed by a plague of sea flies.

A marine craft MU in the area was now unnecessary and 88 MU was officially closed down with an all-ranks farewell dance on 26 February 1946.

There is little sign of the camp now although some buildings at nearby Cuthill Farm could have been the MU stores.

Royal Air Force Tain

A mile or so away to the west, a Tornado approaches in a shallow dive a few hundred feet above the flat pasture land. Puffs of smoke appear as the practice bombs explode near the white targets and the plane climbs trailing a stream of black exhaust smoke. Three other Tornados follow in quick succession but their unearthly racket fails to disturb the sheep and cattle which continue to graze placidly close to the range.

The above incident is an everyday occurrence at the bombing range of Tain, which, due to its close proximity to the large RAF stations of Kinloss and Lossiemouth, and its excellent weather record, is one of Britain's busiest bombing ranges (in the nineties) accepting all sorts of weapons apart from high-level bombing. The area between the Dornoch and Cromarty Firths is unusual for such a northerly latitude with the flat plain covered with fertile fields and trees bearing little resemblance to the stark Highlands a short distance away. The small town of Tain lies at the north east corner of the peninsula and just

Above: "Waterplane leaving Tain" - the original caption scratched into the negative. The aircraft turned out to be a Wight Navyplane No. 129 on the Tain River in 1914, as the lower picture clearly shows the No.129 on the tail. The sight created much interest locally, with fourteen men standing close to the aircraft with others nearby. The lady with the infant in the pram seems more interested in the camera however! *[Tain Museum]*

north east of the town is a 12 square mile area of sandy plain and dunes, now the only permanently manned bombing range in Britain.

In late February 1913 the War Office surveyed a site at Tain for possible use as an aerial Naval base to compliment the Cromarty Firth fortifications but no further action was taken at that time.

In the small Tain Museum are two pictures of a seaplane on the Tain river. Judging by the crowds the plane's presence must have caused some excitement locally. There is no information about this incident in the museum but the No 129 on the tailplane proves that it was a Wight 1914 Navyplane. A photo in the book *'Britain's First Warplanes'* by J. M. Bruce, shows this particular aircraft exhibited at Olympia in March 1914. It first flew on 1 May 1914 and did tests at Calshot in September 1914. By 11 November it was at Fort George where it was reported engineless on 20 December 1914 and wrecked on 30 January 1914. Only two of this particular type of seaplane were built, although improved versions appeared later in the war. There is still no explanation of its visit to Tain which must have been in November or December 1914. At that period the Admiralty were constantly on the look-out for suitable seaplane landing areas and no doubt the trip from Fort George to Tain was one such foray. Tain range was constructed between the wars and used by both RAF and FAA aircraft. There was also a small landing ground which was blocked by cars and poles during the invasion scare of 1940. During the upsurge of airfield construction in 1940 an airfield with three runways was built close to Tain ranges. Reading a contemporary account of wartime airfield construction it would appear that some airfields were built with little or no idea as to their future role and this would seem to apply to Tain. Opening officially on 16 September 1941 as a fighter Sector station to bridge the gap between Scapa Flow and Turnhouse Sectors, Tain's first aircraft were Hurricanes of 17 Squadron. These Hurricanes moved to Catterick in October and were replaced by others of 123 Squadron from Castletown. Despite constant patrolling no action was forthcoming and in March 1942, 123 was replaced by Sea Hurricanes of 801 Squadron FAA. One of the aircraft associated with Tain during that period has been preserved. This is Sea Hurricane 27015 which served with 801 Squadron FAA. After various adventures over the years this aircraft is now at Duxford being restored to flying state.

The Hurricanes were on standby in case of German retaliation against Tain after the Tirpitz bombing raids from the station in the Spring of 1942. Along with Lossiemouth, Tain had been designated as a forward base for bombers attacking the battleship *Tirpitz* when it was based at Trondheim in Norway. For the first operation twelve Halifaxes of 76 Squadron arrived from Middleton St George on 27 March 1942. The first raid on the 30 March was inconclusive and one aircraft failed to return. Another attack on 5 April was aborted due to bad weather and the squadron returned to its home base the following day. On 23 April 1942 twelve Halifaxes returned to Tain and from there carried out two raids on the 27 and 28. A number of

bombs were dropped but no results observed due to the battleship's smoke screen. With the departure of the Halifaxes to Middleton St George and the Hurricanes to Turnhouse, Tain was now left without operational aircraft.

Like a lot of wartime airfields Tain became operational as soon as the runways were completed and before many of the buildings were finished. In June 1942 the writer of the ORB commented:- *"A strong west wind made the aerodrome rather like the Libyan desert with flying sand. There is no doubt that the completion of the station and its efficient appearance has reacted favourably on general morale and discipline. A few months ago it was nothing more than a contractor's dump, with no incentive for smartness':*

During this slack period a Vindicator landed on 23 April 1942 having lost its way enroute from Hatson to Langar. This was the first American aircraft to land at Tain and belonged to *USS Wasp,* part of a task force in the area.

During the early part of 1942 Whitleys of 19 OTU Kinloss sometimes used Tain when their own airfield was waterlogged. There was a Whitley crash on 3 March 1942 and another on 16 March 1942, fortunately without casualties. On 19 May 1942 a B24 which landed was referred to as a civil aircraft in the ORB.

The early summer of 1942 was disastrously wet in the Dornoch area and this combined with lack of aircraft must have lowered the morale of the Tain personnel considerably. The satellite at Fearn was taken over by the Navy and the other satellite at Elgin was now used by Lossiemouth so Tain took on the appearance of a deserted airfield.

However things perked up on 15 June 1942 when Coastal Command Development Unit arrived from Ballykelly with a collection of two Beauforts, two Hudsons, an Oxford and a Wellington. CCDU carried out extensive trials of equipment necessary to the coastal role, hence the variety of aircraft. One of the successes of this period was the development of the Leigh Light. An Albermarle was attached for evaluation but on its first flight on 21 October, 1942, a runaway propeller caused it to overshoot through the invasion obstacles at the end of the runway. Hampdens of 489 and 415 Squadrons called in briefly during the summer on their way to and from North Coates and Wick.

The Armstrong Whitworth Albermarle that overshot the runway at Tain and ended up amongst the anti-invasion defences following a runaway propeller on 21st October 1942. *[Author]*

Flg. Off. J. S. Cummins in Beaufighter 'Eight Ball' of 404 Sqn RCAF at Tain on 29th july 1943.
[Canadian Archives via Chaz Bowyer]

The USAAF had an interest in Tain as an advanced strike base and a party of 144 USAAF personnel arrived in October 1942 to extend the runways with metal plating. FAA aircraft were now using the airfield for night flying and servicing.

The station was transferred to Coastal Command on 22 February 1943 and although no squadrons were permanently stationed there the airfield was used as an advanced base for attacking shipping in the Norwegian area. These squadrons included Beaufighters of 254, Wellingtons of 311 and 347, Hampdens of 405 and Beaufighters of 404. Beaufighters from 144 based at Leuchars were detached to Tain from 8 April to 20 October and during this time made many attacks on enemy shipping in Norwegian waters. Typical of these attacks was an action fought on 21 April 1943. Four Beaufighters attacked an enemy ship of 4000 tons with two escorts. The ship was left listing badly and the escorts were damaged. Two Beaufighters returning to the area in the afternoon were attacked by two BF109s. Hits on one Beaufighter wrecked the radar and wounded the navigator. Limping back to Tain the undercarriage collapsed on landing and the crew just managed to escape before it caught fire.

CCDU left Tain for Dale in South Wales in April 1943. An offshoot of the CCDU was formed as a Torpedo Refresher School in June 1943. This was to keep crews up to date with torpedo training and both RAF and FAA crews used the facilities with *HMS Reading* supplying the Target Towing. On 4 April 1943 two Hampdens of 415 Squadron, AT243 and AT250, collided over the airfield. One landed safely but the other crashed with four killed. Throughout 1943 various squadrons were detached for torpedo training. These consisted mostly of Beaufighters but November saw the first Barracudas of 822 and 829 FAA squadrons.

Unusual visitors from January to March 1944 was 186 Squadron converting from Typhoons to Spitfires VBs before moving to Lympe. The middle of March saw the arrival of 14 Beaufighters of 143 Squadron, 14 of 236, 12 of 254 and 8 Dakotas of 251 with groundcrew. The next day, 17 March, 4 Warwicks of 280 from Thornaby arrived along with 3 Wellingtons from 415 Squadron Thornaby. This was in fact the whole of the North Coates Strike Wing which was apparently going to use Tain as a forward base for a secret mission. No details are available of this operation which was cancelled on 22 March 1944, though it is possible that it might have been an attack on the Tirpitz. Just one of the many costly wartime missions abandoned due to bad planning.

In May 1944 an Airfield Construction Flight from

Liberator II as used by 86 Sqn.

311 Squadron Liberators at Tain in late 1944. *[Zdenek Hurt]*

Oban extended the NE/SW runway with PSP and built diamond shaped hard standings, in preparation for the arrival of Liberators. The first of these, a detachment of 86 Squadron from Keflavik, arrived in June and were very soon in action. One of the first actions by 86 Squadron from Tain was fought on the 26 June 1944 when the crew of Liberator N FL916 spotted a U boat on the surface. Two attacks were made and on the second, three depth charges exploding on the Starboard side of the U boat caused it to turn over and sink. The Liberator had been damaged by gunfire and had to land at Stornoway where it was found that a shell had gone through the main spar.

On 18 July 1944 Liberator F commanded by Squadron Leader Nelms was on patrol roughly halfway between the Lofoten Islands and Jan Mayen island about 1000 miles from Tain. Descending to patrolling height of 200 ft on a clear sunny evening they suddenly saw a surfaced U boat dead ahead about 8 miles away. Squadron Leader Nelms initiated an attack but the U boat immediately crash dived and all the Liberator crew could do was drop a sea marker and start a square search. Two hours later with fuel running low the Liberator was ready to abandon the search when the rear gunner spotted the surfaced sub astern. Squadron Leader Nelms decided to hide in low cloud and dive down to take the U boat by surprise. The U boat remained on the surface to fight it out with his one 37mm and two 20mm guns, opening fire at a range of 1.5 miles using radar directors and proximity and tracer shells. Nelms turned into the attack with his Port wing low in a descending steep curve intended to interrupt the U boat gunners predictions. At 1200 yds the Liberator's front gunner opened fire with his .05 machine guns but they jammed almost immediately.

Nelms proceeded with his attack, dropping six depth charges over the U boat. Only two exploded and apparently caused little damage. There were now only two depth charges left and very little fuel. On the second attack Nelms came in at 150 ft. The front guns jammed

THE END OF A RAIDER...

Three poor quality, but unique photographs of a successful attack on a U-boat by Liberator 'N' of 86 Sqn on 26th June 1944 whilst operated out of Tain.

The picture on the left was taken from the Liberator as the pilot sweeps low over the U-Boat, coming into the attack from astern. By the time the centre photograph had been taken the depth charges have been dropped, the scars of their descent into the water clearly visible in the bottom left of the picture. The U-Boat's wake shows that the vessel was turning to avoid them. The image on the right shows the final result, a successful attack.

The remains of Liberator GRVI EW300 allocated to the Station Flight at Tain.*[Author]*

again but the depth charges exploded and damaged the Uboat. The Liberator was now badly damaged by anti aircraft fire and the starboard inner engine exploded and dropped out. There was nothing to do but ditch and when the Liberator hit the sea it disintegrated with the tail portion breaking off and the cockpit disappearing with the pilot on board. Nelms shot to the surface and grabbed a one man dinghy. Six of the crew were now in three dinghies with two others badly injured some distance away. A few hours later another 86 Squadron Liberator passed overhead but failed to see them despite the firing of all but two of their Very lights. Meanwhile a Catalina of 210 Squadron was sent out to search for survivors but failed to find them. The search was officially called off but 86 Squadron Liberators were asked to keep searching while on patrol. In the early hours of the 21 July a Liberator of 86 and another of 120 located the dinghies and at 09:00 a Catalina of 210 picked up the survivors, The U boat was damaged in another attack but managed to reach harbour safely and survived the war.

In June 1944 the 070°/250° runway was extended to 5900 ft. The other runways at that time were 020°/200° 4300 ft and 130°/310° 3300 ft. Tain's strength was increased by the arrival of 311 Czech Squadron Liberators in August 1944. At this late date in the war it was decided to build two T2 hangars on the south side of the airfield. During 1944 Tain was home to a lot of detachments from other airfields. Of these detachments 206 Liberators from St Eval and 120 Liberators from Ballykelly stayed longest,

harassing Uboats and enemy shipping, mostly at night using Leigh Lights, right up to the end of the war. On 19 September 1944 seven Mustangs, 33 Beaufighters and two Warwicks were diverted in. This was presumably the Banff Strike wing after a Norwegian raid. Seven Halifaxes used the airfield for an operation in October. At the end of the year two Oxfords and five Martinets of a Target Towing flight arrived from Evanton. On 11 January 1945 a Stirling landed after a supply dropping mission in Norway. Frequent visitors at this time were lost B17s and C47s, fooled by the presence of Liberators into thinking that it was a USAAF base.

In March 1945 86 Squadron began to re equip with Mk. V111 Liberators. The last major action of the squadron was on 5 May when Liberator 'G' spotted three U-boats surfaced off the Danish coast. They were already being attacked by a Wellington of 547 Squadron. After being hit by A/A fire the Wellington dived into the sea leaving one airman clinging to a dinghy. Two of the U-boats had now submerged but the Liberator straddled the third with depth charges and it sank leaving forty crewmen in the water. These Germans and the Wellington survivor were picked up by a lightship.

The last days of the war were spent shadowing surrendered U boats. In June 1945 311 Squadron left for Milltown to join Transport Command. 86 Squadron also became a transport squadron at Oakington in August. On 17 August, 519 Met squadron arrived from Wick with Halifaxes, Spitfires and a few Fortresses. It moved to

Tain bombing range in the 1990's. *[Author]*

BOMBING RANGE

DORNOCH FIRTH

Royal Air Force Tain
57° 48' 30" N, 03°58'30"W 0 ft ASL.
Airfield Key
A - Control Tower
B - Bellman Hangars
C - T2 Hangars
D - Blister Hangars

Shaded line denotes line of modern-day road.

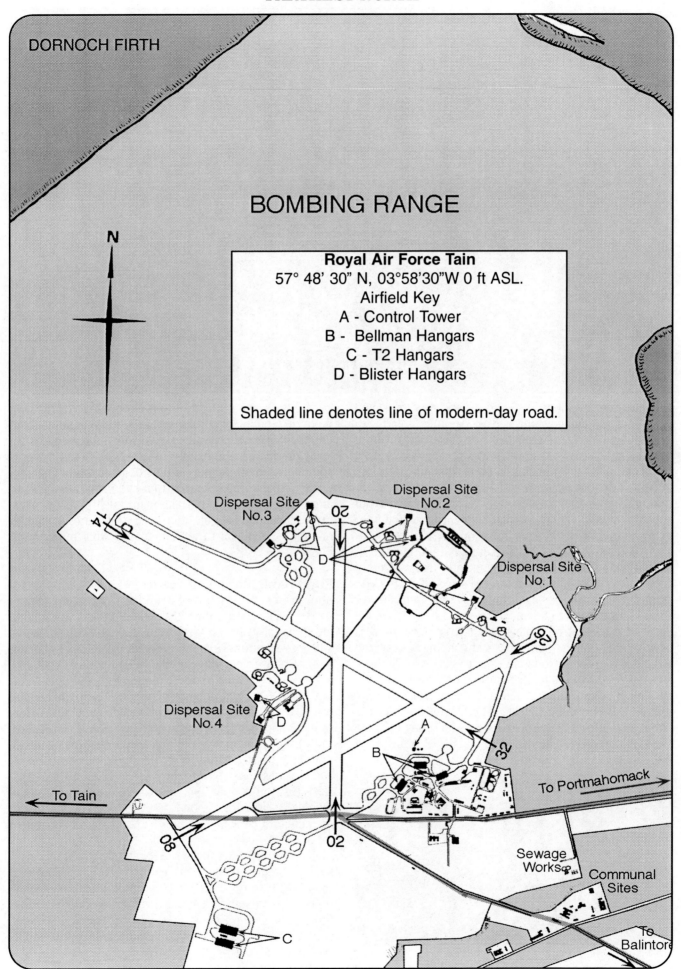

Dispersal Site No.3

Dispersal Site No.2

Dispersal Site No.1

Dispersal Site No.4

To Tain

To Portmahomack

Sewage Works

Communal Sites

To Balintore

Right: The Control Tower of Tain Airfield, still intact in 1990, but now surrounded by sheep. *[Author]*

Below: In the middle distance, behind the derelict buildings lies the RAF camp for bombing ranger personnel in 1990. *[Author]*

Leuchars in November 1945. No 1 TRS, now re-named No.1 Torpedo Training Unit, left for Thorney Island with its Beaufighters Xs in November 1946. Tain now reverted to a C and M basis. Post war Tain was used occasionally by various Coastal squadrons on exercises and also by FAA aircraft from Lossiemouth and Fearn. Tain appeared to have a great potential as an important war time base but for some reason ended up only as a temporary home for many different types of squadrons and aircraft.

After six years of flying operation Tain reverted to its original role as a weapons range and it is now one of the most important ranges for RAF, USAAF and NATO planes. Apart from the targets and weapons control tower there is a helicopter pad and a cluster of huts housing a small permanent staff. The hangars have gone but there is a surprising number of buildings still standing both on the airfield and in the surrounding countryside. A lot of these are now used by local farmers but the Control Tower and the Ops Block are still very much as they were during the war, at least from the outside. The Operations Block is about a mile from the airfield and was built originally for the Tain Sector. The building, built of reinforced

A Fairey Barracuda as used at Fearn *[IWM]*

concrete, is in good condition, although covered with modern Graffiti, and minus doors and windows. The entrance doorway is still marked 'All Aircrew' and this leads down to the miniature theatre with raised balcony so reminiscent of the big wartime bomber bases. The size of the building suggests that Tain had been intended for large scale operations but like many such wartime plans this came to naught, and only this large concrete monolith remains as a monument for what might have been.

Royal Naval Air Station Fearn
About three miles south of Tain and close to the B9166 road to Ballintrae lies the old airfield of Fearn. Built on the level coastal plain the view from the approaching roads still shows quite an intact airfield though it has not been in general use since the end of WW II.

Fearn was built as a satellite for Tain and opened in late 1941. For some unknown reason the original name was Clays of Allen, the name of a small local farm. This rather cumbersome title was soon changed to Fearn after the village of Fearn and Hill of Fearn nearby. As Tain was not being utilised extensively, the RAF hardly used Fearn and so it was transferred to the Navy and commissioned as *HMS Owl* on 5 July 1942. Bomber Command wanted lodging facilities for use on Norwegian operations and ear marked it for 83 Squadron but the Navy refused. So much for inter-service co-operation.

Naval airfields usually had four runways but they had to be content with three at Fearn. The original Tower, a small single storey building with a blast wall, was quickly replaced by a standard naval three-storey building. The three runways, 00°/180° 1180 yds, 050°/230° 1475 yds, and 110°/290° 1260 yds were connected by a 40 ft

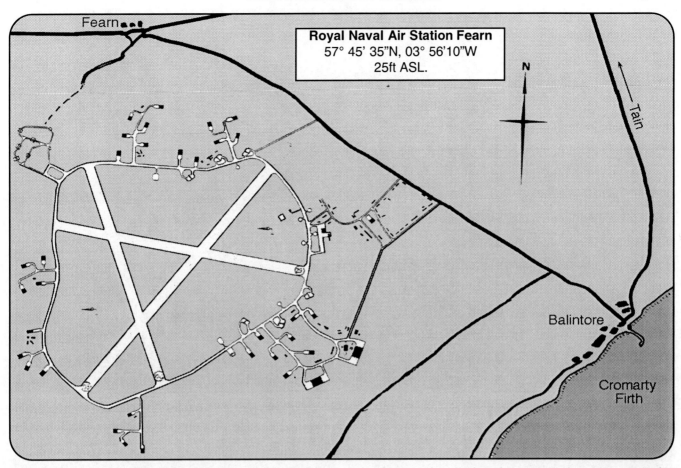

Royal Naval Air Station Fearn
57° 45' 35"N, 03° 56'10"W
25ft ASL.

wide perimeter track. The Navy added five hard standings and clutches of 31 Bellman hangars at various places around the perimeter. There were also two larger 'S' hangars. Domestic accommodation was in four scattered sites to the NE of the airfield in the Tulloch area.

The first naval aircraft to use Fearn were the Swordfishes of 825 Squadron which arrived on 30 September 1942 and departed 9 December 1942. This squadron had just been reformed after being completely destroyed in the abortive attack on the *Scharnhorst* and *Gneusenau* in February of that year for which Lt Cdr E. Esmonde was awarded the VC. 825 was replaced by 819 from Hatson which stayed from 12 December 1942 to 12 January 1943. From 1943

Beech Traveller (also called a Staggerwing in civilian use) communications aircraft at Fearn. [*Mrs E. Hall*].

Fearn was to be employed as a torpedo training unit for the new Fairy Barracudas. The first squadron, 747 was formed on 22 March 1943 and after training moved to Inskip in June. During the next three years 13 other FAA Barracuda squadrons were trained at Fearn before departing to aircraft carriers or shore bases. There was also a Canadian squadron, 825, from 31 August 1945 to 6 November 1945 and a Dutch squadron, 860, from 15 November 1945 to 9 May 1946.

Torpedo training was the main task for *HMS Owl* using Tain range and surrounding waters for practice. The Barracuda had a homing system based on a gyro, information on ship speed and course, and aircraft speed and course, so that if the target took evasive action the torpedo would follow. Flying was generally done in flights of three aircraft although in 1945 this policy was changed to four aircraft in two sections. Radio altimeters were used for flying over the sea. Each course averaged about 30 flying hours per month.

812 and 814 Squadrons arrived in November 1944. Their work up included night anti submarine dive bombing using flares, carrier ranging, squadron formation, and fighter affiliation with Seafires from Evanton. Two aircraft collided during formation flying on 25 November 1944. In mid January 1945 812 moved to Ballyhalbert and from there to *HMS Vengeance* bound for the Far East. At the same time 814 went to Machrihanish and on to *HMS Venerable* also bound for the Far East. It was during December 1944 that problems arose with main spar rivets popping during dives and many aircraft had to be changed as a result. At the end of the war the

Right: Blackburn Firebrand IV

Below: A North American Harvard surrounded by Dutch sailors at Fearn in March 1946. *[Mrs E. Hall}.*

Below right: Beech 18 Expeditor HD763 'F' at Fearn in 1946.
[Mrs E. Hall]

Barracuda squadrons were quickly disbanded but the last did not leave Fearn until May 1946 .

The Barracuda was an extremely ugly looking aircraft and not particularly liked by its crews. Nevertheless they had some successes during the latter part of the war. First in action at the Salerno landings in September 1943 they proved their worth in April 1944 when 42 of them badly damaged the Tirpitz in Norwegian waters. They were later to be used extensively in the Pacific theatre when one of their many successes was the attack on oil installations at Sabang, Sumatra in April 1944.

Although Barracudas were the main aircraft to use Fearn airfield, other types did manage to put in occasional appearances. 828 Squadron brought in its Avengers for a month between February and March 1945. 719 with Firefly IVs re-formed for Strike training in March 1946. The two month training consisted of formation flying, air to sea cannon firing, rocket firing and low level bombing with 25 Ib practice bombs. 736 B Fighter Affiliation unit arrived for a month between July and August 1945. Their aircraft were mainly Seafires but they also had a Dominie and a Beaufighter X.

708 Squadron, the Firebrand Tactical Trials Unit, arrived from Gosport in December 1945. The Firebrand had a lot of teething troubles and 708 was disbanded in March 1946. The Station Flight had various aircraft between 1944 and 1945. These included a Reliant, Swordfish, Tiger Moth and a Beech Traveller. By 1946 the FAA was much reduced in size and many shore stations were closed. These included *HMS Owl* which was reduced to C and M on 2 July, 1946.

In post-war years Fearn airfield was designated as Secondary Landing Ground for Dalcross when that unit was an FTS in 1952 and 1953 but few aircraft appear to have availed themselves of its facilities. The land was then sold to a farmer and also used for motor racing in the Sixties. The Cromarty Firth Development Co bought Fearn in 1974 and plans were made for developing it as the Cromarty Firth Airport. Due to fluctuations in the oil market and the increasing use of helicopters nothing has come of the Airport idea although light aircraft occasionally land there.

The Naval ATC tower is still in good condition beside the remains of the old RAF tower. One hangar and various buildings are still standing and generally speaking this former naval airfield has an air of being ready for action if the need should arise.

Above: Standing stark against the skyline is the Fearn Control Tower in 1990 .
Left: Some of the existing ex-naval buildings. *[Author]*

Chapter Three

THE CROMARTY FIRTH

"For while the tired waves breaking
seem here no painful inch to gain"
Arthur Hugh Clough.

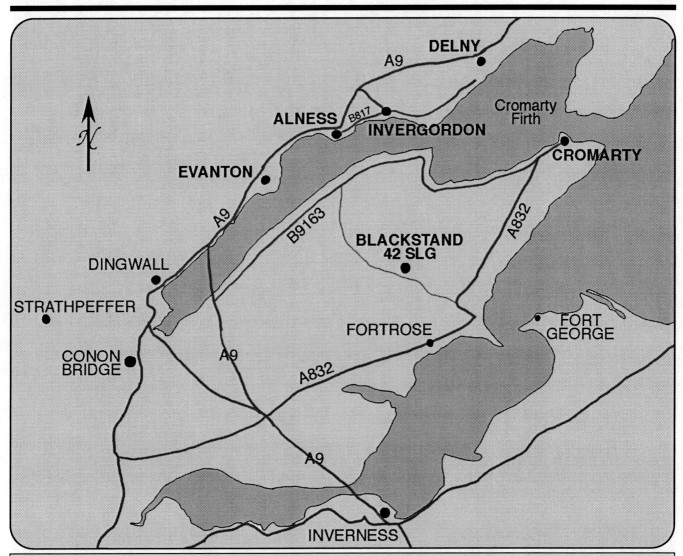

On the A9 five miles further down from where the previous journey ended, a signpost on the left indicates the way to Delny House. The area between this house and the Firth is the site of a World War One airfield used by Navy aircraft from battleships at Invergordon. No relics of this airfield remain.

Two miles west from here, a left turn goes to the town of Invergordon where new dock buildings have obliterated all signs of the old flying boat base.

Carrying on west along the coast road, some remains of the Alness flying boat base including a pier are still visible. Continuing west on the B817, the village of Alness lies eight miles from Invergordon. A large propeller memorial erected to the memory of those who served at local bases during the war is situated in the town centre. Three miles west of Alness, the many surviving hangars and other buildings of RAF Evanton are still very prominent on the left between the road and the sea.

Passing over Cromarty bridge, a left turn takes us onto the B9163. The 23 miles of road to Cromarty passes through the very picturesque Black Isle overlooking the Firth which saw so much flying boat activity during the war. There are no visible remains of the World War One seaplane base at Cromary, but some information can be obtained at the excellent Courthouse Museum and there are military graves in the old churchyard.

THE Cromarty Firth could truthfully be called the cradle

Interested juvenile specators view the busy scene at Cromarty in 1913. On the left, and under way is a Caudron; beached and in the centre of the picture is a Borel seaplane and being pushed by a number of sailors out of the picture on the right is a Farman seaplane. *[Brian Hansley]*

of military aviation in the Moray Firth area. This was due to the presence of the huge naval base built before World War One at Invergordon, where the deep sheltered water of the Firth made it a perfect anchorage for the largest naval vessels. Before the advent of aircraft carriers naval flying was largely carried out by seaplanes. These required coastal bases for servicing and by 1913 the need for such a base in the Cromarty Firth was paramount.

In 1913, *HMS Hermes* was the parent ship for naval flying and on 7 May of that year one of the ship's officers, Lt Cdr A Longmore, was appointed to the command of Cromarty Air Station. This unit existed only on paper and Longmore had the job of finding a site for erecting hangars and a suitable foreshore for launching and retrieving seaplanes. The most suitable area was found to be a piece of ground near Cromarty Coastguard Station on an area of land used by the local fishermen for drying their nets. Just who actually owned the land appeared to be unclear, but an Admiralty letter dated 2 November 1912 authorised the expenditure of £10,000 on the project!

On 4 July 1913 a Bessoneaux hangar arrived after being towed on a lighter from Sheerness. These hangars consisted of a wooden framework covered with canvas and were easily erected by bolting the separate pieces together. Longmore's log of that period makes fascinating reading. Flying was in its infancy and of the 20 naval ratings who arrived in July only half had ever seen an aeroplane before. In fact during 1913 the log constantly refers to fitter and rigger training and also goes into considerable detail about engine and airframe faults and the trial and error methods of rectification.

The first machines arrived by rail and boat and were erected by the semi-skilled hands available. The first seaplane was No 117, a Maurice Farman. This was followed by No 59, a Sopwith biplane, and No 85, a French Borel monoplane.

With these machines Longmore and his other pilots took every opportunity of operating with the Navy during

Lt. Cdr Longmore aboard a Farman.
Right: Short Folder which crashed at Cromarty on 4th September 1914 whilst being flown by Lt. Bowhill.

A 1913 sketch showing the area of Cromarty Naval Base and illustrating the narrow entrance to the channel which gave protection from the elements. *[via author]*

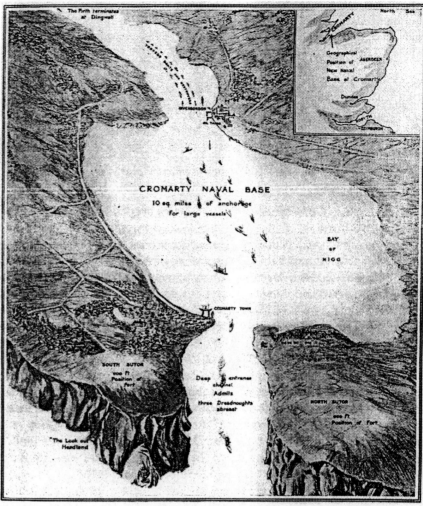

Fleet Exercises. During one of these exercises on 26 July 1913 he spotted a periscope off Nairn and was able to signal its presence by Aldis lamp to a nearby ship. The Navy were impressed by what was probably the first example of air-sea co-operation.

VIP visitors to the Fleet were interested in the seaplanes and keen to have flights. Admiral Jellicoe was delighted with a trip in the little Borel. At that time Winston Churchill was First Lord of the Admiralty and in that capacity made many visits to Invergordon. He was enthralled with flying and took every opportunity to have trips in Cromarty's seaplanes.

Flying and servicing were still very experimental and hazardous. An entry in the log for a weekend in August 1913 sums up the situation perfectly:-

"Saturday August 16th. 'Ratings return from leave 12.30. -3.30 brought Sopwith out but was unable to launch her owing to wheels sticking in the sand, started engine up, found to be running at only 1060 revs. Launched Borel and went off to Nairn with Reese. Did one circle round the games field and then alighted meaning to taxi in towards beach. There was however so many fishing nets, rocks etc that I decided to get into the air again and return. Went to Invergordon and then returned. Engine was not running quite up to the mark. Experienced great difficulty in getting machines in with only a few hands."

"Monday August 18. Sopwith out whole morning trying to get engines to run correctly. Continual trouble with ignition wire breaking off where sweated. Decided to replace large type wire and not to sweat terminal. Borel

oil gauge glass broke while testing engine, replaced with new one. Adjusted top near warp wires. Finished work 5pm."

Cromarty was evidently never intended to be a permanent station and Longmore spent some time in the autumn of 1913 investigating other possible sites. Baltintrail and Nigg were found unsuitable and so was Ferrytown although this was to be a site for a Marine Craft MU in WW II. However the army base at Fort George was considered suitable for both land and seaplanes and preparations were started for eventual removal from Cromarty.

In the meantime the Cromarty seaplanes took part in the autumn Fleet exercises of 1913. A Caudron biplane

Left: Sopwith No. 59 was delivered to Cromarty on 19th July 1913. It was converted into a seaplane.
Right: No. 129 Wight Navy Plane on show at Olympia, London during March 1914.
This machine was wrecked at Fort George on 30th January 1915.

Sopwith seaplane No. 59 taxies across the Cromarty Firth in 1913. *[Brian Hansley]*

flew off from *Hermes* and was housed at Cromarty. Its pilot was Lt Bowhill, later Air Chief Marshal Sir Frederick Bowhill. Another future Air Marshal flying in the area at that time was Lt John Salmond.

Cromarty was used in the round Britain Air Race of 1913 but Longmore only mentions the fact that Hawker called there during the race.

On 10 September 1913 Longmore travelled to Peterhead in *HMS Hermes* and while there selected a site for a future flying boat base. Next day he travelled to Loch Strathbeg which he also found suitable but appeared to be bothered by the wild fowlers on the Loch. This area is now an RSPB Reserve.

Longmore notes in his log for 14 October 1913 that two Marines were sent to Rose Street Iron Foundry in Inverness for instruction on driving motor cars.

By now Cromarty was in the throes of closing. The Bessoneaux hangar was dismantled and transferred by tug to Fort George. The tug Resource landed the advance party and stores at Fort George on 27 October. The rest of the year was spent in moving the remainder of the equipment and aircraft, the task being made difficult by bad weather. About this time fields at Ardersier and Carse of Delnies near Fort

George were inspected as future landing grounds but these were considered unsuitable.

Longmore was now posted to Calshot after handing over Fort George to Lt Oliver on 26 January 1914. He was later to have a distinguished career in the RAF becoming Air Chief Marshal Sir Arthur Longmore.

There is now no trace of the short occupation of RNAS Cromarty. Fort George is even more of a puzzle. Although the RNAS and later the R A F were supposed to have operated from the station during World War One, no records can be found and there are no remains at the present army camp. A letter in the Public Record Office dated 25 June 1918 notes the removal of a 70 ft x 70 ft shed from Fort George to Smoogroo in the Orkneys. The log of Lt Longmore gives a very interesting account of those early flying days but unfortunately the following Commanding Officers appear not to have been such prolific writers.

An unidentifiable DH9 ditching in the Cromarty Firth close alongside HMS Coventry. *[Jack Chapman Collection via R. L. Ward]*

Royal Air Force Invergordon/Alness

Warships at Invergordon no doubt operated seaplanes further inside the Cromarty Firth both during and after World War One. Also, a field at Delny, just north of Invergordon was apparently used as a shore base for RNAS planes from the first carriers. Level fields near Delny would have been the site of the landing ground but there are no traces left of any military buildings though the present Delny House Hotel could have been used as an Officer's mess. Official details of the RNAS presence seem to be non-existent but a report in the *Banffshire Advertiser* of 1 September 1921 refers to a plane (type unknown) which caused great excitement when it force landed at Garmouth en-route from Leuchars to Delny. By the end of the war Delny proved to be too small for expansion and the RNAS activities moved further west to Novar. The *Forres Gazette* of 31 August 1921 reported five planes over Forres en-route to Invergordon. The *Banffshire Advertiser* of 6 July 1922 reported seven planes going to Invergordon with one force-landing at Leith Barn due to a broken prop shaft. This plane was H3540 which was a DH 9A. When Delny closed is in doubt and these planes could have been heading for Novar. Airships were also used in Naval exercises and the R33 was reported operating over the Firth at the beginning of July 1920.

The first recorded use of the Invergordon base by RAF aircraft was in 1924, when the Fishery Board for Scotland requested that an aircraft be used for herring-spotting flights off the north-east coast. Fairey IIID Seagull amphibians were considered for this task but it was realised that they were too small and the larger Felixstowe F.5 flying-boat was selected. After a search at Fraserburgh, Strathbeg and Novar had proved fruitless, moorings were made available at Invergordon. Three Felixstowes, including N4197, operated from Invergordon during July and August, but the project was not judged a success.

The late Twenties and early Thirties saw the development of large flying-boats in the RAF and a detachment of Southampton 11Cs from 201 Squadon operated with the Fleet from Invergordon in August 1929. The next few years saw detachment of Singapores, Londons and Stranraers from 209 and 240 Squadrons.

As these detachments were of a temporary nature during the Fleet's summer cruises, facilities for the aircraft were limited. Personnel were housed in a tented camp and a Signals section with a W/T trailer was provided with manpower from various units. In August 1939 the squadrons on exercise at Invergordon returned to their home base for major servicing while the ground crew remained at Invergordon.

Above: The remains of an unidentified Fairey IIIF being hoisted out of the Cromarty Firth following an accident in the early 1930's. *[Author's collection]*

Left: Felixstowe flying boat at it's moorings in Invergordon Harbour during 1924. The aircraft was used on fishery protection patrols. *[via author]*

Right: Short Singapore K6914 [C} spent it's entire life with 209 Sqn., to whom it was delivered on 1st July 1936 at Felixstowe. It spent three months at Califrana (Malta) in 1937 before being despatched to the colder climes of Invergordon in September 1938.

Left: A close formation of Mk.II Saro Londons of 201 Sqn - K5259 [W]; K5621 [U] and K5262 [Z]
[via Ray Sturtivant]

At the outbreak of war on 3 September 1939 Invergordon was commanded by Gp Capt Croke and had a strength of 250 officers and 269 airmen and civilians (excluding squadrons). RAF Reservists started to arrive, and with bad weather affecting the tents, buildings in the town were taken over as billets with the HQ at a private house, 41 High Steet. The squadrons, operating at that period were 240, flying Londons under the command of Wg Cdr Carter, and 209, flying Stranraers under the command of Wg Cdr Wigglesworth, 209 also looked after

P9630, the first PBY 4 (Catalina), used by the R A F which had been on trials since the summer of 1939. This aircraft, flown by Wg Cdr L K Barnes, came up from Pembroke Dock on 25 September 1939. From Invergordon it flew a reconnaissance, searching for German shipping around Iceland. During this trip the Catalina was forced down by fog in what was then the neutral territory of Iceland but after some diplomatic activity it was allowed to leave and arrived back at Invergordon on 28 September 1939.

For the first two months of the war the flying boats

Supermarine Stranraer K7297 [X] of 228 Sqn. splashing down in 1939.
This aircraft disapeared during a North Sea patrol on 19 August 1939. *[via Ray Sturtivant].*

Saro London Mk.I K5910 [BN:L] of 240 Sqn. is illustrative of the obsolescent flying-boats used by the RAF in the early stages of the Second World War. On the fuselage behind the cockpit is a housing for a torpedo which could be carried to torpedo-bomber units that needed re-supplying.

[via R. C. Sturtivant]

carried out constant patrols but there was also a lot of movement between Invergordon, Shetland and other Coastal bases. The Duke of Kent visited on 28 September 1939 and King George VI arrived on 6 October, 1939 to visit *HMS Sheffield*. The Station ORB also records the visit of a Squadron Leader Vernon of the RAF Pigeon Service who came to discuss the erection of a pigeon loft.

On 23 October, 1939 two Sunderlands of 228 and 240 Squadrons arrived from Pembroke Dock. An HE 111 was sighted on 21 November 1939 but A/A did not fire because of low cloud. The first wartime casualties occurred on 4 November, 1939 when London R' of 240 failed to return from a patrol. On 17 November 1939 another London KS912 crashed at sea but the crew were rescued and landed at Methil by *HMS Imperial*.

In October 1939 two Short S30 Empire flying boats V3137 (ex-G-AFCU *Cabot*) and V3138 (ex- G-AFCV *Caribou*) were impressed by the Air Ministry. Along with Imperial Airways Captains Gordon Store and S G Long and crews they arrived at Invergordon on 21 January 1940. With the Catalina they formed a Special Duties Flight to carry out trials on the early form of A S V. *Caribou* was attacked and sunk by German aircraft while disembarking an RAF radar unit at Bodo in Norway on 5 May 1940, and the same fate befell Cabot the next day. Rumour has it

that broomsticks were fitted to these boats to represent machine guns.

Operations increased with the invasion and occupation of Norway in May 1940. A HE 115 and another Norwegian seaplane passed through Invergordon en route to Helensburgh after escaping from Norway in May.

The early summer of 1940 saw hectic preparations to repel would be invaders. Machine gun posts were set up, trenches dug, road blocks organised and officers ordered to carry revolvers at all times. An exercise on 3 August 1940 involved Army, Navy, RAF and LDV, with the 7th Seaforths from Tain managing to penetrate the defences. There was still time for recreation however and during the summer the camp was visited by the ENSA concert parties 'Wanglers', 'Peaches and Cream' and the 'Troupers'. Accommodation was now a problem and though work had started on brick buildings in August 1940, airmen had to be billeted in local houses and a granary at Inverbraickie Farm. By 25 November 1940 two barrack huts were ready apart from the electricity. It was noted rather sourly in the ORB that *Difficulty in obtaining labour and material was aggravated by usual dilatory ways which characterised building projects*.

During this period constant patrols were carried out over the North Sea but little action was reported. On 3

Seen in happier times - on it's maiden flight from Short Brothers at Rochester, - Imperial Airways' S-30 G-AFCU *'Cabot'* becomes airborne.

Above: Heinkel He 115 (F) 52, with two RAF personnel aboard. On 10 April 1940 this aircraft carried out an attack on the German cruisers Koln and Lonigsberg. This was the first air attack on naval vessels in the history of Norway. RNAF officer Lieut. Offerdal flew (F) 52 to Meikle Ferry on 1 May 1940 and from there was flown the Helensburgh. The aircraft was scrapped without taking part in further operations, although three other Heinkels which also escaped from Norway were used by the RNAF for various operations during the war.

Below: A MF.11 seaplane (built by Marinenes Flyvebatfabrikk) of the Royal Norwegian Air Force which escaped German hands by flying to Invergordon in the spring of 1940. *[201 Sqn]*

Weary crews walk up the Invergordon slipway in May 1940. In the background is the He.115, No.52, which was stolen back from the German authorities in Norway by men of the Royal Norwegian Air Force.*[201 Sqn.]*

July 1940 a Swordfish flying from Aldergrove to Evanton crashed in the Firth and although both crew were rescued they later died from their injuries. A sheep was killed when bombs were dropped on a farm near Invergordon on 25 August 1940. On 15 December 1940 a Sunderland of 201 Squadron crashed on landing. The crew were rescued but the aircraft sank before it could be towed ashore though it was later beached on 28 December.

Christmas festivities for 1940 included a sing song with Cpl Reilly at the piano and Squadron Leader Furths on violin, five a side football, Christmas dinner, children's tea party and a dance.

On 15 February, 1941 a Junkers 88 made a daring attack on the Invergordon base. Diving to 40ft east to west over the oil storage tanks, it dropped two 500 kg bombs. One went through Tank 13, into the next one and exploded without causing a fire, but tons of oil flowed out on to the railway tracks and nearby station. The second bomb went through another tank, but failed to explode after landing in the oil slick. The Junkers made a sharp bank to avoid a church steeple then machine gunned a Sunderland causing slight damage before speeding off. The attack had lasted four minutes without the defences reacting to what was happening. Two civilian workmen on top of the tank when the attack occured slid down to safety. One ran off home while the other repaired to the nearest hostelry for a medicinal dram! The unexploded bomb was defused and the oil hosed into the Firth.

On 3 July, 1941 a Catalina of 209 and one of 240 Squadron departed for Archangel with Sir Stafford Cripps and other officials on board. These aircraft returned a few days later with a Soviet Military Mission. In August 1941 three Catalinas of 422 Squadron arrived from Lough Erne on a secret mission, but packing cases marked S N S O Archangel gave away their destination. Their mission was to transport Hurricane spares and key personnel to Grasna near Murmansk. Flying via Sullom Voe and the Lofoten Islands they landed at Murmansk after one of the aircraft had taken $21^{1/2}$ hours for the trip due to electrical storms. Returning with other passengers one Catalina had to force land at Whallsey in the Shetlands.

In June 1941 4(C) OTU was moved from Stranraer to Invergordon with the officers setting up their Mess in Dalmore House. The OTU had a mixed bunch of aircraft - mostly Sunderlands and a number of unloved Lerwicks.

Ten crews a course were being trained by October 1941. This must have caused occasional congestion in the

Sunderland N9046 from Invergordon. This was the first Sunderland to fight a successful battle with six Junkers Ju88's on 3 April 1940.

L7257 [TA:S] was one of the batch of Lerwick Mk.I flying-boats which served with 4(C)OTU at Invergordon after some use by 209 Sqn....

Firth at times and though the station had no official SLGs, Clachnaharry near Inverness was reported to have been used for some servicing while Catalinas used Urquhart Bay on Loch Ness for circuit and splash training.

In the spring of 1942 it was decided to split up 4 (C) OTU with the initial training of aircrew carried out at Stranraer and operational training at Invergordon. Pilots would do one month's training at each unit while the rest of the crew did only one month at Invergordon. Moving around of aircraft in February 1942 resulted in an Invergordon strength of seven Lerwicks, seven Catalinas, seven Sunderlands, one Singapore and one Stranraer. A Lysander V9857 was based at Evanton. By June 1942 the strength had risen to 17 Sunderlands, 21 Catalinas, 7 Lerwicks, two Stranraers and one Singapore. Apart from training, the OTU aircraft did various other odd jobs during this period. On 13 February 1942 several flying boats visited Dornoch for War Weapons Week. On 21 April 1942 three Sunderlands flew to Loch Lochy with 35 Commandos on board each aircraft. This was to give the troops training in embarking and disembarking from flying boats. On 16 May 1942 three Lerwicks did a formation fly past for Warships Week.

By summer of 1942 the OTU was producing on average 22 trained crews a month. The flying boats were anchored in the north and south "Trot" in the Firth from Invergordon to Alness - about $2^{1}/2$ miles. Daily servicing was carried out from a floating dock at Dalmore Pier. A slipway had been built at Alness at the end of 1941 and because of lack of space at Invergordon this slipway and the flat area around Alness Point was now used for major servicing. 30 hour inspections were done at anchor but the boats were beached for 60 and 100 hour inspections. The Alness base, now named 5 FBSU, (flying boat servicing unit), had four hangars which could hold three Sunderlands each while hard standings could accommodate other aircraft. For night flying the flare path was in the centre of the Bay with four 'Runways' one for each of the compass points. Early in the war the flare path lights were lit from a flare tied to a broom handle held

The unofficial Station Crest of RAF Alness with it's motto 'OGAW DELPUS' (Oh Gawd Help us) reflects with feeling the adversity felt by ground crews!
[C. Wood]

from a speed boat. Later on battery operated lights were used and navigation lights were positioned at Invergordon, Saltburn and South Sutor.

A tragic incident occurred on 25 August 1942. The Duke of Kent, who took a keen interest in RAF affairs, was due to visit the troops in Iceland, and a flight from Invergordon was organised for this purpose. A Sunderland of 228 Squadron flew from Oban to Invergordon where the Duke came aboard after travelling up from London by train. The weather was dull and overcast with drizzly rain and after take off the Sunderland flew at about 800 ft northwards over the sea. This would have been the proper course to follow but for some inexplicable reason the aircraft turned inland and in the heavy mist and rain crashed on the mountain Eagh Rech (Eagle Rock) above the village of Berriedale. All the crew perished apart from the rear gunner, Flt/Sgt Andrew Jack. Although badly injured he managed to make his way down the hill but it was not until the following day that he staggered into a croft cottage and safety. At the subsequent Court of Enquiry the pilot was found solely to blame, but to this day it remains a mystery why an experienced pilot should have wandered so far off course at such low altitude in conditions of poor visibility.

The last Lerwicks were disposed off to 422 RCAF Squadron Lough Erne in July 1942. These aircraft had never been successful, and unpleasant handling characteristics including lateral instability and a vicious stall had made them unpopular with the aircrew. Stranraers and Singapores also left and the OTU now used only Sunderlands and Catalinas. By the end of 1942 the serviceability record was appalling, with only four servicable Sunderlands out of a strength of 17 in December of that year. The situation improved in 1943 and with sufficient buildings in use at Alness, the station officially became RAF Alness from 10 February 1943.

Training accidents were frequent. In January 1943 a Sunderland crashed on the flare path and another was sunk in a gale. In April a Sunderland and a Catalina broke from their moorings and sank. In May a Catalina sank after a heavy landing. The standard OTU patrol was now 17 hours and a landing in darkness after such a long trip could be hazardous. No less than three Sunderlands crashed on the flare path in the last week of November 1943. Probably the most spectacular accident happened on 22 November 1944 when Sunderland DD851 had a starboard inner engine failure on take off. When the blazing engine fell out, the aircraft crashed on the railway line two miles north east of Invergordon. There were no survivors.

Training and operations continued throughout 1944 with one different operation in October when nine Sunderlands of the OTU and four from 201 spent three weeks ferrying time expired airmen from Keflavik in Iceland. Sunderlands and Catalinas were now the basic aircraft at Alness. There were however occasional odd visitors such as a Kingfisher on 5 December 1943, two Mariners on 10 August 1944 and a Coronado on 6 September 1945. A Northop seaplane also dropped in at

Above: H.R.H. The Duke of Kent in 1940.
Below: The route of the Duke's ill-fated Sunderland

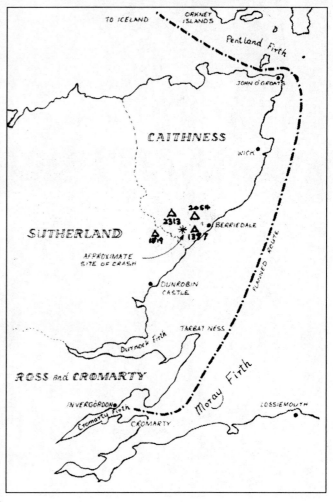

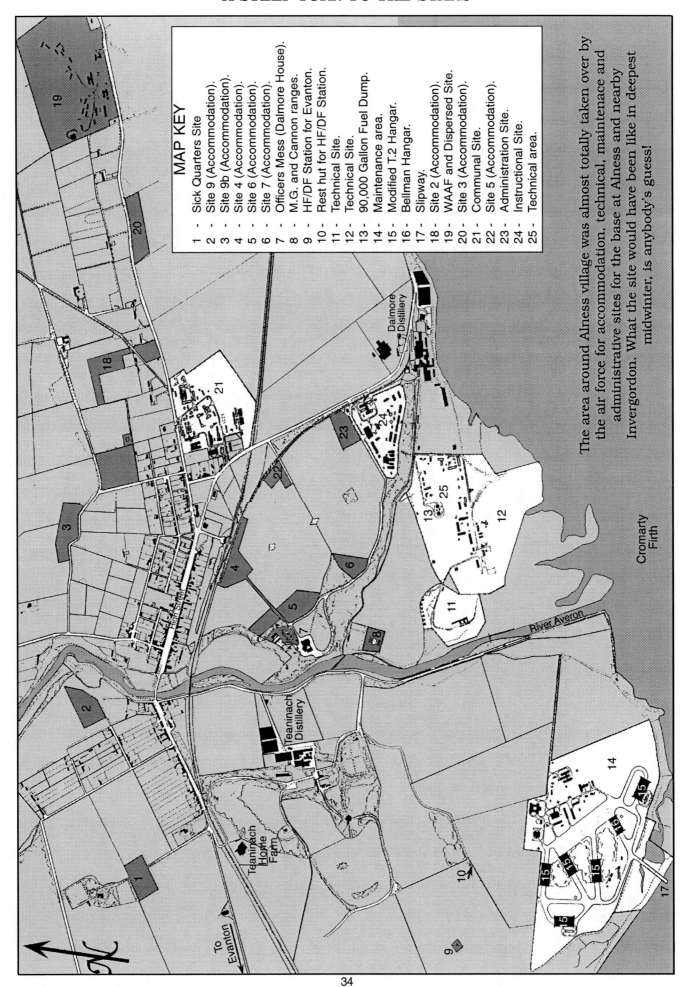

MAP KEY

1 - Sick Quarters Site
2 - Site 9 (Accommodation).
3 - Site 9b (Accommodation).
4 - Site 4 (Accommodation).
5 - Site 6 (Accommodation).
6 - Site 7 (Accommodation).
7 - Officers Mess (Dalmore House).
8 - M.G. and Cannon ranges.
9 - HF/DF Station for Evanton.
10 - Rest hut for HF/DF Station.
11 - Technical Site.
12 - Technical Site.
13 - 90,000 Gallon Fuel Dump.
14 - Maintenance area.
15 - Modified T.2 Hangar.
16 - Bellman Hangar.
17 - Slipway.
18 - Site 2 (Accommodation).
19 - WAAF and Dispersed Site.
20 - Site 3 (Accommodation).
21 - Communal Site.
22 - Site 5 (Accommodation).
23 - Administration Site.
24 - Instructional Site.
25 - Technical area.

The area around Alness village was almost totally taken over by the air force for accommodation, technical, maintenace and administrative sites for the base at Alness and nearby Invergordon. What the site would have been like in deepest midwinter, is anybody's guess!

Saro Lerwick L7257 [TA:R] of 4(C)OTU sunk at its moorings at Invergordon on 11 November 1941 during a gale ...

...and is seen here in the process of being retrieved by the men of 56 Maintenance Unit from the waters of the Cromarty Firth, using oil drums as a pontoon, in December 1941
[Ian Angus]

Alas poor Lerwick...!

During the salvage process, a bulkhead burst and the tail rose to the surface. The only thing to do was to tow the aircraft out to deeper water so that it could be turned upright and towed back!

Right: The remains of Lerwick I L7257 [TA:R] being removed on a 'Queen Mary' transporter and sent to Greenock for repairs. The aircraft was finally struck off charge on 4 February 1942 as being uneconomical to repair!
[P. H. T. Green collection]

Right: Sunderland Mk.V ML778 [TA:P] of 4(C)OTU had started life as a Mk.III aircraft. In May 1951 it was sold to Aéronavale (the French Navy) for further service.
[via R. C. Sturtivant]

Below: The substantially-complete remains of Catalina I Z2141 [QL:A] of 413 Sqn., based at Sullom Voe, which sank at its moorings at Invergordon on 10 November 1941.[Ian Angus]

various times during the war. Training continued after the war ended but in 1946 it was decided to move the OTU. The first choice, Killadeas on Lough Erne, proved to be unsuitable and the OTU finally moved to Pembroke Dock on 15 August 1946. Although no longer a permanent base Alness was used by Sunderland Squadrons during Fleet exercises. During 1947/48 the RAF auxiliary boat Bridlington' was based at Invergordon and used as a radar and torpedo target. Alness flying boat base was closed in January 1957 when the last of the Sunderland squadrons were disbanded.

After the demise of the flying boats Alness continued to operate as a unit, albeit of a maritime nature. 1100 MCU operated target tugs and ASR launches from part of the old Alness station. With the disbandment of the Royal Air Force Marine Services in 1986 the maritime operations necessary for the ranges in the Cromarty Firth were taken over by a civilian firm which operates from the same buildings as 1100 MCU. In the Eighties some RAF buildings are still intact near Dalmore Distillery and the concrete bases of many more are scattered around the Alness area. The pier and flying control tower are still in existance and nearby on the beach are two massive concrete blocks $3^{1}/_{2}$ ft high $7^{1}/_{2}$ ft diameter and 75 yds apart. These were probably used for beaching the Sunderlands and are likely to remain forever as a poignant reminder of the big flying boats which had their home here for so many years.

A fine airborne shot, probably taken in late 1945, of Sunderland Mk.V SZ568 [TA:C] of 4(C)OTU. This 'boat' went on to serve with 235 OCU and was not struck off charge until October 1956.

Left and below: Two views of the hull of Catalina AH531 [TA:K] of 4(C)OTU, which sank in a gale on 5 September 1942, being lifted onto the slipway. This 'Cat' was, not surprisingly, then Struck Off Charge. *[Ian Angus]*

Below left: The primitive control tower on the end of Alness pier, still in existence in 1990. *[Author]*

Not the best of pictures maybe, but nevertheless the only one located that shows the much-modified and somewhat basic control tower at Invergordon, seen in April 1945.

Right: An aerial view taken in the late 1990's of the former RAF Station at Alness, on 42 acres (17ha.) of which contractors began a £1.3 milion project in February 1997. A new access road off the A9 was built, and drainage and electrical services were installed during the six-month contract. Further development as a strategic industrial and commercial site will take several years.

Below: On 8 May 1995 a Monument to those who had served at RAF Invergordon and Alness was unveiled in the town of Alness.

The monument consisted of a Catalina propeller salvaged from the Firth and mounted on a pole in the form of a cairn, flanked by a pair of flagpoles. [Author]

Royal Air Force Evanton

If we must all be gunners
then let us make a bet
We'll be the best damn gunners
that left this station yet !
George Harding RCAF

About six miles west of Invergordon on the north coast of the Cromarty Firth is the small town of Evanton. Between the town and the coast is a conglomeration of hangars and buildings with the outlines of runways on the grass area beside the sea.

These are the remains of an airfield which probably has the most varied history of any in the Moray Firth. The Navy, when at Invergordon, needed a shore base and this was at first Delny just north of Invergordon. As Delny could not be enlarged for bigger aircraft, a new grass airfield was constructed near Evanton and opened in 1922. It was originally called Novar as the land had belonged to the Novar Estates. Novar in the Twenties and Thirties was used by aircraft from the Home Fleet when they were based at Invergordon during their cruises in April and October. Most of the servicing was done at weekends with the aircraft flying off to the Fleet on Monday mornings. At that time FAA aircraft were serviced by RAF personnel with detachments to Novar from Leuchars which was a RAF training unit for FAA aircrew. Charlie Wood, now deceased, recalled being on this detachment in 1929. There were very few buildings on the camp and the RAF brought their own signals vehicle for T19 and T21 transmissions. This was powered by a 9HP Austin engine which usually seized up by the end of the detachment. They also had a Leyland workshop lorry with sufficient equipment to do most repairs.

The aircraft using Novar at this period included Darts, Bisons, Blackburns, Ospreys and Flycatchers, mostly from the carriers *HMS Argus* and *HMS Furious*. Later on the camp was used for armament practice training for Nimrods and Ospreys.

August 1937 saw a new era starting at what was now RAF Evanton with the formation of No 8 Armament Training camp, although the FAA continued to use the airfield for aircraft of 800 and 820 Squadrons of *HMS Courageous* and 801 and 822 Squadrons of *HMS Argus* during the closing months of 1937. The new buildings were not ready until November 1937 and the first course for flying instructors for air firing commenced on 29 November 1937. At the same time Heyfords of 6 and 99 Squadrons from Finningly and Mildenhall flew in on

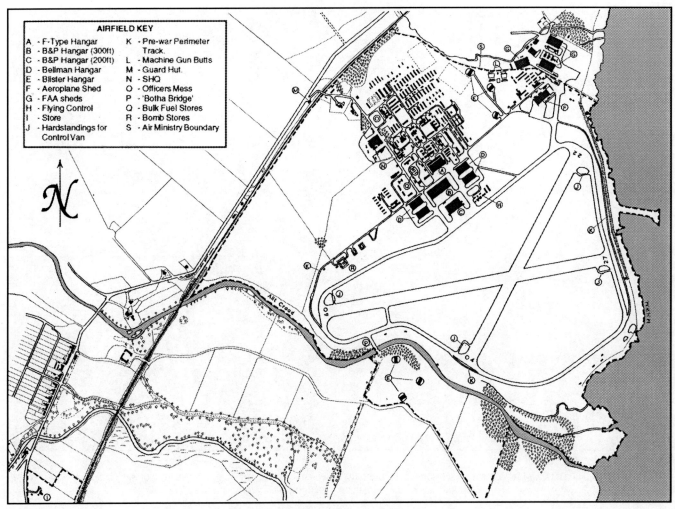

AIRFIELD KEY

A - F-Type Hangar
B - B&P Hangar (300ft)
C - B&P Hangar (200ft)
D - Bellman Hangar
E - Blister Hangar
F - Aeroplane Shed
G - FAA sheds
H - Flying Control
I - Store
J - Hardstandings for Control Van
K - Pre-war Perimeter Track.
L - Machine Gun Butts
M - Guard Hut.
N - SHQ
O - Officers Mess
P - 'Botha Bridge'
Q - Bulk Fuel Stores
R - Bomb Stores
S - Air Ministry Boundary

Royal Air Force Evanton in it's final stage.

detachment. This was to be the pattern for the next couple of years with detachments from at least 24 different squadrons plus training units using Heyfords, Wellesleys, Whitleys, Battles, Blenheims and Hampdens. The FAA continued to use the airfield up to the outbreak of war and Evanton personnel refuelled the flying boat visitors at Invergordon from 50 gal drums transported up the Firth in barges.

Despite the intense flying there were few accidents and probably the worst of these was caused by an "Act of God". In January 1938 a gale blew up, and as the camp staff were returning off the last train from Inverness they witnessed a scene of chaos. The wind was lifting the aircraft off the ground and rotating them on their tail wheels, with pickets being ripped out and propellers windmilling. One Wg Cdr was frantically trying to tow an aircraft with wheels spinning on the wet grass as they were being blown towards the Firth. Virtually all the aircraft were damaged. On 25 and 26 February most of the station's aircraft were involved in an unsuccessful

search off the west coast of Scotland for a Wellesley of the Long Range Development Flight. On 24 March 1938 Heyford K6860 of 102 Squadron crashed after engine failure.

Tain range was used for firing and there was also an emergency landing ground at this range. The ELG staff were responsible for drogue recovery and a high speed launch patrolled for air sea rescue. The target tugs were Fairy Gordons mostly of rather ancient vintage. Their Panther 11A engines had a habit of shedding tappet

Opposite: HMS Furious, one of the early aircraft carriers, steaming along the Cromarty Firth. *[G Garvock]*

Above: A low-level aerial view of Novar Camp taken sometime during the nineteen-twenties. The 'temporary' nature of the location can be seen by the lack of any permanent structures! *[J. McAdam]*

Below: The ugly Avro Bison - in this case N9966 - inside one of the canvas Bessaneaux hangars at Novar in 1927. Note the grass floor! *[J. McAdam]*

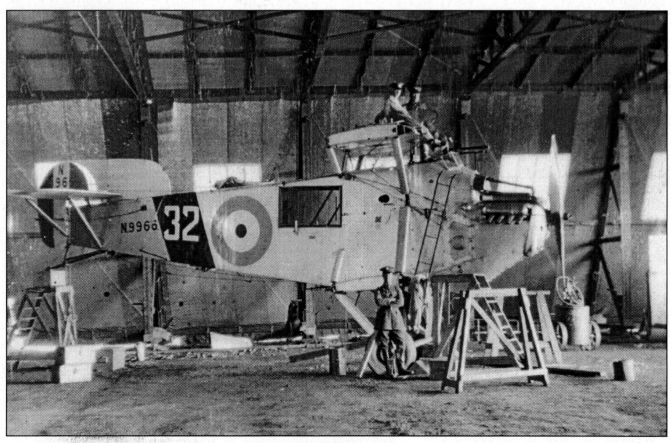

Images of Novar!

Top: another aerial view, showing the larger canvas hangars.

Above: a plethora of uniforms!. Two groups pose for the 'Camp Portrait'

Above left: A decidedly 'Heath Robinson' aircraft re-fuelling rig at Novar 'sometime in the 1930's
[R. L. Ward]

Left: A Walrus of 421 Flight comes to grief in 1923. [R. L. Ward]

Fairey IIID as used by the Fleet
Air Arm at Novar in the 1920's
[J.McAdam]

covers which flew over the crew's heads and sometimes hit the rudder. Three drogues were carried and these were paid out for firing practice and later dropped for retrieval by the drogue operator. It could be a dangerous business as some trigger happy pilots hit the target tugs instead of the drogue. For this onerous job, fitters and riggers got 1/- a day flying pay.

During the Thirties the RAF produced a series of public Air Days usually co-inciding with Empire Day. The 1939 Empire Air Day was to be the last pre war event and 78 RAF stations were opened to the public throughout the country. Of these, Evanton was the farthest north and created quite a stir with approx 9,000 spectators and a mile long queue of cars to the main gate. The local newspaper, the *Ross Shire Journal*, devotes five columns to the event starting off by stating that:

"Chief interest in the whole of the north of Scotland centred at Evanton, Ross-Shire, the size and importance of which Air Base must not be mentioned in public print."

Whether because of this censorship or ignorance of aeronautical matters the reporter goes on to describe the afternoon's events without actually mentioning the types of aircraft involved though these would probably have been the Gordons plus visiting bombers. Dummy bombing and machine gun attacks, formation flying and

flypasts thrilled the crowd but the main event of the afternoon was the arrival of a Spitfire (referred to by the reporter as a "Spitfire Bomber"). One of the early Spitfires, it was flown by Squadron Leader Stainforth of Schneider Trophy fame from Netheravon via Driffield, Turnhouse and Montrose. Quoting the *Ross Shire Journal*:

"Like an eagle but growing bigger and bigger as it approached, the Spitfire sped towards the aerodrome". Having landed *"...the intrepid airman with admirable coolness threw back his overhead protection and climbed easily out of the machine"*. After being welcomed by the station Commander Wg Cdr Busk, the pilot was presented with a haggis on a silver salver decorated with the Seaforth tartan. The pilot presented the CO with a Wiltshire ham and in return got a bottle of whisky. At a news conference afterwards the Squadron Leader declared *"I am grateful for the haggis but I am not sure what to do with it. I do know what to do with the whisky"*. After three quarters of an hour on the ground the Spitfire left for home and the display continued with a final set piece bombing of the airfield.

A delightful picture of a pair of
Fairey IIID's - S1527 '7' and S 1332
operating from Novar.

Handley Page Harrow '31' seen flying from Evanton in the late 1930's on gunnery training duties.
[B Hansley]

Hayfords were common visitors to Evanton in the thirties, this being a machine from 'A' Flight of 10 Sqn.
[Flight]

Westland Wallace target-tug K4344.

by the CO. This was later replaced by a Magister.

In December 1939 a detachment of Blenheims from 64 Squadron arrived for fleet protection. For this purpose they were fitted with four machine guns in a pod under the fuselage. The Blenheims stayed for a month and during this period there was also a detachment of Hampdens from 106 Squadron. In February 1940 the FAA officially occupied the lower part of the camp for reserve aircraft storage, disembarked aircraft, minor repairs and inspections. In February 1940 the unit was re-named No.8 Bombing and Gunnery School.

The occupation of Norway and Denmark by the Germans in the spring of 1940 brought all north east airfields to a renewed state of readiness. Apart from the

Above: Heyford K5196 of 99 Sqn with damaged rudders at Evanton in 1938.
Below: Hampden L4070 of 83 Sqn at Evanton during April 1939
[P H T Green Collection]

Apart from the many types of bombers constantly on the airfield Evanton also had the odd unusual visitors. These included Hectors of 612 County pf Aberdeenshire Aux Sqn, a bright red Percival Q6 personal transport of the air Minister Lord Londonderry, and an Ensign which took the full length of the airfield to land, sliding across the wet grass with wheels locked.   Squadrons continued to visit for armament training but on the outbreak of war in September 1939 No 1 Air Observers School arrived from North Coates. This was now re-named No 8 Air Observers School, flying Harrows, Henleys, Wallaces and Battles. The trainee gunners were taken up about five a time in Harrows, taking spells at the guns firing at ground targets or drogues towed by Wallaces and Henleys. The first gunner's course started in October 1939 and passed out a month later with a total of 768 flying hours. Other aircraft on Evanton in the early months of the war included a HP 42 for use as a unit's transport aircraft and a Tutor for use

Aircraft 'incident's continued to happen at Evanton.

Below: Caught in a gale during 1940, this Hawker Henley was tipped onto it's nose.

Left: An unidentifiable Westland Lysander suffered undercarriage collapse in September 1942.
[B *Hawsley*]

continuing pressure to produce more gunners, five Battles and two Harrows were got ready for operational use in the event of an invasion when they were to fly to Dishforth. Fortunately these ancient aircraft were not called upon for operations. Lysanders of 614 Squadron arrived in June 1940 for army co-operation training. The old Wallaces were exchanged for four Battle tugs from Jurby. Although the emphasis was still on gunnery training the School now did bombing training also using Harrows fitted with five sets of bomb sights.

The first 25 WAAFs arrived in December 1939. One of these (now Mrs McGregor residing in Stonehaven) recalls how they were at first shunned by the airmen and it took a long time for them to be accepted. Later in her stay she remembers cooking for Sir Stafford Cripps before he left for Russia.

In the spring of 1941 the venerable Harrows were replaced by Blackburn Bothas. These aircraft may have

The crest of No.8 Air Observers School, Evanton.
The motto translates as 'Labor will learn expertness'

been relatively new but they had already been discarded as operational aircraft after serving with only one squadron, 608. Underpowered and underarmed these planes were now relegated to training schools of the RAF. Fifty Bothas had arrived at Evanton by April 1941 and very soon they developed an evil reputation for those who had the misfortune to fly them. Their lack of power was bad enough on large airfields but used on a small area like Evanton bounded on one side by the sea and on the other by wooded hills this could be lethal.

In March 1942 Wimpey Construction started building runways which were finished in the autumn. Due to the limited space only two rather short runways were constructed, 1233yds at 270° and 970 yds at 220° As these were not even at right angles these were soon problems with cross winds. Hangars were also built - two Boulton Paul, four Bellman, one F and six blister type. The airfield was on a lower level than the building site which caused problems when towing aircraft. A bridge had to be built to connect the dispersals with the hangars and this was called the Botha Bridge. With the considerable amount of bombing and gunnery training now being carried out, and other airfields vying for space, new ranges were opened up. One of these was Coull Links north of Dornoch. Six dummy tanks were positioned as targets and the Bothas would fly parallel with the coast so that the trainee gunners could fire broadside at them. On 7 April, 1943 the AGS had 36 Bothas, 18 tugs and a DH60 on its strength. The Lysander tugs were gradually being replaced by Martinets which were purpose built for the job.

Royal Air Force Evanton, photographed from 8,000ft in 1942. *[B Hansley]*

October. The ORB notes (sighs of relief all round!). The Botha had been one of fortunately relatively few WW II aircraft which was a complete failure in everything it did. Of the many Botha accidents at Evanton twenty had been complete write offs and apart from the casualties the effect on the training programme must have been significant. Another unusual aircraft to arrive in the summer of 1943 was a Avro Manchester, forerunner to the world-famous Lancaster. This however was never to fly again having been obtained for ground instructional purposes. Probably the largest aircraft ever to use Evanton was a USAAF B17 which landed there after getting lost en route from the USA to Britain. Before leaving it was daubed "Evanton Babe".

Nevertheless these new aircraft had their share of problems with two unexplained engine failures and drogue hang ups which could be fatal to the crewman even if the aircraft was not dragged into the ground. Apart from aircraft faults accidents were caused by low flying. It would seem that Polish pilots were addicted to this pastime and in July 1943 Sgt Modrzeywski was put under close arrest after hitting the water of Loch Fleet in his Marinet. He was later de-moted and given 35 days detention. The station still got the odd aircraft such as a Tutor K3294 which arrived on 21 April, 1943. No reason was given for this detachment. In the summer of 1943 it was decided to replace the Bothas with Ansons fitted with Bristol turrets. The first Ansons to arrive were grounded for lack of spares for their turrets and the ORB for 10 July 1943 states that the Bothas were to be retained indefinately. This must have caused some consternation but by August the Ansons arrived to stay and the Bothas started to leave, the last one on 20

The unit strength on 4 April 1944 was 28 Ansons, 20 Martinets, one Master II and one Magister. At that period the strength of personnel at Evanton was 1340 RAF and 39 WAAF. By now the surplus of trained aircrew necessitated the closure of many training stations and 8 AGS was one of them. The last course, No 138, a polygot collection of British, French, Norwegian, Czech, Polish and Belgian aircrew passed out on 18 August 1944. The station was now handed over to a Care and Maintenance party from Dalcross but a new chapter in its history was about to unfold.

Miles Martinet target tug as used at Evanton

This Evanton-based Blackburn Botha ditched into the Cromarty Firth on 9th Sepember 1943. The aircraft was towed ashore and beached at Invergordon, from where the RAF removed all that was salvagable.
[B Hansley]

The Naval section of Evanton had been expanded in 1943 to form a Class B repair yard and as it was a satellite of Fearn it was named *HMS Owl II*. The whole station now came under Naval control being commissioned as *HMS Fieldfare* on 8 October 1944. Originally only minor inspections were carried out but the aircraft repair yards task was Cat B (a total strip down) maintenance. Evanton handled Swordfish, Barracudas, Travellers, Harvards, Seafires, Walruses, Avengers and other types from the FAA units at Twatt, Hatson, Machrihanish, Fearn and Crimond, as well as from carriers. One Traveller was used as an Admiral's Barge; the others were stored in crates, eventually being assembled, flown to Donibristle, embarked on a carrier, and pushed into the Clyde estuary. Many Barracudas flew straight to Evanton from their factories. They were either scrapped at Evanton or Donibristle, the only parts salvaged being the brand new engines. There were still RAF in the west side of the camp until June 1945. A large building programme at the end of the war produced a new Naval camp at the cost of £2,000,000. As often the case when the Navy took over RAF camps, or indeed vice versa, some of the alterations appeared to be rather unnecessary. For example, the ATC tower was converted into a three storey Naval type like a ship's bridge. A lot of different types of aircraft were constantly flying in or out or doing test flying with the many surplus Navy pilots at the end of the war used for the ferrying jobs. In 1946 a Lancaster carrying spare crews succeeded in landing on this small airfield. After the advent of jet aircraft Evanton's short runways became unsuitable and the ARY closed in March 1948. It would appear with hindsight that the extensive building work carried out post war was never properly utilised. There were sufficient living quarters for 150 officers, 2369 other ranks, 17 WRNS officers and 458 rating WRNS. All this was now vacant although some of the hangars continued to be used for storing engines and other spares. In mid 1955 a detachment of the USAAF 28th Weather Squadron moved in and stayed for eleven years conducting high altitude weather research using balloons.

Unlike most abandoned airfields Evanton managed to retain a lot of its buildings including the large hangars. These have now been utilised by a number of local industries and form a thriving industrial estate. The runways are intact although the land has reverted to farming. Other buildings still standing include Naval Married Quarters and near the shore a pillbox with a pitched roof, probably disguised as a dispersal hut.

Although not an operational station, Evanton played an important part in the training of both RAF and FAA aircrews from the end of WW I to the end of WW II. It probably played host to more different types of aircraft and squadrons than any other airfield in the Moray Firth. In the same area Evanton was the only station to have had an Empire Air Day, was the first station to have received a Spitfire, went from Naval ownership to RAF and back to Navy, and of course had the doubtful distinction of being the only station in the north east to fly Bothas.

Some of the building at Evanton that survive into the 1990's
[Author]

Chapter Four

AROUND INVERNESS

"We are but warriors of the working day
Our gayness and our guilt are all besmirched
With rainy marching in the painful field"

Shakespere: Henry V Act 4, Scene 3

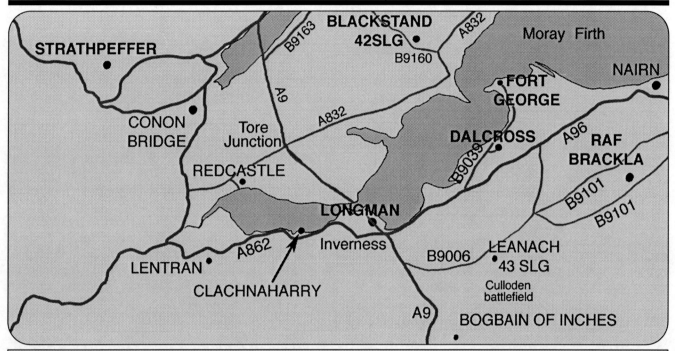

Ten miles from Cromarty on the A832 lies the town of Fortrose. On the top of the plateau about a mile north of Fortrose is the site of the wartime Blackstand SLG.The site is unmarked but can be investigated from a farm lane on the north side of the road. Various buildings including a Super Robin hangar still exist but are rapidly deteriorating. The bays west of Fortrose were occasionally used by RAF flying boats pre WW2.

Eight miles west of Fortrose on the A832 is Tore Junction. Three miles west of this a side road on the left goes through a forest containing the remains of WW2 77 Maintenance Unit Advanced Ammunition Park. A few bomb storage huts still survive but the area is difficult to investigate.

Turning left at Muir of Ord the A862 (formerly the main North road from Inverness) passes Lentran House about five miles west from Inverness.This old people's home housed a WW2 maintenance unit and a couple of RAF huts still survive. Clachnaharry Bay, immediately west of Inverness, was occasionally used by flying boats before and during WW2.

The old Inverness airport at Longman ,east of the town,has all but disappeared under industrial buildings but one or two RAF buildings still remain. Leaving Inverness by the A96, the present Inverness Airport (Dalcross) lies five miles to the east. Ex RAF hangars and buildings are still in use beside more modern erections. Near the terminal is a statue of Capt Fresson,the founder of Highland flying. North of Dalcross is the army base of Fort George.This has an excellent museum but there is no trace of the seaplane base situated there during 1914/15. Returning to Inverness, a left turn leads to Culloden battlefield. Although well signposted with a thriving visitor centre, there is no mention of the WW2 SLG of Leanich which occupied the fields to the south. Two small huts on the north side of the road and another two a field's length south are all that remains of this small airfield.

East from Culloden the B9006 leads on to the B9090 which passes Brackla Distillery, about three miles from Nairn. The level area between the distillery and the River Nairn was the site of the WW2 Brackla airfield. Little remains here also, apart from a broken up perimeter track. From Brackla the B9101 leads into the village of Auldearn where a large wooden building was once part of RAF Kinloss Sgt's Mess.

The area between Evanton and Inverness is unsuitable for airfields but various items of aeronautical interest have occurred in the vicinity of the Highland capital over the years.

Although aeroplanes and airships must have been a fairly common sight around Inverness during WW I they were obviously becoming scarcer in later years as the following extract from the *Inverness Courier* of 22 April 1919 shows :-

Visit of Aeroplanes
"For the first time for many years Inverness was 'visited' on Sunday afternoon by an aeroplane. That is to say it passed over the town at quite a low altitude, so that the noise of its propeller attracted everybody's attention. The day was calm and sunny and excellent views were got across. It came up from the south and after circling over the town sped south westwards. An hour or so later a second aeroplane followed the same route but at a higher altitude. It is said that the machines came from Edinburgh and were bound for Oban. A telegram states that two Handley Page aeroplanes left Andover on Saturday on a trip round the UK and arrived at Belfast on Sunday evening."

Although the inhabitants of Inverness did not realise it they were witnessing an epic flight on that April day. Major Keith Park had taken off from Andover in a HP/400 F3750 named *'Last Days'* with nine of a crew on a round Britain trip. They had landed at Edinburgh and after over flying Inverness had flown down the Great Glen and on to Belfast where they had to land on a wharf at Harlands and Wolff's shipyards due to bad visibility at Aldergrove. They eventually completed the circuit of 1880 miles in 28 hrs and 30 mins at an average speed of 66mph. There is no mention of a second aircraft but its possible that the Inverness reporter may have been mistaken. Keith Park was later to have a distinguished wartime career becoming Air Chief Marshal Sir Keith Park.

Clachnaharry
Just west of Inverness is the surburb of Clachnaharry distinguished only by a small pier. The sheltered waters of the Beauly Firth to the north of Clachnaharry have been used occasionally for flying boat operations over the years.

The first flying boat to use Clachnaharry was the

Handley Page 0/400 'Last Days'

Saro Cloud G-ABXW *'Cloud of Iona'* which was tested on the Inverness Stornoway route at the end of 1934. During the second world war Sunderlands from Alness occasionally used this area for servicing presumably when their home base was overcrowded. During the Wings for Victory Week in 1943 a Singapore was anchored at Clachnaharry and visitors ferried to and from the flying boat for half a crown a head.

An unusual visit is recorded in an article from the *Northern Chronicle* of Wednesday 1 November 1933:

"Colonel Lindbergh and his wife arrived at Inverness about 4pm on Wednesday in their seaplane, having flown from Galway in Ireland in 3hrs 40 mins. The machine landed in the Firth near North Kessock and taxied to a buoy, where a rowing boat, in which there were Customs officials, was waiting. It was later moored to a buoy further up the Firth.

Colonel and Mrs Lindbergh were rowed ashore to south Kessock, where a number of people had congregated. They were met by Capt. Fresson, manager of Highland Airways Ltd. Colonel Lindbergh stated that they had encountered a strong head wind and that the weather was extremely cold. They were evidently very pleased with the warm reception accorded them. In the course of their flight from Ireland two stays snapped, and these were repaired by craftsmen from the Rose Street Foundry. Asked what their next objective was, Colonel Lindbergh would offer no explanation. They left Inverness on Thursday about 1.30pm."

The visit would have occurred during one of the

Clachnaharry Pier, 1989. *[Author]*

Col & Mrs Lindbergh with
Lockheed Sirus floatplane

many pioneering flights made by Col and Mrs Lindbergh in their Lockheed Sirus floatplane.

Inverness Flying Boat

Many British towns have given their names to aircraft but there are few of Scottish origin. Lerwick and Stranraer come to mind but it is less well known that in the Twenties a flying boat was named Inverness.

In 1922 a German firm, Rohrbach Metallflugzeugbeau started a branch in Copenhagen - to circumvent the ban on building of planes in Germany. The British government became interested in their designs, and in 1924 ordered two Ro IV flying boats. They were supposed to be built by William Beardmore & Co Ltd at Dalmuir on the Clyde but in fact the first machine was built in Berlin and assembled in Copenhagen. This aircraft was then flown to Felixstowe for trials on 18 September1925. Extensive tests soon established that the flying boat was just about useless for the long range reconnaisance role envisaged by the makers, but even so the second aircraft was still completed on the Clyde in 1928. This aircraft proved to be no better than the first and the MAEE at Felixstone decided to scrap them both in April 1929.

Why were the aircraft named Inverness? No one knows, but it was probably just a name plucked from the air, and it is doubtful if the capital of the Highlands would wish to be associated with such a pair of extremely ugly and utterly useless aircraft.

Flying Fleas

The small town of Conon Bridge, 20 miles north west of Inverness seems an unlikely spot for aviation pioneering, yet it was here in the Thirties that an unusual aircraft was built and flown.

During the Thirties there was a craze for building Flying Fleas. The Mignet Pou-de-Ciel (Sky Louse) was of French origin and must surely have been one of the most unlikely flying machines ever built. Plans were easy to obtain and with few restrictions on flying at that time all sorts of people had a go at building a plane of their own. In 1936 the veterinary surgeon at Conon Bridge, a Mr Murray Lamb, had had enough of a succession of fast American cars so he decided to build a Flying Flea.

He commissioned Frazer's Coachbuilders of Dingwall to make the airframe, and a Mr Menzies to do the metal work such as the undercarriage legs, engine mountings and controls.

When the machine was finished the owner had to do his own test flying as no local pilots were available, or willing, to take this rather unorthodox machine into the air. Mr Lamb apparently made a few trips but one evening in a field at Cleethorpes Farm near Maryburgh the Flea failed to clear a dyke and was badly damaged in the ensuing crash. Unlike many Flea pilots Mr Lamb escaped unhurt but seemed to lose interest in aeronautics after this incident.

The fate of this machine is unknown but there is a picture of it outside a hangar at Longman, and the plans were supposed to be still in Frazer's garage at Dingwall in the Fifties. The sons of Mr Frazer and Mr Menzies remember the Flea with nostalgia and still have photos of it while it was in its prime.

The less-than successful Inverness flying boat

Flying Flea G-ADWX with builders at Dingwall in 1936. Note the unusual towing arrangement! *[Murray Fraser]*

Lentran House, 79 Maintenance Unit

Lentran House stands in wooded grounds about five miles west of Inverness on the south side of the old A9 road. The former hotel, now used as an old people's home, seems an unlikely base for an RAF camp, particularly a Maintenance Unit.

Why Lentran was chosen as a site for an MU is not known although the presence of a Signals unit nearby at Bunchrew may have had some influence on the decision. On 1st July, 1941 two officers and eight airmen arrived to set up a HQ in Lentran House. On 3 July 1941 Flt Lt Grimes arrived from 11 MU Dumfries to take command of Lentran (now 79 MU). It was noted that the MU would be used by the RAF stations at Lossiemouth, Kinloss, Invergordon, Wick, Castletown and Skaebrae. More personnel arrived in August 1941 and excavations were started for a Bellman hangar. Camp defence was not overlooked as the Station Operations Record book for 7 August, 1941 noted that wooden clubs were to be issued for this job. By 1 September 1941 the strength was two officers and 91 airmen and preparations were started on a hutted camp. The Bellman was completed on 30 November 1941 and the huts in June 1942. Airmen now moved into the huts from billets in Inverness.

The MU was apparently a storage unit for spares of various aircraft such as Hurricanes, Spitfires, Catalinas and Hampdens. The ORB gives no details of particular items but August 1942 records 1033 Receipt vouchers and 2779 Issue vouchers which denotes quite a busy unit. Sect Off Mitchell was the first WAAF to arrive on 18 December, 1943 and by May of the following year there were 17 WAAFs on the unit strength. February 1943 saw a guardroom, fire shed, dope room and MT bays erected. May 1943 had a record 11,268 demands. During Wings for Victory Week in June 1943 the unit raised £378-9-0 (£3-11-4 per head). There were now 36 WAAFs on the station strength and the CO, Flt Lt Brown, was promoted to Squadron Leader.

With the increasing work load more storage space was required and in the spring of 1944 three Blenheim and four Spitfire packing cases arrived and were converted into huts by local labour. In June 1944 there were 79 RAF and 50 WAAF on the strength. During that month £600 (£5 per head) was raised by the unit for Salute the Soldier Week.

The autumn of 1944 saw a lot of improvements on the camp. A new Nissen hut was erected and radios were supplied for the recreation hut which was decorated and furnished by the camp personnel. A dance band of two RAF and a WAAF was formed and dances were held regularly. A field behind S H Q was used for games and the unit football team joined the Inverness League. In May 1944 another hangar (an old Bessoneaux) was erected.

Lentran House, 1989. *[Author]*

Now overgrown and forgotten - two views of the Bomb Store, RAF Redcastle. *{author}*

With the run down of the European War in the spring of 1945 a more relaxed atmosphere prevailed. Rambling and Cycling Clubs were formed and ENSA shows visited regularly. A VE day picnic was washed out but the disappointed airmen and women got free tickets to an Inverness cinema. Peacetime procedure was now in operation with Wednesday afternoon games, 36 hour weekend passes and one church parade a month. The VJ picnic was also cancelled by rain and again everyone got free tickets to the cinema. On 15 August 1945 a farewell concert was held. September saw a gradual posting out of all personnel and 79 MU disbanded officially on 27 September 1945.

Although only a small unit 79 MU was obviously very busy storing and issuing aircraft spares (mostly engines) for just about every type of aircraft operating throughout the Moray Firth and further afield. A couple of ex RAF huts are still in use behind Lentran House but few if any of its present occupants will know of its busy wartime role.

Redcastle

Directly north from Lentran across the Beauly Firth lies the small hamlet of Redcastle. In a wooded estate nearby can be found various buildings which by their shape, and the fact that they are partly covered by grass turfs, look very like the old Anderson shelters. In fact these are the remains of a WW II ammunition dump, No 77 Maintenance Unit Advanced Ammunition Park. (AAP) .

With millions of tons of ammunition being produced during the war, storage became quite a problem. Apart from large storage depots, smaller dumps had to be found, reasonably accessible to the user units but isolated enough for safety in case of accidents. In the early part of the war there was a complicated system of sending ammunition from factories to different depots which could involve nine stages of handling. It soon became obvious that this was highly inefficient and from 1941 onwards it was more usual to send the ammunition from the factories direct to an AAP, many of which were built all over the country. Redcastle was the furthest north of the AAPs and the choice of this remote area would have made sense at the time as there was a small railway station at Kilcoy about a mile away. This railway line which closed in 1963, ran from Fortrose to Muir of Ord and could therefore be used to transport bombs and depth charges to Alness and Evanton on the Cromarty Firth. Coastal stations required much less ammunition than Bomber units and the capacity of Redcastle was officially 5 Kilo-Tons (calculated on minimum safety distances). This would be normally be between 500 and 1000 tons of explosive. Like other AAPs built at the time Redcastle would have consisted of shelter type buildings scattered throughout the woods and connected by sawdust or woodchip roads.

These huts are now the only remains of a unit which played an important though largely unrecorded part in the WW II air activities from the Moray Firth.

Royal Air Force Blackstand

It seems that around 1937 a number of RAF flying boats - possibly Singapores - visited Fortrose Bay, for a number of local people remember the crew being billetted in their homes. Whatever happened there may be uncertain, but it is known that eight miles north-east of Inverness and close to the small town of Fortrose on the south coast of the Black Isle lies the site of 42 Satellite Landing Ground known officially as RAF Black Isle but also called Blackstand or Fortrose.

SLGs were sited in some peculiar places but few as odd as Blackstand. Blackstand Farm which was requisitioned for the construction of the SLG was situated

Left: RAF Blackstand - also known as Blackstand Farm.. RAF personnel and vehicles in evidence.

Below: Defiant L6936 of 2AGS undergoes maintenance away from Blackstand in 1944. *[Ian Angus]*

on a plateau ovelooking the Moray Firth. The site could not by any stretch of the imagination be described as level but nevertheless after an inspection on 9 May 1941 the firm of Messrs Rendall, Palmer and Tratton (the contractors for all SLGs) started removing fences and stones, laying drainage, and grounding telephone wires on the nearby roads. A 1100 yd runway was marked out and a HQ planned in a requisitioned farm cottage. Until huts were built personnel were to be billeted in Fortrose. Blackstand was to be a satellite for 46 MU at Lossiemouth and the CO of that unit inspected the site on 1 July, 1941. Progress was slow due to the shortage of labour but by the end of July it was nearly completed. An Anson piloted by Flg Off Harris made a trial landing on 12 August 1941 and on the 22 August, 1941 42 SLG was officially opened with the arrival of two officers, two NCOs and 22 airmen. The airfield was still incomplete and in September 1941 additional land from the farm of Upper Raddery was requisitioned for runway extensions. Fuel for the unit was supplied by RAF Evanton and guards by the 6th Battn. Cameron Highlanders. Blackstand was intended as a storage area for 46 MU's Beaufighters with a total capacity of between 50 and 60 aircraft. With all the aircraft stored in the open, camouflage was a problem especially as SLGs were supposed to be secret, and had to be referred to as airstrips. No control tower was built and not even a wind sock was allowed. When aircraft were due to land an airman burnt some gunpowder in a stove to show the wind direction. The spring of 1942 saw work starting on hard standings for medium sized aircraft but it is noted in the ORB entry for August 1942 that some of these hard standings were sloping, thus causing aircraft

towing accidents. A fire tender arrived in March 1942 and also a two ton roller for flattening the mole hills on the runway extension. By April, 1016 yards of boundary fence had been erected.

Accommodation was still a problem and in May 1942 Braelangwell House was inspected as a possible billet. In January 1942 SLGs were declared prohibited areas for aircraft other than those belonging to their parent MUs after it was reported that aircraft from Dalcross had been using Blackstand. When an aircraft was coming in to land

Warning still intact, Blackstand 1989. *[Author]*

Above: Church Parade, Blackstand 1944

Below: The same building in 1989. *[Author]*

A number of buildings survive at RAF Blackstand, including both timber and brick structures.

Below: Remains of some of the old RAF buildings at Blackstand, as photographed by the author in 1989.

at Blackstand an airman had first to run out and chase off the sheep and cattle, but this was a minor hazard. Pilots intending to use the strip were encouraged to walk over it beforehand for familiarisation purposes. New pilots obviously had problems. Regular users made a habit of landing up hill regardless of the wind direction. By aiming the aircraft from the bottom corner diagonally to the top far corner the worst that could happen was a sideways slip with the nose over the boundary fence. Despite these natural hazards few accidents seem to have occurred and the only one reported in the ORB was a collision due to a skid between Beaufighters EL445 and EL533 on 10 November 1942. After the need for camouflaging became less important Sommerfield tracking was laid, supposedly by 40 London evacuees.

Beaufighters were the main aircraft to be stored, although a Halifax landed in August 1942 but did not repeat the venture. After open storage for $2^1/2$ years a Super Robin hangar from RAF Lossiemouth was erected in March 1944. This could accommodate one Beaufighter

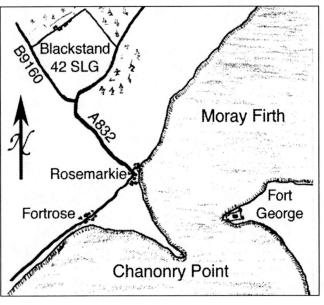

and two Defiants. 1944 saw the largest build up of aircraft with a total of 117 in July. After VE Day in 1945 storage gave way to salvage with a party from Bristols helping to remove servicable spares before breaking up the remainder. The last aircraft, two Warwicks, flew out in October 1945. The small number of airmen based at Blackstand obviously assimiliated well with the local civilians. Probably the only official parade was held in Fortrose for VE day and a farewell dinner was held in the town when the strip closed. After the war Blackstand was occupied by the Forestry Commission. A lot of trees were planted but the Commission have now left the site. RAF relics remaining include the hangar and a few brick built buildings of indeterminate use. One building had apparently been a stone bothy with a rather incongruous brick extension. Still legible after 40 year's weathering is a stencil 'Oil Store' on a wooden door. Blackstand in its day performed useful service for its parent unit 46 MU but at the present time it is hard to imagine that an airfield had ever existed on the site.

Royal Air Force Longman

The area to the east of the town of Inverness is now (in the Nineties) known as the Longman Industrial Estate. Covered by numerous factories, stores and industrial buildings, with further land emerging from infill of the Firth, it is very difficult to imagine an airfield on the site. Longman Fields, as this area was originally called, was at one time an execution ground and even in the 1930s it was just a flat piece of open ground. In 1932 Highland Airways Ltd. proposed an airmail/newspaper service between Inverness, Wick and Kirkwall and Capt E E

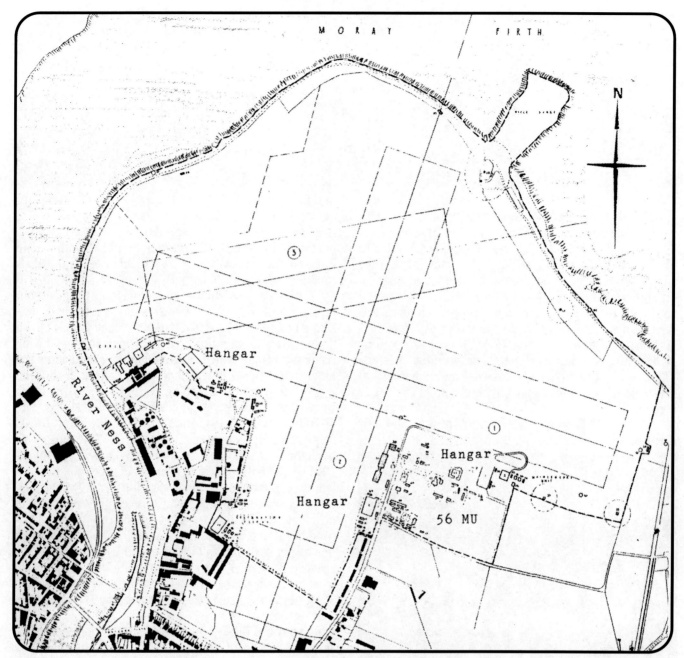

Royal Air Force Inverness (Longman) 57° 28'00"N 01°14'00"W. 8ft above sea level

Fresson asked Inverness Council if they would consider turning Longman Fields into a Municipal Airport. Capt Fresson was an experienced aviator with a great enthusiasm for extending flying throughout the Highlands so he soon persuaded the council of the benefit of his ideas. The first flight from Longman by Fresson was on I5 August 1933 and Inverness Municipal Airport was officially opened by the Duke and Duchess of Sutherland on 17 June 1933. Being close to the water's edge, flying boat operations were envisaged but these came to nothing although a Saro Cloud landed in August 1933 with spectators from the Isle of Man for the Highland Gathering. On 8 May 1933 an Orkney service was started with a Monospar ST4 and later a D H Dragon. They did a return service each weekday stopping at Wick and connecting with south bound trains at Inverness. On 29 August 1934 the first regular internal airmail service was started. The small airline prospered and expanded its routes to include Renfrew, Perth, Sumburgh and Aberdeen. It now merged with Northern and Scottish Airways to form Scottish Airways using DH. Dragons and a General Aircraft Monospar. The outbreak of war in September 1939 caused a temporary cessation of civilian flights from Longman.

At first the RAF appeared little interested in Longman. A Hart from 603 Squadron was reported landing on 17 June 1933 and in May 1939 an all yellow Piper Cub of the Inverness Civil Air Guard arrived. In 1940 Lysanders from 614 Squadron arrived for army co-operation work and in August of that year 14 Gp Communication Flight moved in with Dominies and Oxfords. 614 Squadron also operated some Rocs for dive-bombing demonstrations.

Longman's civilian hangars [Inverness Museum]

Royal Air Force Longman was officially opened on 1 April, 1941 with Squadron Leader Whitehead as CO of an airfield practically devoid of aircraft. 614 Squadron was now re-numbered 241 Squadron and started converting to Blenheims, finally leaving Longman in August 1941. They were replaced by 309 Squadron which continued army co-op and coastal patrols. Dalcross was now being opened and a lot of Longman personnel were involved in this operation. As the airfield was so under used the Ferry Pool at Prestwick flew up one-Oxford, four Masters, one Manchester, two Hurricanes and later four more Masters. These were picketed in the open while awaiting transit to Lossiemouth and Kinloss which were temporarily water logged.

On the 12 February some excitement was caused by a Hurricane's guns being fired in a hangar, fortunately

One of 614 Sqn's Lysanders

causing no casualties. The next day a Blenheim crashed at the mouth of the River Ness and on 31 March 1942 a Hurricane spun into the sea near the airfield.

Although Dalcross had tarmac runways it became water logged in April 1942 and the Defiants of the AGS had to operate from the relatively dry grass of Longman. During this period it is noted that Perkins Diesel engines were carried in the rear seats of Defiants from Longman to Wick. A Reliant and an Argus were stationed at Longman about this time probably for communication purposes. The end of April and beginning of May 1942 saw the arrival of various Chesapeakes (or Vindicators as the Americans called them). These came from Hatson and belonged to a US battle fleet in the Shetland area. On 18 May 1942 Lord Louis Mountbatten arrived in a Lockheed Electra. At this

period there seems to have been some disagreement between the army and the RAF as to the importance of Longman and the army seemed unwilling to allocate personnel for its defence. An exercise in September 1942 involved the embarking of troops in three flying boats (Sunderlands) near the airfield.

1943 saw only minor operations from Longman but in July of that year a RAF Communication Flight was formed to fly weekly trips to Orkney calling at Castletown if necessary. Another unit based at Longman was 70 Wing Calibration Flight which calibrated local ground and naval radar units. This was reformed as 526 Squadron in June 1943 but continued doing the same work using Blenheims, Oxfords, Dominies and Hornet Moths. The ORB for 19 July, 1943 notes that a RN Capt Briggs inspected a helicopter of 526 Squadron. This must have been the first helicopter seen in the area. On 19 January 1944 a USAAF B24 en route from Gander became lost and landed at Longman. A difficult feat but the crew managed the even more difficult exercise of taking off again the next day. On 21 January 1944 a Dalcross Anson LV127 overshot in heavy rain and crashed into a blister hangar destroying itself and an Oxford with the loss of one life. A short time earlier the same day another Anson had overshot and crashed into an earth bank north of the Slaughterhouse guard gate. On 21 August 1944 a JU88 flew over Inverness. The next day Spitfires of 13 Gp Comm flight patrolled the area but the enemy did not return. The severe weather of January 1945 closed most of the airfields in northern Scotland but by dint of rolling the snow Longman managed to stay open. On 14 April 1945 a B17 arrived from Polebrook but only stayed a few hours. This aircraft, 338130, was a veteran of 78 missions. On 1 May 1945 526 Squadron was disbanded and absorbed into 527 at Digby. Three Dominies of 527 were left at Longman until the squadron was disbanded on 15 April 1946. A lodger Naval communication squadron 762 left for

A US Navy Vindicator visited Longman during 1942

Stranraer K7300 at Longman after being salvaged from Invergordon in 1941. *[Ian Angus]*

Donibristle on 27 July 1945. New year 1946 saw the lifting of restrictions on civilian flying and the Inverness routes started again using captured German JU52s later superseded by Dakotas. Longman was now considered too small for safe operation of commercial aircraft and all flying was moved to Dalcross re-named Inverness Airport in 1947. Although wartime flying activities from Longman were on a smaller scale than many other airfields one lodger unit contributed a very considerable amount to the war effort. This was 56 Maintenance Unit which was responsible for salvaging wrecked and damaged aircraft throughout the Highlands.

The combination of high mountains, treacherous weather, inexperienced training crews and old aircraft ensured a constant catalogue of crashes throughout the war. The MU's job was to find and rescue survivors, collect bodies and if possible salvage at least some of the aircraft. This unfortunately was rarely possible and the salvage crew's job was then to remove or bury the wreckage so that the crash would not again be reported by passing aircraft. For various reasons wreckage was often left on the site and remains to this day in remote parts of the Highlands. 56 MU was formed on 18 November 1940 and officially started work on 1 January 1941. At first the work was contracted out to Barrie & Co Dundee and was civilian manned with a RAF CO Fit Lt Whiting. Although the Queen Marys and other transport were housed at Longman, a lot of the MU's work was carried out in Inverness at both Strothers Lane and Farraline Park. The offices were adjacent to the Little Theatre and Police Station building while the vehicles had servicing undertaken at McRae & Dick's garage by MU personnel. A Mess was provided in the Northern Meeting Rooms while there was a Salvation Army hut at Charlie's Cafe.

The first aircraft worked on included Hurricanes, Masters, Wellingtons, Spitfires, Whitleys, Moth, Magister,

The inboard section of a mainplane of a Boeing B-17 Flying Fortress salvaged from Kinloss in September 1941. *[Ian Angus]*

Two views of 56 MU salvaging a Catalina which sunk at moorings in Sullom Voe on 25 November 1941. *[Ian Angus]*

Blenheim, Anson, Lysander, and Harrows. Of these some were repaired on site, others returned to factories and others scrapped. As the work load increased a party of re-inforcements arrived from 63 MU Carluke in April 1941. In September 1941 the MU had 106 aircraft of which 88 were repaired either on site or in factories. On 9 September 1941 the MU received its first Fortress AN536 which necessitated manufacturing special equipment for its transport by road from Kinloss. This was the one which had returned to Kinloss badly damaged after the abortive raid on the German battleship *Von Scheer.*

The MU also dealt with flying boats. On 13 September 1941 a London with four bodies on board was recovered from the Cromarty Firth and towed five miles before beaching. A Stranraer was recovered in October 1941 and the gales of November made more work for the MU when a Lerwick was sunk at Invergordon and four Catalinas sank at Sullom Voe. The Lerwick salvage was particularly tricky as the hull overturned before it was towed into Invergordon and dispatched for repair to Greenock. The work of the MU was extremely varied. A lot of engine repair work was carried out on Wellington engines while in December 1941 they moved a barrage balloon from Invermoriston to Inverness. On 8 January 1942 a party of 20 airmen commanded by Flg Off Jones recovered four bodies from Whitley NI498 of 19 OTU which had crashed in snow on Carn Choire Mhoir. From January 1942 the MU started work on Hudsons in conjunction with Cuncliffe Owen at Wick. Throughout 1942 most of the MU's work was on Wellingtons from 20 OTU either at Longman or Lossiemouth. A Wellington missing since January was found near Braemar on 22 February and the MU had the job of removing eight bodies and wreckage in April 1942. From 12 March 1942 the MU was reconstructed into five Salvage Sections and a repair section for aircraft repair on site for Hudsons, Spitfires and Bristol types.

On 30 April 1942 Whitley Z6641 force landed on a sandbank half a mile from Inver. The MU dismantled it and floated the pieces to the mainland on rafts. On 10 August 1942 Whitley Z9468 was dismantled on site (Sarclett) and sledged across bogs to waiting vehicles. The unit strength around this period was 400 personnel. On 8 November, 1942 Spitfire BR256 was salvaged from 2300

Engine of Sunderland ML858 on St Kilda, after crashing in July 1944

ft up on Lochnagar. On 11 December 1942 Wellington L7867 was found to be impossible to salvage at 3500 ft up on Ben Alder. On 23 February 1943 two officers and 43 men salvaged Whitley LA837 from the Cromdale Hills. February operations included salvaging a Swordfish, two Catalinas and two Sunderlands from the Cromarty Firth and a Sunderland TG686 from as far north as a lake in the Faroes. The problems of finding crashed aircraft in even moderately wild country are well illustrated by an operation on 11 March 1943. A party set out to search for an Oxford N7236 supposedly crashed 12 miles south of Elgin. This aircraft was not found but the searchers found another Oxford N7435 which had been missing since 1940. March operations in 1943 included a Sunderland, Catalina, and Botha from the Cromarty Forth, a Whitley off Nairn and another Whitley off Foula in the Shetlands. For this latter job the salvage party arrived by RAF boat to Foula. After dismantling the aircraft the remains were transported by barrows and trollies to the jetty. From there the wreckage went by punt to the "Maid of Thule" which took it to Scalloway in three trips. In May 1943 a party camped out near Clunas while recovering the wreckage of Whitley BD295.

On 22 July 1943 a party set out to salvage Vickers Wellington L7867 which had crashed on Ben Alder on 10 December 1942. The salvage party camped out five miles from the wreck and after dismantling the aircraft the remains were carried by 25 mules of the 52nd Indian Division to the waiting three tonners. The job was completed on 3 August 1943. No reason has been given for this elaborate operation when a lot of other wrecks were left untouched.

On 26 August 1943 a Hampden which had crashed 1500 ft up Ben Loyal was removed by horse and sledge. On 12 October 1943 Oxford HM724 crashed at 3759 ft on Braeraich. At first this wreck could not be found due to low cloud but when it was discovered parts of it could only be recovered using an Army Mountain Battery based nearby. The current salvage projects in October 1943 were Whitley EB386 and Hampden P1207; both off the Aberdeenshire coast between low and high water - the latter in a minefield. On 14 November 1943 Wellington HF746 crashed on Ben Rinnes and although the MU removed most of the wreckage, some small parts remain to this day.

One of the most difficult salvage jobs for the MU was that of a Boeing B-17 which in January 1944 crashed in Loch Quoich after running out of fuel on its way to the USA. Lying in 60 ft of water 200 yds off shore it took a month's work to salvage. In December 1943 an Oxford force-landed, on Askerry Island. The pilot was rescued after being ten days marooned but waves crashing across the island made the aircraft Cat E before the salvage party could get ashore in March 1944. Even an RN LCT had been unable to land.

In June 1944 a JU188 was recovered with the help of the Canadian Forestry Corps sledges and tractors. In July, Catalina JX273 crashed and became a total wreck on Watersay. A 12 man party recovered guns and wreckage

Above: Hudson V9177 fuselage salvaged by 56 MU. *[Ian Angus]*

Below: Longman airfield , as seen in the 1950s, prior to the grass landing field being turned into an industrial site. The dotted line denotes the old pre-war area occupied. *[Inverness Museum]*

The site of Longman airfield as seen from a Dragon Rapide in September 1991. Some old RAF buildings are visible in the middle left. *[Author]*

between the road and the sea. Using two 22 ft boats the operation took 22 days.

One of the most bizarre operations carried out by 56 MU occurred in July 1944. On the 7th a Sunderland ML858 crashed on the lonely island of St Kilda, the furthest west of the British Isles. A 12 man salvage team arrived on board HMS *Phrontis* on the 10th July. Having found the wreck, attempts to blow it up failed as the explosives merely punctured the skin. The party now dug 37 holes 8 ft by 8 ft by 4 ft deep in which they buried the engines and small airframe parts. The large parts of the hull and mainplanes were inverted and painted brown so that over-flying aircraft would not mistake it for a new crash.

Another crash occurred at Foula on 29 July 1944. The Canso 11062 had to be cut up and slid down a hill for removal. During the six months from September 1944 to March 1945 the average strength of the unit was 88. It is noted in the January 1945 ORB that Sunderland H6006 had to be abandoned after being swept away from its position underwater. During the same month Wellington LR140 was partially salvaged off Lossiemouth and Liberator FL949 was partly buried where it had crashed on Hoy. Later on in February/March a seven man team spent five weeks carrying this Liberator wreckage down the hill and into a bog at' the bottom. In April 1945 a B17 which had crashed on Beinn Eadorra was broken up and the wreckage rolled down the hillside. A member of the team was injured by an oil cooler during this operation. Liberator EV955 was cut up and salvaged from Tain beach in May 1945. This proved to be the last salvage job for 56 MU which closed officially on 30 June 1945. Any work outstanding was now cleared by a detachment of 63 MU at

Dalcross. McRae & Dick was de- recquisitioned on 11 October 1945 and the unit finally closed on 18 October 1945.

The history of the flying squadrons of the RAF has been well documented over the years and it seems a pity that units like 56 MU have been practically forgotten. The men of these units did a magnificent job rescuing crews and salvaging aircraft from the most remote and inhospitable parts of the British Isles.

Apart from their technical skills, great ingenuity had to be used in organising methods of transport and salvage, and this often meant that aircraft which appeared to be a total loss were returned repaired for further action. 56's residence at Longman must have played an important part in the RAF's war effort.

The airfield at Longman has, in the Nineties ,vanished under a maze of factories and industrial buildings. A close search will reveal a few original airfield buildings but the sights and sounds of aircraft have long since become memories of the past.

Royal Air Force Dalcross

Although not a particularly large town, Inverness has long been regarded as the capital of the Highlands. During the Thirties most towns of any size constructed their own airports and in the case of Inverness flying commenced at Longman. It was soon obvious that Longman was too small and too close to Inverness for expansion so Capt Fresson, the energetic pioneer of Highland Airways, started to look further afield for a new site.

Capt Fresson was at this time living at Mid Kerrigan, Dalcross, about five miles east of Inverness, and this was the area he decided would be most suitable for his new

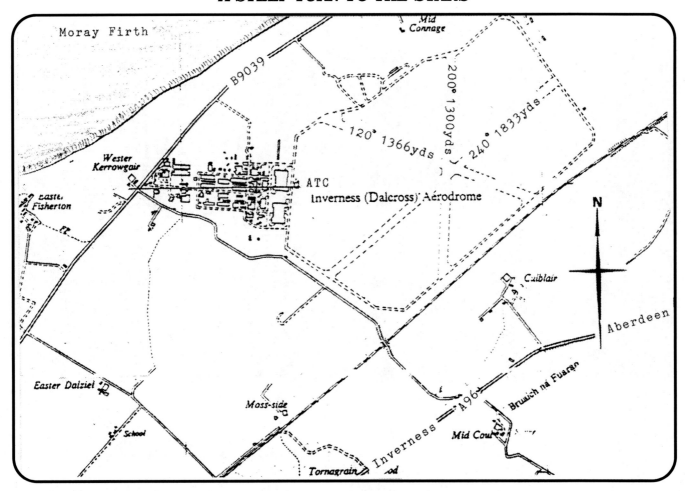

Royal Air Force Dalcross 57° 32' 32"N 04°03'08"W. 45ft above sea level.

airfield. Shortly before the outbreak of war in 1939 he was approached by the Air Ministry who were also looking for an airfield site. The Dalcross area seemed to be what they wanted but Capt Fresson wanted guarantees that his own flying interests would be protected after the RAF moved in. With the outbreak of war, work commenced and almost immediately Capt Fresson was evicted from his own house which was soon surrounded by airfield buildings.

Aircraft started flying from Dalcross in the summer of 1940 when a flight of 614 Squadron Lysanders did anti-invasion patrols around the coast. It became obvious that the airfield was susceptable to flooding - something Fresson had worried about - so it was closed while runways were constructed.

Although the airfield was not complete, No 2 AGS moved in with Defiants and Lysanders on 5 July 1941. There was a shortage of drogue operators for the Lysanders and 30 men were sent to Evanton for training. A Lysander crashed on the airfield in October and a Defiant crashed at Elgin the following month. Dalcross was also used by aircraft from other units such as the Whitleys of 19 OTU. The runways were not completed until October 1942 and during periods of wet weather Dalcross aircraft had to resort to the RLG at Brackla or even sometimes to the dryer grass field at Longman. Three training turrets were erected on the ground for training gunners against aircraft circling the airfield. The Defiant had not been a great success either as a fighter or as a trainer and 13 crashes are recorded during their stay at Dalcross. One of these landed on a sand bank in shallow water and had to be towed off by horses after a failure of the tractor in May 1942.

April 1942 saw the Lysander target tugs being replaced by the more modern Martinets TT1. The ORB records the fatal crashes of two Tutors in June and July 1942. Even at this stage of the war Tutors must have been

Lysander of 2AGS Dalcross. *[V.L.Winterburn]*

A pair of air-to-grounds showing the airfield at Dalcross. Above: A vertical picture, taken in May 1942, with the runways still under construction.

Right: Slightly overshooting the turn onto Finals! Dalcross as seen from an Avro Anson heading out over the Moray Firth.
[D. L. Winterburn]

in the vintage aircraft category. A detachment of Oxfords from No 1 FTS Montrose arrived in April 1942 and more Oxfords arrived in October to form 19 (P) AFU. Accommodation for the new flying pilots was in Nissen huts some distance from the flying site and 50 lady's bicycles were issued for transport.

By April 1943 Martinets had completely taken over from the Lysanders. The AGS now had 13 Ansons in place of the Defiants which were being disposed of and had all gone by the end of 1943. A Tutor was still recorded on the strength so presumably it was a station hack.

The AFU's first fatalities occurred on 19 December 1942 when Oxford BC 240 crashed at Cawdor. During 1943 the AFU faced considerable problems in the use of relief landing grounds which were necessary for the proper training of pilots. Leanach, Brackla, Forres and Elgin were all within range but there seems to have been constant disagreements between stations and Commands as to their use by different aircraft. Judging by contemporary reports a standard flying policy between the stations just did not exist. Problems at the end of 1943 were also caused by huge invasion exercises being carried out in the Culbin Sands area. This curtailed low flying considerably. Possibly because of all the distractions the AFU closed on 21 February 1944 with all the aircraft flying to 21 AFU at Wheaten Aston.

During 1942 Dalcross had a detachment from 309 Squadron now flying Mustangs. It was during this detachment that one of their pilots made a remarkable long distance flight. Flt Lt Lewkowitcz, a fully qualified engineer, had calculated that a Mustang could fly to Norway and back on a mission. Group HQ had ignored his request for a proving flight so on 27 September 1942 he set off without permission for Stavenger where he attacked enemy positions before returning safely to Dalcross - a round trip of 700 miles. For using his initiative Lewkowitcz was both reprimanded and commended and as a result of his experiment Mustangs began to attack more distant targets.

In 1943 there were short detachments of some front line squadrons such as 88 with Bostons, 63 with Mustangs and 652 with Austers. The AGS still carried on its training role though for some reason in 1943 the station helped to re-train redundant WAAF balloon operators as flight mechanics.

By May 1944 the establishment was 34 Ansons and 27 Martinets. By now the Ansons would fly in formations of three or four aircraft in order to economise on Martinet towing time. By the end of 1944 the need for air gunners was not so great but despite this the Ansons of the AGS were replaced by Wellington Xs, and later 16 Spitfire Vlls were used for cine gun attacks. The establishment at the end of 1944 was 27 Wellingtons, 26 Martinets, one Master and one Magister.

Harry Bourne, who now resides at Bridport, was a W/O pilot at 2 AGS during 1944 and 1945 when he flew Ansons, Masters, Martinets, Spitfires and Wellingtons. He recalls a frightening experience in a Martinet when lightning struck the towing cable dissolving it in a ball of flame. Another time he had to land hurriedly at Lossiemouth downwind against other aircraft due to engine trouble. A couple of rocker box covers had fallen off.

In December 1944 nine Halifaxes of 102 Squadron and 15 of 42 Squadron were diverted in after Ops. These were probably the largest aircraft ever to use Dalcross. By now the gunner's courses included French, Polish, Belgian, Norwegian, Dutch and Danish airmen. Contemporary reports conclude it was a happy unit and on VE Day there was quite a celebration. A huge bonfire fuelled by chairs and tables eventually burned down the main electrical cables. The CO. Gp Capt Crawford, chased

Defiant marked '42' departs Dalcross aboard a 'Queen Mary ' trailer courtesy of 56 MU. [Ian Angus]

Oxford NM609 of 8 FTS. For some reason the aircraft has been parked without chocks!

the culprits but being reputably the shortest officer in the RAF he failed to catch them. Nevertheless there were no repercussions.

The summer of 1945 saw a gradual run down of the unit. There were however still enough aircraft to participate in a Battle of Britain display on 15 September 1945 when 1500 people turned up to see Wellingtons, Martinets, Spitfires, Tempests, Lancasters, Halifaxes, Magister, Oxford, Anson, Sea Otter, Hurricane and Warwicks. Training finished in October 1945 and the remaining Wellingtons and Martinets were ferried away.

In January 1946 122 Squadron brought its Spitfires from Wick, re-numbered to 41 and moved to Wittering in April 1946. Dalcross was still the HQ of 13 Gp which kept its Comm Flight there. With the departure of the RAF, civil flying started again in 1947 in what was now Inverness Airport.

The run down of the RAF after 1945 was halted temporarily when the Korean war started in 1950. With the threat of this local war spreading, the shortage of trained aircrew had to be quickly rectified, in some cases by training National Service aircrew. For this training many more flying schools were needed and quite a few RAF stations were re-activated for this purpose.

One of these stations was Dalcross which by 1950 was being used, albeit on a limited basis, as Inverness Airport. On 26 February 1951 a Flt. Lt Moore, one SNCO and two airmen formed the advance party to re open the former RAF airfield. Many of the old RAF buildings were either uninhabitable or occupied by squatters and at first the advance party had only one hut and ate at the Ship Inn Ardersier. Some airmen were later accommodated at the army camp at Fort George. On 14 March 1951 S/L Riley arrived with 65 other ranks. By then the old NAAFI was back in use but all ranks shared the same mess. The accommodation situation was so acute that some postings to the unit were held in transit at RAF Lindholme.

8 FTS, as Dalcross was now to become, operated Oxfords and the first two of these aircraft arrived on 10 April, 1951. By the middle of June, 15 more Oxfords had arrived and also a new CO Gp Capt Barrett. More airmen continued to arrive and the first course of cadet pilots (42) started training on 21 July 1951 after their initial training on Chipmunks at Booker.

By September 1951 8 FTS had a strength of 912 airmen and 61 Oxfords. The unit was well enough established to be able to hold a Battle of Britain Open Day on 15 September 1951. 28 Oxfords flew in formation

forming the letters RAF and then there were displays by Shackletons, Vampires, Meteors and Sea Furies. A crowd of 2500 attended but it was noted that although the war had been over for six years photographs of aircraft were still forbidden.

A new NAAFI was opened in February 1952 but accommodation was still rather primitive. Jock Wilson, now living in Derby, recalls the shock of arriving from the heat of Singapore to the cold wind swept wastes of Dalcross. In order to keep warm, chocks and wheel covers were burned in the hut stoves.

On 29 November 1951 Oxford HN310 crashed killing the pilot Flg. Off Johnston. On 6 December 1951 Oxford V3910 went missing and was not found until 19 December 1951. The crash occurred on Maol an Tailleir where the terrain was so rugged it took 16 men working in relays to carry down the body of the pilot.

On 1 April 1952 the ORB records Oxford DF467 missing and on 19 August 1952 V4192 also went missing. The ORB does not record the fate of the two pilots.

Another Battle of Britain At Home was held on 20 September 1952 and despite bad weather 4000 people attended. Aircraft flying included Seafires, Fireflys, Harvards, Vampires and a Washington. By November 1952 the aircraft strength had risen to 65 Oxfords, 5 Chipmunks and one Tiger Moth.

A new Astra cinema was opened on 6th January, 1953 with the appropriate film 'Angels one Five: The severe gales of January 1953 did some damage but all the aircraft were safe. Oxford HM745 crashed in the Cromarty Firth killing the pilot on 19 June 1953.

Dalcross hangar packed with Oxfords of 8 FTS in September 1952. [R Hendrey]

By now Dalcross had its own pipe band, in time for the Coronation celebrations. The Queen arrived in a Queen's Flight Viking on 6 August 1953 when she was going to receive the Freedom of Inverness.

By late 1953 the need for the emergency flying schools had ceased and the last course, No 36, of NS pilots passed out on 7 October 1953. All aircraft were ferried away on 29 November 1953 and the RAF left Dalcross to resume its peacetime role as Inverness Airport.

Since the Fifties Inverness Airport has been built up gradually into a small but busy airport linking the capital of the Highlands with London and the south as well as the Western Isles and Orkney and Shetland. British Airways are the main carriers but visiting aircraft are plentiful and RAF aircraft often take advantage of the local good weather when southern airfields are fogbound. A modern reception hall and other buildings have been added over the years but quite a few old RAF buildings are still intact and some still in use.

During August 1963 Dalcross regained some of its wartime memories when the airfield was used as a base for filming '633 Squadron: Even at that time servicable Mosquitos were difficult to obtain but six did arrive, although five was usually the maximum number airborne. A B25 Mitchell and a Brantly helicopter were used for the

flying sequences mostly in the Great Glen and Glencoe. The filming took a month and at the end of it everyone concerned was entertained to a huge barbecue. Champagne and lobsters were flown up from England for the occasion in a Meteor which had to be flown at 8000 ft to avoid the champagne bottles bursting.

Dalcross airport marked its 50th anniversary with an airshow on 26 August 1990. Over 12,000 people attended to watch flying displays by a wide variety of aircraft ranging from a SE5 replica to a Nimrod from nearby Kinloss. A fitting finale for the first fifty years of a small but active airfield.

During 1994/95 extensive buidling work was carried out at Dalcross. A new Control Tower was erected on the southside of the airfield and the old tower demolished to make way for larger handling areas necessary for bigger aircraft expected at this thriving airfield.

In 1996 'Easy Jet' started cheap, no frills flights into Inverness from Luton. These were to prove very popular, and when Air UK started it's Stansted/Inverness service the future of London flights from Inverness seemed secure. However, at the end of 1997 BA changed it's flights from Heathrow to Gatwick and started using the smaller BAe 146. The reason for this moved seemed very obscure to the air-minded Highlanders. Worst still was to

Celebrations at Dalcross!

Above: A Cessna tows a banner over the airport celebrating 50 Years of an Airport in the area. *[Author}*

Above left: Richard Fresson, son of the late Captain E.E.Fresson OBE (left) assists Peter Clegg, Chairman of the Fresson Trust (centre) with the unveiling of the statue of Ted Fresson.

Left: The overall scene with DH Rapide G-AIDL DH60 Moth G-AAWO and Dan-Air 737 in the background at Dalcross in September 1991.

come when Air UK stopped it's Stansted flights and Easy Jet threatened to do the same. This came just when Dalcross had started a huge modernisation programme on it's reception area. At the time of writing the future of the largest Highlands airport seems very uncertain.

Royal Air Force Leanach

Culloden Moor outside Inverness is the site of the last battle to be fought in Great Britain. Some would say that this battle fought between the English and the Scots should best be forgotten but recently the site has become a tourist attraction with a large information building, shops and cafe. The mass graves of those who fell are scattered over a wide area and most are marked with the names of different clans.

To the east of the battlefield a brick built hut is rather incongruous in this setting. The method of building defines its origin as wartime military, and it is in fact a Flight hut -the last remaining relic of Leanach airstrip, 43 SLG in W W 11. Trees planted during the last few decades have considerably diminished the open ground but there can never have been much space for even a small airfield. Leanach was selected as an emergency airfield by Highland Airways when they commenced flying from Longman in the Thirties. They also sometimes used Bogbain of Inshes farms - a few miles further west. Situated on a high plateau it was more likely to be clear when the low lying Longman suffered from fog. On 18th

August, 1939 Hampden L4179 of 106 Squadron crashed in a plantation at Culloden while flying from Waddington to Evanton.

Highland Airways used Leanach for diversion purposes up to and after war commenced. When 46 MU at Lossiemouth required another SLG the Leanach site was requisitioned after a trial landing on 10 May 1941.

On 17 May 1941 the site was inspected by Flg Off Freeor and Mr Potts of Rendell Polman and Tritton the contractors. They agreed that it could accommodate 50 aircraft. In July 1941 work commenced on grounding telephone wires, removing hedges and fences and requisitioning Clava Lodge for accommodation. On an inspection on 4 August 1941 the runway NE/SW had been harrowed and seeded but the building work was held up due to lack of "brickies' Gp. Capt. Shaw inspected on 29 August 1941 and by then fuel, rations and barrack services had been organised with RAF Dalcross. By October 1941 the HQ offices had been completed and Clava Lodge occupied. On 20 October 1941 an advance party of P/O Horscroft, one NCO and 12 airmen arrived to take over. P/O Horscroft was the first pilot to land on the new airstrip on 25 September 1941. In the latter part of 1941 Leanach was used by a DH89 from Inverness and a couple of Tutors from Dalcross. As the secrecy of storage SLGs was paramount, action was taken to ensure that only aircraft of 46 MU could use the airstrip facilities.

By the early part of 1942 Hurricanes and Spitfires of 46

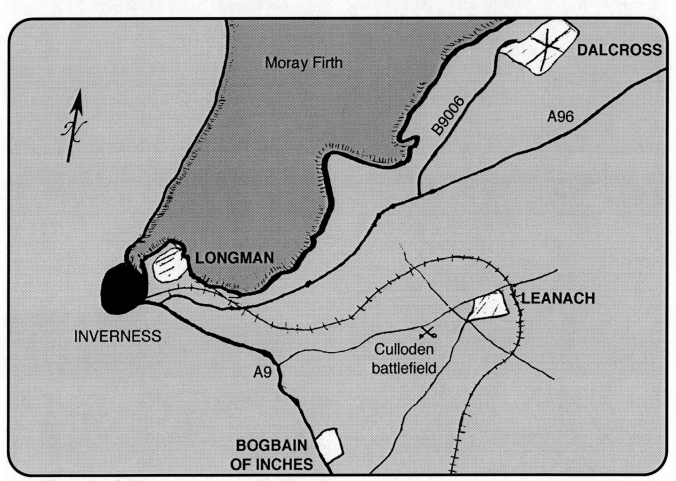

Site at Leanach

Fell at Culloden! The remains of Shackleton XF710 after crashing on 10 January 1964. *[John Chartres]*

MU were being stored north of the B9006 in a field bordered by a wood. Aircraft landed across the second wood between the road B851 and the River Nairn. Gaps can still be seen in the stone walls and hedges. The possibility of storing larger aircraft was now investigated and the Chief Test Pilot of 46 MU, Flt Lt Haines landed an Anson on 20 May 1942. Accompanied by ATA pilot Capt Heering he later landed a Wellington 1C. Conditions were marginal and only selected pilots were allowed to land Wellingtons when they did arrive. The wet grass surface could cause problems and the normal practise was to bring the aircraft in under power about 2mph above stalling then dropping immediately over the hedge and praying hard. A certain Alistair Liddell, cousin of Ian Munro of Leanach Farm is supposed to have flown a Spitfire through the central arch of Culloden Viaduct about this time.

By 12 October 1942 the army accommodation at Culloden Tea Rooms was assessed for use by the RAF Regiment. Leanach continued in its role as storage unit for 46 MU with the main aircraft now being Beaufighters. Although aircraft had been using the strip for a while the SLG was not 'officially' opened until 1 June 1942. At this time there was a staff of three NCOs and 31 airmen.

19 (P) AFU at Dalcross had no relief landing grounds early in 1943 and it was arranged for their pilots to use Leanach for simulated night flying in their Oxfords. This was done by using sodium flares on the ground while the pilots wore blue tinted goggles. Dalcross started operating in this role on 6 June 1943 and it was soon obvious that this was interfering with the MU's storage facilities. Because of this and also the inability of Leanach to take the larger aircraft now being handled by 46 MU, the MU party left for their new SLG at Dornoch on 11 October 1943. 19 AFU continued to use Leanach until it was disbanded on 25 February 1945. The SLG does not appear to have been active after that date.

Although Leanach ceased to be used for flying when WW II ended, Culloden Moor was to be the scene of a serious air crash on 10 January 1964. On that night Shackleton MkIII XF710 of 120 Squadron Kinloss experienced an engine fire while flying near Inverness. The fire rapidly got out of control and when the engine fell out the pilot had to crash land on the nearest available piece of level ground. This happened to be Culloden Moor and although the aircraft was destroyed on impact all the crew escaped unhurt. A quite spectacular ending to aviation at Culloden.

Royal Air Force Brackla

Two aerial photos of Brackla taken in 1946 show the small airfield literally covered in aircraft and a quick count reveals 335, mainly Halifaxes and Warwicks. This period was the heyday for Brackla as far as aircraft numbers were concerned although few of these aircraft would ever fly again.

Brackla, situated beside the B9990 road about three miles south of Nairn, was never intended to be used as an operational airfield and in fact when the land was requisitioned in May 1939 it was to be the site for No. 11 filling factory for bombs and shells. However the flat ground in the loop of the River Nairn seemed to be a good place for a landing strip and during 1940/41 it was built up as an RLG by MacAlpines at a cost of £890,000. A main

Sole relic of RAF Leanach in 1990. *[Author]*

runway of bar and rod tracking ran N/S for 1150 yds, and there were also two grass runways E/W 1250 yds and NE/SW 2000 yds. A concrete perimeter track surrounded the airfield with 30 diamond hard standings in five dispersal groups leading off the track. Two T2 hangars were built at the north end of the main runway and two more near the technical site north of the Distillery and Brackla House which was apparently not used by the RAF Accommodation and administrative buildings were located in ten different sites east of the B9090 and scattered about the fields in the usual wartime pattern.

Flying started at Brackla when 2AGS at Dalcross began to use it as an RLG for their Defiants and Lysanders in July 1941. During the winter of 1941/42 it was used extensively when their parent base at Dalcross became badly water logged. On 29 December 1941 Whitley K9029 of 19 O T U Kinloss crash landed on fire but the crew escaped unhurt. Another Whitley K9017 crashed in an adjoining wood on 9 January 1942 and all five crew members were killed. By now Brackla had become an RLG for 19 OTU and in May 1942 the runways were wire meshed and the N/S runway extended to 1450 yds. 19 OTU continued to use the SLG with their Whitleys and Ansons throughout 1942 and 1943. Other aircraft came in occasionally and it is noted in the Kinloss ORB for 2 December 1943 that three Dakotas and three Horsas had landed at Kinloss en route from Langar to Brackla. This was probably part of the pre-invasion exercises carried out in the Moray Firth area.

During 1943 Brackla, in common with other SLGs was shuffled about between various units although 19OTU maintained a parent role even when none of its aircraft were actually using the strip. At this period some of the unused accommodation was occupied by the army.

2 AGS Dalcross returned in December 1943 this time with Martinets and Ansons. As 19 OTU were not using the airfield 19 (P) AFU used it as an RLG for its Oxfords from December 1943 to February 1944. The OTU gave up Brackla on 27 April 1944 and Oxfords from 14(P) AFU Banff used it as an RLG from June to September 1944. Situated in a quiet country area Brackla at this time seems to have been a popular posting. Bill Short, now residing in Morecombe recalls meeting his future wife there and they both preferred it to the more disciplined Kinloss.

By December 1944 the end of the war was in sight and it was obvious that there was a surplus of trained air crew in the RAF. Various units were formed into Aircrew Allocation Centres where the surplus aircrew would be selected for other jobs and also be prepared for eventual release. Brackla was one of the stations selected for this job and it must have been quite a shock to the first aircrew - especially those from overseas - when they arrived in the

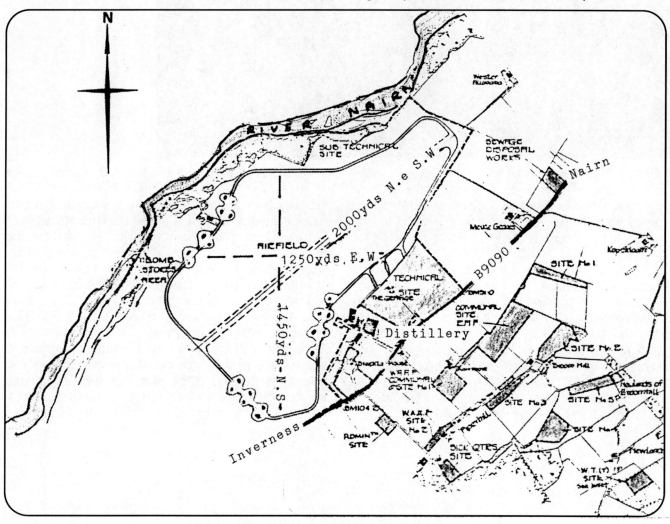

Royal Air Force Brackla. 57° 32' 30"N 03° 54' 38"W. 82 ft above sea level.

Aerial photo of Brackla in 1946, covered with Halifaxes awaiting disposal.

bitterly cold winter of 1944/1945. LACW Clarke (now Mrs Lane of Aberdeen) remembers arriving at the AAC and being given the job of starting a library. As the sites were so scattered a bike was a necessary issue. The AAC appears to have been a relaxed sort of unit but after a few months it was moved to Catterick.

Extract from Oct 1944 Issue of Tee Emm, the RAF Training Memorandum:-

'At Brackla the bundles of round and square pegs are sorted out so that they can be fitted into the approrpiate holes without the aid of a sledge-hammer. There are sports of every kind from football to fishing, and from clay pigeon sgooting to darts; the food is good and so is the local beer; there are discussion groups, lectures of all sorts by all sorts of experts; and above all NO BULL... No one stays at Brackla longer than a month'

Brackla now entered its last period of activity when 45 MU Kinloss took it over as 102 Sub Storage Unit in 2 February 1945. The airfield was to be used as storage and scrapping unit and the first of 130 Halifaxes arrived on 7 February 1945. Some Halifaxes were prepared for the French Air Force but the majority were scrapped. Many more Halifaxes and Warwicks flew in later but by the end of 1946 when the unit closed they had all been broken up and sold to the scrap merchants.

At present it is hard to realise that over 300 large aircraft were once parked on what are now farmer's fields. A few small buildings and parts of the perimeter are all that remains of this once crowded parking area. A few miles from Brackla, in the village of Auldearn, a large wooden hut, now being used as a shed, has been identified as part of the old Officers Mess from Kinloss.

Chapter Five

MORAY

In cottage gardens, sweet flowers drink
Last dregs of colour from the fading light,
Their scent floats on the dusk, to link
With the now distant thunder of the engines
In a strange deceit;

As if the world went well...

'Sound in the sky' 1943

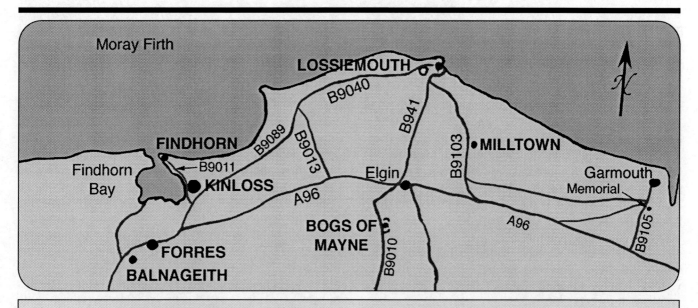

Two miles west of Forres on the A96 beside a 'Little Chef' restaurant, is a memorial cairn erected to the memory of those who served at RAF Forres. The remains of the airfield are still visible on the south side of the road. In Tolbooth Street in the centre of Forres is a plaque placed on the site of a Whitley crash in 1940.

RAF Kinloss is well signposted on the B9089 east of Forres. A diversion north on B9011 ends at the village of Findhorn the scene of some RAF flying boats' visits in 1937. This road passes the end of the main Kinloss runway. A lot of flying activity can be seen from here but parking is not encouraged. The B9089 passes through the main Kinloss camp with buildings both sides of the road. On the south side is Kinloss Abbey containing many RAF graves. The area past the camp on the north side was, in the early war years, a 'Q' site for Kinloss, but nothing now remains. The B9013 goes south to the A96 and Elgin.

At the west end of Elgin a right turn on to B9010 goes past the old airfield of RAF Elgin (Bogs of Mayne).

Some buildings are still standing and there is a well preserved 20 OTU badge mounted at the centre of the camp.

The town of Lossiemouth lies six miles north of Elgin on the A941. The town and RAF base are very close but best views of flying activities can be seen from the coast road B9040 near Covesea lighthouse. In the centre of the town at Lossie Green is a small plaque dedicated to the eleven victims of a Wellington crash in this area in 1945.

The B9103 east of Lossiemouth passes a churchyard containing many RAF and Naval graves. On the same road, three miles from Lossiemouth is RAF Milltown airfield, now a wireless station and closed to the public. The village of Garmouth is three miles further east. Outside the village on the B9015 on the roadside opposite Connagedale Farm is a small white cross erected to the memory of a pilot killed in a Hurricane mid-air collision over this spot in 1941.

The B9015 meets the A96 at village of Mosstodloch.

The county of Moray in the Nineties has one of the largest concentrations of air power in the UK at the RAF stations of Kinloss and Lossiemouth. Both these stations will

celebrate their 60th anniversaries in 1999 but there was flying activity of sorts in the county long before 1939.

As early as 13 August 1913 the *Forres Gazette*

7th August 1913 - near Elgin. A Farman being flown by Capt. Dawes of the RFC is seen en route Montrose - Nairn.
From a painting by the Author

reported on what was the first sight of an aeroplane at Forres. This was a flight from Montrose to Nairn by a Capt Dawes of the RFC and an NCO, name unknown. The Farman biplane had a slight mishap at Johnshaven but landed safely at Keith for re-fuelling before passing over Orton, Elgin and Forres to land at Nairn golf course. The return journey the following day was witnessed by vast crowds including Prince Wilhelm of Prussia who was staying at the Imperial Golf Hotel. About this period there are reports of seaplanes on Lochindorb, a loch south of Forres. The island with its ruined castle in the centre of the loch would have made flying rather hazardous and obviously nothing came of this venture.

Moray must have been overflown by Naval planes during and after World War 1 and the Forres Gazette gives various reports of aircraft and airships during Naval exercises at Invergordon.

It was during one of these exercises that the first aircraft crash occurred in Moray. In September 1929 a plane from HMS Argus landed near Duffus with engine trouble and another plane coming to its assistance hit a stone dyke which tore off its undercarriage. The aircraft was completely destroyed but the pilot was unhurt. As often with newspaper reports of that time no details of the aircraft were given but it was probably a Fairy 111F belonging to 441 Fleet Reconnaissance Flight which was serving on HMS Argus at the time.

A more pleasant incident had occurred in September 1927 when a plane actually landed in Cooper Park, Elgin. The DH60 was piloted by Flt. Lt. David D'Arcy A Greig who had spent some of his youth at Spynie Farm House and was

educated at Elgin Academy. He had flown north to visit some friends at nearby Westerfolds and then used his plane to go shopping in Elgin much to the excitement of the local inhabitants. De Arcy Greig was later to be one of the famous Schneider Trophy team in the early Thirties.

The first recorded aircraft landing in the Kinloss area was a D.H.60 Moth belonging to a young army officer of the KOSBs stationed at Fort George. On his way to spend the day at Findhorn Yacht Club in 1933 he landed his plane near Langcot House, the present residence of the Kinloss CO. This young officer, R. Speir was later to join the RAF and reach the rank of Wing Commander. His widow still lives in Nairn and takes a keen interest in ATC activities. Before the advent of either RAF Kinloss or Lossiemouth, one aspect of flying had been investigated in the Moray area. In June 1935 the Elgin and District Gliding Club was formed by a number of local enthusiasts with one Slingsby Primary Glider. The first flight was made by the President Mr A Buchan jr. Apparently various areas were used for take offs and

The first aircraft to land in the Kinloss area - a DH60 pilotted by G. Speir.
[Mrs Speir]

Short S18 and Blackburn Perth
in Findhorn Bay
[G. Fraser]

landings including Sherriffmill, Pittendreich and Pluscarden. The club was obviously very popular and it was reported in the local papers of 20 July, 1935 that an 83 year old Elgin lady, Mrs Barren, wished to join after experiencing the thrill of her first aeroplane flight.

The outbreak of WW II curtailed civil gliding but after the war the Navy operated a successful club from Milltown. When the Navy left and Milltown was taken over by radio aerials the RAF moved the club to Kinloss but retained the name Fulmar Gliding Club. The civilian Highland Gliding Club used the old airfield at Dallachy for their operations. but have now moved to a field at Birnie.

Flying boats also came to the Moray area albeit briefly just before World War II. Old photographs show two flying boats in Findhorn Bay and these can be identified as the Short S18 'Knuckleduster' and a Blackburn Perth. They belonged to 209 Squadron which was the only squadron to operate the S18 for trials in the Thirties. The S18 had a top speed of 150mph, a range of 850 miles and could carry 1000 lbs of bombs or an 18" torpedo. Defensive armament consisted of three machine guns. Despite providing valuable experience in handling monoplane flying boats the S18 project was cancelled and this single aircraft ended its days as an instructional airframe at Cosford in 1938.

What were they doing in Findhorn Bay? There is no record in the Squadron ORB so it can be presumed that they were investigating the bay as a possible flying boat base. During the Thirties the flying boat played an important role in the expanding RAF and new bases were required around the coast of Britain. Obviously Findhorn Bay was unsuitable and the flying boats left never to return.

Royal Air Force Forres (Balnageith)

Apart from the two large bases of Kinloss and Lossiemouth there were four smaller airfields in Moray. Approaching Forres from the west the first of these airfields was Balnageith which is still very noticeable after passing over Findhorn Bridge.

The unusually large area of flat ground is still devoid of hedges and would seem to be a perfect spot for an airfield. The Air Ministry must have thought so in the early war years when the farms in the Balnageith area were requisitioned and developed into a satellite for Kinloss. The grass airfield was marked out for three runways - the longest NE/SW passing dangerously close to Forres town. The other two runways formed an unusual arrangement of a cross over the centre of the main runway. These were probably only used if there was a cross wind on the main runway. A T2 hangar plus technical buildings were located on the east side with domestic and administrative buildings in the fields further east. Sixteen hard standings were constructed down the side of the River Findhorn with a short connecting perimeter track leading to the west end of the main runway. Forres possessed fewer buildings than most satellites probably because the close proximity of the main base Kinloss made transport of men and materials a fairly easy matter.

Before the airfield came into full operation the local town of Forres was the scene of a horrific crash on 7 November 1940. For no apparent reason Whitley N1440 dived from 1200 ft straight into the town centre. The aircraft which was completely destroyed, demolished the rear of two houses. Miraculously there were no civilian casualties but the RAF crew of six all perished. A plaque commemorating this incident was erected in 1989. RAF

Short S.18 over Findhorn Pier. [G. Fraser.]

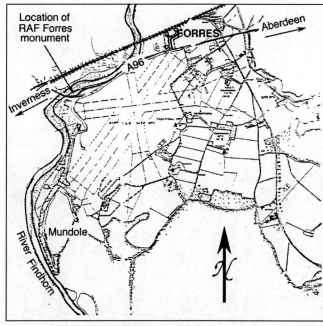

Royal Air Force Forres.
57° 35'53"N, 03° 38' 39"W. 50ft above sea level.

Above: Whitley N1412 on Forres airfield 1941.

Right: A somewhat battered Whitley at Forres.

Forres became officially operational on 3 January 1941when Kinloss was unusable due to snow, ice and water logging. 'D' Flight Whitleys became permanent residents on 30 April 1941 and 'C' Flight on 13 May 1941. The rest of 1941 was spent in intensive flying which badly damaged the grass surface. By January 1942 Forres was itself waterlogged and the Whitleys had to be diverted to Brackla for training. This happened just after a detachment of 614 Squadron Blenheims had used the airfield for army co-operation training.

Early summer 1942 saw Forres aircraft go into action against a German target. 'Bomber' Harris was determined to release huge raids on German targets but in order to make up the magic figure of 1000 he had to scour the OTUs for aircraft flown by instructors and half trained crews. Forres contributed 12 Whitleys which flew to Abingdon on 24 August 1942. From there they bombed Bremen with the loss of one aircraft and crew taken prisoner.

The Whitley had been a reasonably good bomber in its time but those which formed the OTUs were veterans of many actions and were generally in a poor state of repair. This factor combined with inexperienced crews, poor weather and the local mountainous terrain, made flying from Forres extremely hazardous. Whitley N1373 stalled and crashed on the approach to land on 18

February 1942 killing six of its seven man crew Retired agricultural engineer Bill Shepherd remembers an incident in 1943 when, after scrabbling into the air the Starboard engine cowling fell off. They managed to bring the aircraft back safely. Some time later he had an even closer brush with death in somewhat unusual circumstances. Their crew had been doing their pre-flight checks when an irate Aussie crew claimed the aircraft had been allocated to them. The RAF crew left them to it but minutes later it crashed with no survivors, near Altyre, shortly after take off. Not all accidents happened in the air however. There was one spectacular explosion in August 1944 when Whitley D819 blew up outside a hangar due apparently to a fitter cleaning an engine with petrol while an electrician was fiddling with the electrics.

By the end of 1944 the need for aircrew was decreasing and Forres was reduced to Care and Maintenance on 22 October 1944. The buildings were then used to house POWs and later members of the Polish Army. Quite a few of these Poles settled in the Forres area rather than return to Soviet-occupied Poland.

There was still some flying activity in the area from a concrete strip on the Mundole side of the field in 1960. This was used by a local businessman. Some old RAF buildings still stand on the dispersals and one or two have been converted to dwelling houses. Despite encroaching building from Forres and a small housing estate on the Mundole side Balnageith still looks like an airfield and it is easy to imagine the hive of aircraft activity which occurred there during the war years.

In 1996 a group of local people decided that a

Whitley and crew, RAF Forres 1941. [RAF Kinloss]

Dummy camp at Forres with T2 hangar and Whitleys of 19 OTU. *[PRO]*

Two photographs of the memorial cairn at Forres. In the background can just be made out some of the old RAF buildings on the edge of the airfield. *[author]*

suitable monument should be erected before all traces of this airfield vanish completely. Practical and financial help was soon forthcoming and the monument, a stone cairn and plaque, was erected at the roadside near the Findhorn bridge and overlooking the old airfield.

On May 29 1997 the monument was unveiled by the Lord Lieutenant of Moray, Air Vice Marshal G. A. Chesworth CB. OBE, DFC. JP in the presence of a large crowd of local people and ex-members of RAF Forres. A flypast by a Kinloss Nimrod and a Tiger Moth completed the ceremony. All the airfields in Moray now have appropriate monuments to record their past achievements

Royal Air Force Elgin (Bogs of Mayne)

About three miles south west of the town of Elgin at a cross roads on the narrow B9010 road is an earth mound surmounted by a large concrete 20 OTU crest. This is the most tangible reminder of the old Elgin airfield also called Bogs of Mayne.

During the hey day of civil flying expansion in 1934 Elgin Town Council considered an application from Highland Airways to develop an area at Wester Manbeen farms for use as a stop on the Aberdeen/Inverness route. Nothing seems to have come of this idea but obviously the level farm lands attracted the attention of the Air Ministry so that when RAF Lossiemouth was built, Bogs of Mayne was also developed as a Satellite Landing Ground. Completed by the Royal Engineers at the beginning of June 1940 the airfield was immediately obstructed because of the invasion scare. The actual airfield was laid out between the River Lossie and the B9010 road with landing areas north/south 1400yds. east/west 1250 yds, and south east/north west 1100 yds. A perimeter track with 18 hard standings was laid out parallel to the River Lossie. The two farms of Wester and Easter Manbeen were left intact but soon became surrounded by huts and technical buildings. Two hangars, a B1 and a T2 were built at the south-west corner of the airfield. The bomb store site straddled the southern end of the main landing strip. Domestic and administrative buildings were scattered in sites throughout the fields to the west. There were 15 sites in total which makes Bogs of Mayne very well equipped for a Satellite role although expansion of the airfield may have been mooted at some time.

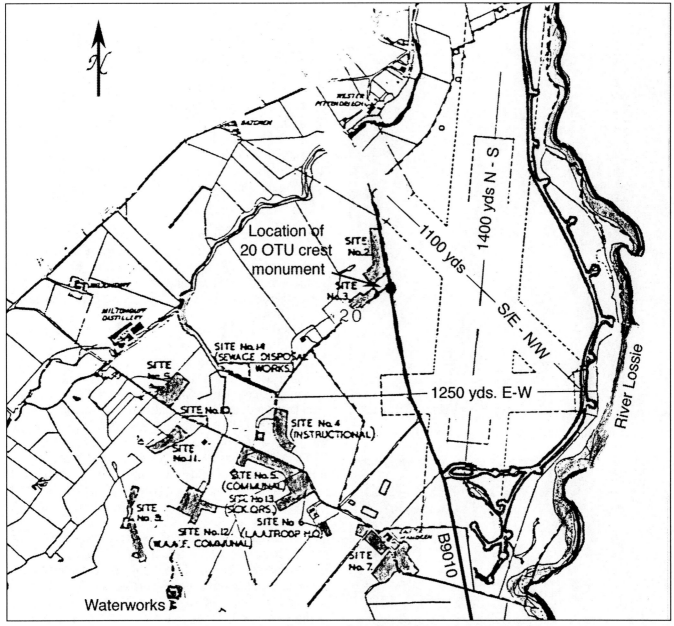

Royal Air Force Elgin 57° 37'30" N 03° 20'15"W. 100ft above sea level.

To relieve the congestion when 20 OTU arrived at Lossiemouth, 57 Squadron Blenheim detachment moved to Bogs of Mayne in August 1940 and continued their anti-shipping operations from there until leaving for Wyton in November. The Blenheims of 21 Squadron also used Bogs of Mayne in 1940 as did the Lysanders of 614 Squadron based at Longman. After the German air attacks on Lossiemouth in October 1940 a detachment of 232 Squadron Hurricanes from RAF Skitten arrived for air defence duties. This detachment left for Montrose in April 1941 without having made any contact with enemy aircraft. Between April and September 1941 Bogs of Mayne was also to have detachments of Hurricanes of 17 Squadron from Sumburgh and Castletown. These later moved to Peterhead, Skaebrae and Tain.

During the stay of 17 Squadron two of its Hurricanes collided near Garmouth. One pilot baled out safely but the other, Sgt May, was killed in the crash. Local residents erected a small white cross at the roadside near the place of the crash and this cross can still be seen near Connagedale Farm.

20 OTU started using Bogs of Mayne on a permanent basis when 'A' Fit Wellingtons moved in on 18 April 1941. In June of that year a sodium flare path was installed for stimulated night flying - a necessity because of the' limited hours of darkness in those northern latitudes. The build up of flying training continued throughout 1941 and 1942. Wellingtons and Ansons of 20 OTU were the main users but Whitleys of 19 OTU Kinloss were occasional visitors. One of these, a Whitley V P499, overshot when attempting to land in the early hours of 20 March 1942. After stalling, the aircraft crashed into trees and burst into flames 200 yds from Mayne House. The six man crew were all killed. It is possible that parts of this aircraft are still embedded in the surviving trees. The couple of tiny wooded hills in the vicinity were obviously hazards of the training crews

Heavy landing by a Hurricane EF:R of 232 Squadron.

and one was nick-named "Gremlin's Roost" probably by crews who came too close to the tree tops for comfort.

During the summer of 1942 Bogs of Mayne was used as a departure point for 20 OTU Wellingtons going to English bases to take part in the early 1000 bomber raids. 14 Wellingtons with two Ansons for ground crew left for Stanton Harcourt on 26 May 1942, and after raiding Cologne returned on 3 June 1942. 12 Wellingtons and a Harrow left on 24 June 1942 and after losing an aircraft over Essen returned on 28 June 1942. Eight Wellingtons and three Ansons left for Snaith and returned on 29 June 1942 with one aircraft lost over Bremen. The last trip consisted of 11 Wellingtons which left on 10 September 1942 and returned on 12 September 1942 after a raid on Dusseldurf from Elsham Wolds.

Normal flying training took its toll of aircraft and crews. On 8 May 1942 Wellington 28852 crashed while overshooting killing one crew member. On 20 July 1942 Wellington HT 867 crashed on airfield buildings killing the pilot. Only one crew member survived when on 6th August, 1942 Wellington R 1480 crashed near D Fit dispersal after its Port wing caught fire causing the structure to collapse. Throughout 1942 and 1943 the units's ORB recorded numerous crashes, overshoots and belly landings.

During 1943, Oxfords of 19(P) AFU Dalcross used the airfield for a short period. This was the time when SLGs were being swapped around between parent airfields as different Commands wrangled over their allocation.

It was during 1943 that 20 OTU was granted its official badge. The Lossiemouth CO asked the W/O I/C Workshops, W/O W G Horner to manufacture replica badges for Lossiemouth and Bogs of Mayne. A Cpl Michelmore drew the badges on a plaster cast which was used to make a mould. This was filled with re-inforced concrete, allowed to set for seven days and primed for fourteen days before erection.

The Lossiemouth badge has disappeared but it says a lot for its excellent construction that the Bogs of Mayne

badge is still in perfect condition. Recent enquiries have cast doubt on wether there were two badges. There is proof of a badge positioned near the flagpole at the entrance to Lossiemouth, and one theory is that this badge was moved to Bogs of Bayne when the Navy took over Lossiemouth. A local farmer, Mr Joughan, moved the badge to it's present position in 1968 - but by the early 1970's it was in a rather neglected state, so I ltook on the job, cleaning and painting it for a few years until RAF Lossiemouth took on the task, and now keep it in excellent condition.

On 23 January 1944 Wellington HE541 was on a fighter affiliation exercise from Bogs of Mayne. During a dummy attack by fighters the Wellington made a medium turn to starboard but failed to recover and crashed on Elgin Golf Course about 300 yds west of the Club house, killing all six crew members. The crater caused by the crash can still be seen.

The constant flying plus water logging played havoc with the surface of the airfield. Some bar and rod tracking

The cross at Connagedale Farm site of the Hurricane crash.

[author]

A Wellington and groundcrew of 20 OTU at the Bogs of Mayne. *[J.C.Lawson]*

had been laid, but in the autumn of 1944 a full bar and rod system was installed. Mr Lawton, now residing in Durham, recalls arriving at Bogs of Mayne in a party of 30 from 5016 Airfield Construction Squadron 5351 Wing normally based at Liberton near Edinburgh. Six weeks had began allocated for the job but by working from 8 am to 7:30 pm the work was completed two days ahead of schedule. As a reward the WAAF adjutant laid on a party for the squadron in the NAAFI. Further work had to be carried out on the tracking in March 1945 but with the end of the war the airfield went to C & M on 24 June 1945. At its peak strength at the end of 1944 there were 1087 RAF and 234 WAAF on the unit.

On 28 July 1944 Bogs of Mayne was taken over by 46 MU as Sub Storage Unit specialising in the storage of Lancasters and Harvards. When the Navy took over Lossiemouth in July 1946 the MU still carried on with their disposal of aircraft either by flying out or scrapping. No 105 SSS came under the control of 45 MU Kinloss in January 1947 and probably ceased shortly afterwards.

The airfield has now been dug up in a series of gravel pits though the perimeter track is still largely intact. The hangars and tower have vanished but quite a lot of buildings are still in use by local farmers while ruins of others abound in the fields and woods. Of these the Decontamination Centre, built of solid concrete is intact and used as a builders workshop. Perhaps the most interesting relic is the Waterworks. Bogs of Mayne was unusual in that it had its own waterworks consisting of a concrete dam across a small stream and an underground pumping station. This was apparently abandoned with the rest of the station in 1947 but a few years ago a local man managed to get the pumps working and now uses the water for his fish farm located in what were the WAAF quarters. A good example of swords into ploughshares.

Bogs of Mayne airfield, with a number of aircraft visible. They are awaiting scrapping - the date is 26 August 1946.

Right: Old RAF Buildings Bogs of Mayne 1991 . *[author]*

Below: The Interior of the waterworks engine room. *[author]*

Bottom: Bogs Of Mayne 1991. *[author]*

Royal: Air Force Milltown

During WW II a lot of the major airfields in Britain developed "Q" sites in order to divert possible enemy air attacks. Situated a few miles from the airfield, the "Q"! sites were basically dummy airfields equipped with a lighting system which could be operated during an air attack and theoretically divert the raiders from the main target. How effective these diversions were is not known.

RAF Lossiemouth developed a "Q" site on some level farmland at Milltown three miles S.E. of Lossiemouth. On 27 October 1941 this "Q" site was abandoned and a start was made on developing the area as a proper airfield. Three runways were laid out; 054° 1900 yds, 114° 1540 yds and 175° 1400 yds. Twenty seven hard standings were constructed around the perimeter track and two hangars a TI and a BI were built. There where the usual technical and administrative buildings with domestic sites scattered in the surrounding fields. Milltown was intended to house a Coastal Command OTU with a secondary facility as a Bomber Command advance base to be used instead of Peterhead. The necessity for another airfield in this already crowded area cannot have been of any great urgency as it was not expected to be completed until April 1943. By then the original plan for a CC OTU had been abandoned and on 14 June, 1943 Milltown became a satellite for 20 OTU's Wellingtons with C flight moving over permanently on 5 September 1943.

For the next year the whistling roar of Wellingtons was a familiar sound around Milltown as more crews were trained for Bomber Command. Accidents were frequent but fortunately most of them were of a relatively minor nature such as undercarriages collapsing. One serious accident occured on 25 October 1943 when a Wellington crashed on overshooting killing the four crew. Another crashed in the sea on 26 May, 1944 close enough to the shore to leave the fin protruding above the shallow water. Gliders, probably Horsas, came for Exercise Tyndall in December 1943. The airfield was also used for diversions and it was noted that four Stirlings ex ops came in on 20 October 1943. On 28 July 1944 a Liberator FL930 from 86 Squadron landed when it was unable to reach its home base of Tain after two engines were badly shot up. Eleven

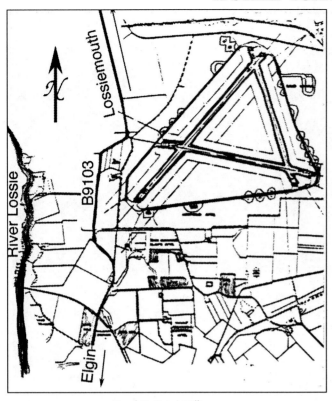

Royal Air Force Milltown
57° 40' 38"N 03° 13' 38"W. 12 ft above sea level.

Lancasters diverted in on 27 August 1944.

By the autumn of 1944 the need for trained aircrew was decreasing and Milltown was given up by 20 OTU on 1 September 1944. The station was now taken over by Coastal Command and the first squadron to arrive on 15

September 1944 was 224 with Liberators MkVIs from St Eval. 224 was tasked to seek and destroy U-boats and shipping off the Norwegian and Danish coasts. 224's patrols started well with Liberator 'R' damaging a U-boat on the 18 September and 'C' sinking a U-boat on the 19 September. Another was sunk on the 29 September by Liberator 'A'. Co-operating with a Wellington of 407 RCAF squadron one of 224's Liberators damaged a U-boat on the 30 October. The fine weather caused Milltown to be used for a lot of diversions in the winter of 1944/1945 when bases farther south were fog bound. Three Lancasters from 44 Squadron and two from 207 came in on 25 October, 1944 and 14 Lancasters from 97 Squadron Coningsby landed on 13 December 1944. On 21 December, 1944 dense fog down south caused massive diversions and Milltown played host to 21 Lancasters from 617 Squadron Woodhall Spa, 7 Lancasters from 189 Squadron Fulbeck, 9 Lancasters from 227 Squadron Balderton, 4 Fortresses from 214 Squadron Oulton and 5 Liberators of 223 Squadron from Oulton. A 502 Squadron Halifax made an emergency landing on 15 October, 1944 after flak from a ship being attacked off Norway ignited a flare in the bomb bay and caused a bomb to hang up.

Milltown played its part in the sinking of the Tirpitz when along with Lossiemouth and Kinloss it was used as forward base for the Lancasters of 617 Squadron. Twelve Lancasters took off on what was to be an abortive mission on 29 October 1944 but their raid on 12 November 1944 was to succeed in finally sinking the *Tirpitz*.

On 14 November 1944 a Liberator of 224 Squadron failed to return after being attacked by enemy fighters. The crew of another Liberator saw a pall of smoke rising from the sea but there were no survivors. 224 started converting to MkVIII Liberators on 27 November 1944 and were out of line on training until 27 December 1944. With their new aircraft 224 continued their shipping patrols

Two views of Liberator GRVIII from 111 OTU with slight undercarriage trouble 17 October 1945.
[via V. Griffen]

224 Sqn aircrew pose on and in front of one of their Liberators at Milltown - around July 1945. *[via W Moses]*

with four more attacks in March and April. On 5 May 1945 Liberator T' with the squadron Commander Wg Cdr. Ensor as captain was patrolling the Inner Kattagat for escaping subs. Four U-boats were seen and one was sunk. This was the second U-boat kill for Wg Cdr. Ensor, his first being in November 1942. Their last wartime operational sortie was flown by Flt Lt Pretlove on 2 June 1945. Their total wartime score was 11 U-boats destroyed and three shared.

One of Milltown's runways was closed for repair in January 1945 and the Liberators of 224 had to go to Lossiemouth for loading. The favour was returned in February when Lossie runways were being repaired and their Wellingtons used Milltown for circuits and training. The end of the war in Europe saw the arrival of 311

Squadron Liberators. This Czech squadron which had been previously on anti sub work from Predannick in Cornwall and Tain, was now taken over by Transport Command and used Milltown to convert to Liberator Mk Vis. Their short period of transport work had mostly been used to carry Czech forces back to their homeland and they were disbanded in February 1946.

224 departed for St Eval in July 1945 and were replaced by 111 OTU from the Bahamas with Liberators and Halifaxes. 1674 HCU also arrived at that time also with Liberators. These were the last RAF units to use Milltown and were disbanded when the Navy took over in 1946.

Milltown now became HMS Fulmar 11, a satellite of HMS Fulmar at Lossiemouth. A mirror landing installation was installed so that student pilots could carry out MADDLs (Mirror Aerodrome Dummy Deck Landings). The first squadron to use the airfield was 767 with Seafires, Fireflys and Harvards. These were later joined by the Seafires of 766. The Lossiemouth Handling Squadron operated Meteor TT20s from there between 1958 and 1962. During the period of Naval occupation Milltown was used by various FAA squadrons such as 736, 738, 759 and 764. These operated a variety of aircraft including Buccaneers, Sea Furies, Sea Vampires, Sea Hornets, Hunters and Scimitars. During 1952 and 1953 Milltown was used for all Fulmar flying training when the Lossiemouth runways were being repaired.

On 5 July 1948 two Seafires of 767 Squadron based at Milltown collided near Glenlatterach Reservoir south of Elgin. One pilot was killed but the other baled out safely. The crankshaft, propeller hub and other wreckage still lie on the hillside near the Reservoir.

The RAF still used the Milltown occasionally for exercises. Hercules were there in 1968. From March 23 until April 2 1971 seven Harriers of 1 Squadron operated with the support of nine Hercules, three Andovers, seven Argosys and a Belfast. Four Harriers of 1 Squadron came for Exercise "Snowy Owl" in the spring of 1972.

With the RAF returning to Lossiemouth in September 1972 Milltown relinquished its Naval role. A detachment of Harriers with Hercules support were probably the last aircraft to use the runways in the spring of 1973 during Exercise "Skyrut': The Fulmar Gliding Club moved to Kinloss in 1976 and Milltown was officially

RAF Milltown, as seen from the air in 1946, before the Navy moved in.

The remains of a Seafire, Glenlattrach 1990. *[author]*

closed for flying on March 1977.

The station now became a radio transmitting site of 81 Signals Unit and the airfield was soon covered with a forest of aerials. As Milltown is now also used by a RAF Regiment unit it is virtually a closed area and little can be seen of present operations or former RAF buildings.

The Moray Spitfire

A Spitfire for £5,000 would be a real bargain in 1998, yet that was the price quoted in 1940 when communities throughout the country were asked to contribute as much as possible for the purchase of extra Spitfires for the RAF

Like other communities Moray rallied to the cause and with many fund raising activities in the autumn of 1940 produced the necessary £5,000 for one of the famous fighters. In recognition of the efforts a Spitfire was named "Moray" and a scroll commemorating the event still hangs in the office of the local newspaper *"The Northern Scot"*.

The history of many of these named aircraft has not been recorded but we know quite a lot about "Moray". 'A Mk VB Spitfire W3773 took the name, when it left the factory at Castle Bromwich on 22 August 1941.

On 7 September the Spitfire was flown to Hornchurch where it joined 54 Squadron. During the next ten days it was flown by various pilots without seeing any action but on the 17th, "Moray" was the mount for Sqn Ldr N. "Fanny" Orton, a renowned fighter pilot with at least 17 kills to his credit. The operation was one of the "Circus" type where the Spitfires protected Blenheims attacking factories at Lens and Bethune in France. During the attack the British planes were set upon by ME 109s and in the confused fighting which followed Sqn Ldr Orton was shot down. No trace of the pilot or plane has ever been found but another pilot saw a ME109 being shot down by the Sqn Ldr.

"Moray's" life was short - a mere nine flying hours, but even that brief life was sufficient to strike a blow against the enemy and the people of the county of Moray can be justly proud of their very own Spitfire.

The Moray Spitfire

Chapter Six

ROYAL AIR FORCE KINLOSS

They go among the wandering stars,
And the glory gathered clouds divide
Before the broad-winged shining cars
Whereon the new knight errants ride;
Distance and time, and ancient fears Have been forgot;
Storm and the sea, the old barriers, control them not.

Neil East

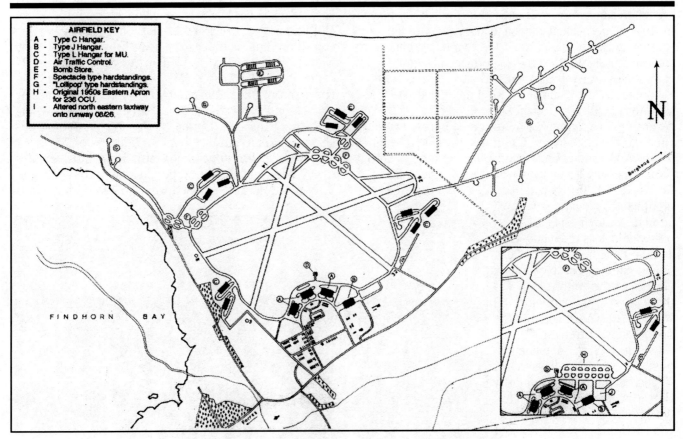

Royal Air Force Kinloss 1944. The inset shows changes made up to 1958.
57° 38' 45"N 03° 33' 45"W. 19ft above sea level.

A couple of miles east of Forres on the A96 a large group of buildings can be seen about half a mile to the north. At first glance this looks almost like a small town but a closer look reveals the fact that it is a large airfield. Most of the buildings are camouflaged to merge with the landscape but one large hangar painted "hemp", Nimrod aircraft of the same colour and several red brick buildings stand out against the green forest background. At present this airfield of Kinloss is the fourth largest in the UK with four resident Nimrod squadrons and a constant stream of NATO visitors.

When the RAF Expansion Period started in 1937 many new airfields had to be built to house the increasing number of aircraft. At that time Kinloss was a flat area of fertile farms bordered on the north seaward side by heath and sand dunes. When surveyers arrived in 1937 it was soon obvious that they had found a perfect site for their requirements. The farms of East Langcot, Doon Park, Kinloss House and parts of Cullerne, Muirton and Rose Valley were requisitioned and by 1938 work was in full swing, filling ditches, removing trees and hedgerows and levelling the ground. Some of the farm buildings were demolished but others such as Langcot House and Kinloss House were retained for use by the RAF.

The airfield was laid out with three runways - 208° 1400 yds, 263° 2000 yds, and 321° 1400 yds, surrounded by a perimeter track and hard standings. The landing area was on the level Kinloss plain, hangars and technical buildings on the south side, and domestic and office buildings further south where the ground sloped

Before flying could commence, the airfield site had to be cleared - clearance of Muirton Wood in 1937 [Bill Shand]

upwards. Kinloss was a mixture of permanent buildings such as three C type hangars and temporary accommodation, mostly wooden huts. Even at this period in 1938 a permanent station had been envisaged for Kinloss and with this in mind the temporary huts were laid out in a similar pattern to a permanent station.

Kinloss was officially opened as 14 Flying Training School under the command of Gp Capt P. Peck DSO, MC on 1 April 1939 - some might say an appropriate date. The advance party of airmen arrived from Montrose two days later and the first aircraft, Oxford N4584 piloted by Flt Lt Widdowson, landed on 9 May 1939. According to an old station messing account there were 257 airmen living at Kinloss on 1 July 1939 and it cost £413-13-10 to feed the month's aggregate of 7307 airmen, which is not as parsimonious as it sounds when at that time beef was $4^{1/2}$d a pound and a loaf cost 1d a pound. At the outbreak of war there were 400 airmen, 50 soldiers, 20 WAAFs and 10 boys on the station strength.

The FTS was intended to operate 38 Oxfords and 26 single engined aircraft mostly Harvards, but also a few obsolete Hinds and Audaxes. Pilot training was carried out throughout the summer of 1939

but with the declaration of war on 3rd September the station went on a war footing. Aircraft were hurriedly camouflaged, blackouts were enforced, uniforms worn and gas masks carried at all times. Shortly after the war commenced the station had its first crash on 15 Sept. 1939 when Cpl Happell was killed in Audax K5207. On 28 September, 1939 Oxford N4758 crashed killing the two crew. During the autumn of 1939 more aircraft, mainly Ansons and Harvards, arrived to increase the training capacity of the unit. During this period the station was also used as an advance base for Whitleys of 77, 10, 51 and 102 Squadrons operating North Sea patrols. Spitfires of 609 also came for a short period at the end of the year. Two more Harvards crashed with the loss of their pilots

RAF Kinloss, as photographed by the German Luftwaffe on 2 October 1939. [via Wg Cdr Chris Birks]

Left: Harvards replaced Harts at 14 FTS during the autumn of 1939.

Below: For twin-engined training Airspeed Oxford's were used by 14 FTS. *[RAF Kinloss]*

in December 1939.

The first WAAFs had arrived in the autumn of 1939 to be viewed with some mistrust by the all male establishment. Mrs Ross, now residing at Locherbie, was one of these WAAFS. She remembers especially the severe winter conditions made worse by their primitive quarters. She also recalls that Plt Off Hillary (the future author of *"The Last Enemy"*), did his training at 14 FTS although he does not mention it by name in his book.

During this period, training crews were liable to use any level field in the vicinity for practice landings. So common was this in the area around Fochabers that local people still think that it was an official landing area!

Despite the severe weather at the beginning of 1940 flying training carried on but with the invasion of Norway and Denmark in April 1940 a change of role for the station was initiated.

Changes in RAF policy caused 14 FTS to depart for Cranfield on 20 April 1940. On 17 May 1940 a new unit, 19 Operational Training Unit, was officially formed. Operating Whitleys for training night bomber crews, this was to be the major unit at Kinloss for the remainder of the war. Detachments of Hampdens of 50 Squadron and Whitleys of 77 and 102 during this period used Kinloss as a base for attacking targets in Norway.

It was at this time that another unit arrived at Kinloss. This was 45 Maintenance Unit which was to receive aircraft from the makers and prepare them for squadron use. Although officially opened on 6 April, 1940 the MU did not receive its first aircraft until May due to their hangar accommodation on the north side of the airfield not being completed. At first the MU dealt with Oxfords and Hawker biplanes but by June 1940 it started to specialize in Halifaxes, Whitleys, Wellingtons and Spitfires.

June 1940 was a period of upheaval on most RAF units throughout the country and Kinloss was no exception. The arrival of the OTU caused severe accommodation problems as much of the domestic site was still in the process of being built. Kinloss in June 1940 was bursting at the seams but still had to accommodate 100 men of 88 Squadron evacuated from France after losing their Battles and equipment. Fortunately they stayed only briefly before going to Driffield to re-form. Many local buildings had to be commandeered for accommodation. These included such unlikely places as Glenburgie Distillery and a local church. By 12 June 1940 the number of airmen on the unit had passed the thousand mark with 300 soldiers and 40 WAAFS. The airmen's numbers had increased to 1500 by the end of July.

With the threat of a German invasion now imminent a defence system for the camp had to be set up and by August 1940 the perimeter had been wired, pill boxes and trenches prepared and facilities provided for fire fighting and anti gas precautions. 292 A/A battery had arrived in April but by the summer all personnel had to be ready to act in a defensive role should the need arise. The defence of the station was organised by an ex Boer War army officer and very soon airmen were training for the unaccustomed roles of machine gunners, guards and fire fighters. The aircraft of the OTU, were, on the receipt of code words "Julius Caesar", to be made ready to attack any enemy attempting to land on the nearby coast.

When it was formed in May 1940 19 OTU had on its

Whitleys of 19 OTU bask in the glow of a sunset.
[RAF Kinloss]

Left: A 19 OTU Whitley is dismantled after making a crash-landing at Wick in November 1940. *[Brian Hansley]*

Below: Whitley P5064 'G' of 502 Sqn crashed two miles east of Kinloss after take-off for night flying, 5th November 1940. *[RAF Kinloss]*

strength 48 Whitley Mk Ills and 16 Ansons. These aircraft had been obtained from many different operational squadrons as could be seen from the varied camouflage schemes ranging from the all black of night bombers to the normal green and brown day colouring. The first course of 13 pilots, 12 AGs and six Air Observers started on 15 June 1940 and the second course of 11 pilots, six AGs and six Observers commenced on 29 June. On 29 July 1940 the first crews to complete the course went to 78 Squadron then operating Whitleys from Dishforth. The busy flying programme was soon marred by casualties. All the crews were killed when Whitley P5006 crashed on Ben Aigan on 23 October 1940 and Whitley H9031 crashed in the sea on 5 November 1940. Nine more aircrew lost their lives when P5064 crashed on 5 November 1940 and N1440 on 7 November 1940. The latter aircraft crashed for no apparent reason in the centre of Forres. Training aircraft

were not even safe from friendly aircraft as the crew of N1505 found out on 25 November 1940 when they were attacked by two Hurricanes but managed to land with undercarriage up at Wick.

There was probably good reasons for the Hurricane pilots being trigger happy as at that time there were fears that the Germans would use captured British aircraft to penetrate UK airspace. In his book *"Sky Spy"* Ray Holmes recalls being ordered from Castletown, where his 504 Squadron was based, to intercept a strange aircraft near Kinloss. Approaching the aircraft he found it was a Whitley and though the pilot did not fire the colours of the day he did give him a friendly wave. On returning to base Ray Holmes was informed that the Whitley had turned and set off for German occupied Nonvay. No official information has ever been given about the truth or otherwise of the captured aircraft stories.

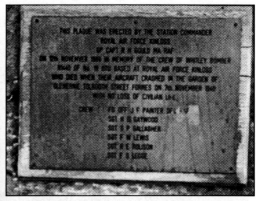

Left: the ruined buildings in Forres following the crash of Whitley N1440 in November 1940. *[A. Grant]*
Above: The commemorative plaque marking the sad event. *[Author]*

By the end of 1940 45 MU had 45 aircraft in storage but during the year they had dealt with a variety of aircraft including obsolete types like Wallace, Harrow and Envoy. They now processed Whitleys, Halifaxes, Spitfires and Wellingtons in a K type hangar on the main site and two L type hangars on No 4 site.

The severe weather of January 1941 caused problems with snow, ice and floods, and at the end of January the new SLG at Forres had to be used. In this hectic period the ground crew's job in keeping the aircraft flying was never ending. Jim Ritchie, now residing in Kent, recalls arriving at Kinloss in October 1940 as a 17yr old airframe fitter straight from Halton and probably the youngest airman on the station. Shift work was the norm with a rather disorganised system where an airman could work from 8am to 5pm, then Ilpm to 3am, and back again at 8am. An 80 to 100 hour week was common. Weekends off were unknown but if a major servicing was completed in nine days, the tenth day was free. Like most airmen Jim Ritchie got no leave in his first year at the unit and had not even been given a 48hr pass.

During the first half of 1941 the Whitley IIIs were gradually replaced by 1Vs and Vs. The new aircraft with only 200 to 300 hours on the clock should have been more reliable than the ancient IIIs but in the early months they gave a lot of trouble and the 800 men in the maintenance hangars had their work cut out just to keep them flying. For the first year of flying by the OTU, 60 Whitley accidents of various categories had occurred and it is noted in the station ORB that flying hours per fatal accident was 3141. In January 1941 a new flare path of 27 lights was erected but this had to be relit if the wind changed as the airfield was still grass. During this period a Q site (dummy airfield) was laid out at Rose Valley which had been used as a bombing range and it is believed to have been ear marked as a possible site for a satellite airfield for Kinloss or Lossiemouth. The extremely boggy terrain ruled this out however. Retired Wg Cdr Ken Greene who farms at Lower Hempriggs, east of Kinloss, recalls an incident while serving as a Signals Instructor on the OTU. On 27 July 1941 his Whitley K9033 had just taken off on the second circuit of a circuits training programme when at 02:35 the Starboard engine failed. The next thing Ken knew was his head hitting his radio and on moving back to investigate he found the aircraft filling with water. All the crew got out safely into their dinghy and were soon picked up by a launch from Burghead where they were taken to the Commercial Hotel for a medicinal dram. The Whitley still lies in Burghead Bay about a mile from Ken's farm.

In September 1941 Kinloss was the base for an attack on the German battleship *Admiral Von Scheer* at anchor in Oslo harbour. The squadron selected for the operation was No. 90 based at Polebrook and the only RAF squadron to have Flying Fortresses at that time. Their first operation to Wilhelmshaven in July had been a failure but high hopes were held out for the Oslo trip. Four Fortresses - AN525, AN532, AN533 and AN535-complete with ground crew arrived at Kinloss on 5 September 1941. On their first attempt to bomb the Scheer the Fortresses failed to find the target but bombed the secondary target from 30,000 ft. Returning to Kinloss they had to wait for more bombs from Polebrook before trying again on the 8 September. Of the four aircraft which set out, AN533 'N' vanished without trace, AN532 'J' returned with bombs due to heavy cloud making bombing impossible, and AN525 'D' was shot down by Me 109s, crashing in Norway - the first B-17 to be shot down during the war. After abandoning his sortie Sgt Wood, the pilot of AN535 'O' jettisoned his bombs and climbed to 34,000 ft. Oxygen

Fuselage of Fortress AN535 'O' being removed by 56 MU after it's crash landing at Kinloss in September 1941. *[Ian Angus]*

A pair of aerial photographs of RAF Kinloss, taken by the Luftwaffe, 14 March 1941 showing the amount

problems caused one of the crew to pass out and when the aircraft descended to 29,000 ft it was attacked by an ME 109 and a gunner was killed. By now the cabin was full of glycol smoke and the astrodome had to be jettisoned. With one engine stopped and two damaged, and aileron controls shot away, the pilot fought to keep control with elevators and rudder. Jim Ritchie remembers seeing the Fortresses returning with the badly damaged aircraft skidding across the airfield, but fortunately not catching fire. 90 Squadron did a few more operations but the Fortresses were never a success and the RAF were not to use them again until a later version had been produced.

1942 started with a Whitley being fired on by a convoy in the Firth - the Navy never seemed to get out of the habit of firing on everything that flew. On 6 January 1942 Whitley N1498 crashed in snow 2000 ft up on Carn a Choire Mhoir 17 miles south east of Inverness. There were no survivors and 42 years later volunteers built a memorial cairn at the site where some of the wreckage still remains.

In March 1942 Kinloss was one of the bases used for attacks on the German battleship *Tirpitz* anchored in Asen Fjord. Twelve Halifaxes of 35 Squadron took part in an unsuccessful attack on 30 March 1942. Two aircraft failed to return from this trip and two were also lost when

of overlay, the Luftwaffe camera's generated. The aircraft is flying to the top of the page. *[both Ian Keillar]*

35 Squadron attacked again from Kinloss on 27 April 1942. Of these two, one, W1048 crash landed on a frozen lake. When the ice thawed the Halifax sank and remained on the bottom of the lake until 1973 when a RAF sub aqua team brought it to the surface. After dismantling it was taken to the RAF Museum Hendon where it is now on display.

In June 1942 the aircraft and crews of 19 OTU had their first taste of operational flying. The early 1000 bomber raids required many OTU aircraft to make up the numbers and 19 OTU sent twelve Whitleys and crews to Abingdon from where they made an attack on Bremen with the loss of one aircraft on 24 June 1942. Apart from the visiting squadrons the normal routine for 19 OTU in 1942 was intensive flying training, with, unfortunately a higher than normal quota of accidents. The unit strength by the end of the year was 50 Whitleys, 15 Ansons, a Defiant and two Lysanders. The constant circuit flying was playing havoc with the grass airfield and there was great relief when concrete runways started being laid in the Autumn of 1942. The job was carried out by a USAAF Engineer unit which also built the runways at Lossiemouth during the same period thus giving them valuable experience for the massive airfield building

Halifax W1048 salvaged from a Norwegian lake in 1973. *[Aeroplane Monthly]*

programme in east Anglia. The glaring white concrete was camouflaged by spraying it with tar, laying down wood chips and spraying this green.

During 1941 and 1942 45 MU had expanded considerably. It now occupied eleven hangars around the airfield plus many hard standings stretching through what is now the Findhorn Foundation and out into the woods of Roseisle. Fields were also requisitioned on the south side of the airfield where the married quarters are now situated.

In the summer of 1941 the SLGs for storing aircraft were opened at Dornoch and Kirkton across the Moray Firth in Easter Ross. The MU was now dealing with Spitfires, Wellingtons, Whitleys and Halifaxes. The MU also housed a detachment of civilians from Marshalls of Cambridge which repaired aircraft beyond the capacity of unit repair. Without this detachment many aircraft would have had to have been sent south.

By early 1943 there were over 2000 airmen on the station and this had risen to 2,700 by September. The messing account ledger for that period contains some interesting figures such as an airman's ration entitlement of 1/7 per day. An airwoman on the other hand was only entitled to 1/4. No doubt some Whitehall bureaucrat had decided that females needed less food than males. This was a very busy year for flying but despite the pressure of training the station was able to produce a formation of 27 Whitleys taking off at one minute intervals for a Wings for Victory show on 29 May 1943. The station ORB records more crashes and accidents than any other activity. A combination of worn out aircraft, inexperienced crews, bad weather and inhospitable terrain was a recipe for accidents and many air crew were lost before ever becoming operational. Perhaps the most bizarre accident occurred on 19 October 1943. Whitley N1369 was just starting its take off run for a night flight when the pilot aborted after experiencing a severe bump. Thinking he had burst a tyre he flashed his Aldis lamp through the window and found to his surprise that there was an Anson sitting on top of his fuselage. This Anson, DJ104, had landed squarely on top of the Whitley and both had to be towed away locked together. No one was hurt but it must have been an interesting Court of Enquiry.

Whitleys and Ansons had been the mainstay of the OTU since 1940 but they also had other aircraft for fighter affiliation. Until the middle of 1943 this work was carried out by a Defiant and four Lysanders. These aircraft were then replaced by six Martinets and later still by five Hurricanes. Master IIs were used in late 1944. Apart from the training aircraft there was a hack Oxford in Maintenance Flight and 1681 Bomber Defence Training flight had Tomahawks. The CO had a Tiger Moth which was replaced by a Magister in 1941. This was the aircraft that one CO was reputed to have used to drop hand grenades in Burghead Bay. The dead fish were later picked up by an ASR launch. Despite the fact that training units were being run down in 1944 due to a surplus of aircrew, 19 OTU actually replaced its aging Whitleys with Wellington Xs in October. The ground crew had done their Wellington training at 20 OTU Lossiemouth earlier in the year. During the four years that 19 OTU had used Whitleys they had lost 123 aircraft, 67% of that type lost in Scotland.

On 31 August 1944 Lancaster PD259 of 463 Sqn, RAF Waddington crashed at Cairn Dulnain north of Kingussie, killing all seven crew. Recovering the bodies was the first major task of the newly-formed Kinloss Mountain Rescue team. A lot of wreckage remains on the site to this day.

Throughout 1944 Kinloss was used a diversion airfield for many bomber squadrons, mostly Lancasters and

Hitching a ride! Anson aboard Whitley N1269 at Kinloss - 19 October 1043. *[Sqn Ldr Beeby]*

Sqn Ldr Gibbons and ATC examine the wreckage of 463 Sqn Lancaster PD259 which crashed at Tomatin on 31 August 1944, during an expedition to the site in June 1994 . The squadron code J:OI in red, outlined in yellow is clearly visible on the piece of fuselage the party is supporting. [J Gibbons]

Halifaxes, returning from bombing raids on Europe. Lancasters of 9 Squadron also used Kinloss as a base for attacking the German battleship *Tirpitz* in October 1944, in conjunction with 617 Squadron from Lossiemouth and Milltown. Stirlings from the "Moon" squadrons 138 and 161 from Tempsford frequently landed at Kinloss after long trips to drop supplies to resistance fighters in Norway.

Kinloss reached its peak man power of 3,000 in April 1944 but thereafter the numbers declined and on VE day 1945 there were 2,448 of all ranks on the station. VE day was celebrated by a parade and a day off. The last day exercise of 19 OTU was flown on 1 May 1945 and the last night exercise on 13 June 1945. The aircraft were now dispersed to MUs at Bicester and Little Rissington. The station was officially put on C and M on 13 June 1945. On the 28 June 1945 a farewell dance for the OTU staff was held in one of the MU's hangars and a few days later special trains transported all OTU personnel south.

During this early post-war period the busiest unit at Kinloss was undoubtably 45 MU. Thousands of surplus aircraft had to be disposed of, mostly as scrap, and 45 MU played its part, firstly with Ansons, Halifaxes and Warwicks. Parking space was a problem and soon every spare hard standing throughout the station and surrounds was occupied by aircraft awaiting the axe. The satellite airfield at Brackla was also used for storage and at one time there were more than 300 Halifaxes parked on this small field. It is believed some of these Halifaxes were refurbished for the French but the majority helped to swell the coffers of the scrap merchants. A Warwick crashed killing the two crew in December 1945. The remains of engines and other parts are still visible on the crash site in Culbin forest. Another Warwick had crashed in the sea eight miles north of Covesea Lighthouse on 16 November 1945. Three crew were killed but the other two were rescued by the crew of the fishing boat Lazerous. The cook of the Lazerous was unfortunately washed overboard and drowned shortly after the rescue.

The end of the excitement of the war years and uncertainties about future service in the RAF did not help morale in 1945 and 1946. Nevertheless Kinloss appears to have been a reasonably happy unit. At one time the airmen's mess food was supposed to be the best in the RAF, and for those who still complained, egg, bacon, sausage and chips could be had for 1/6 in a Forres cafe. Not too cheap when one considers the average airman's pay of 28 shillings a week. In June 1949 the RAF Flying Review published an item on Kinloss in the series "What the stations are like". After describing the many social activities at Kinloss the article ends :- "It is a happy station; it has more hours of sunshine throughout the year than any other in the British Isles; it has an outstanding flying record, and unrivalled sporting and social facilities':

With the war ending in 1945 many airfields closed almost overnight with squadrons and units being dispanded as quickly as possible. Some stations had however been ear marked for peacetime roles and Kinloss was one of them. Apparently the Navy had wanted the base but ended up instead with Lossiemouth. Despite the disbandment of the OTU there was no dramatic reduction in manpower and in 1946 the strength had only fallen to 1300. Kinloss moved into Coastal with the arrival of 6 (C) OTU from Silloth on 19 July 1945. This unit's Wellington Mk.10s were replaced with Warwicks in October 1945. Demobilization played havoc with training during this period and both instructors and pupils were liable to depart suddenly half way through a course. The OTU which was re-designated 236 OCU on 1 August 1947, had a mixed bag of Beaufighter Xs, Mosquito VIs, Lancaster IIIs, Brigands and Buckmasters. There was also a Spitfire for fighter affiliation.

Kinloss had Battle of Britain At Home days in 1948 and 1949. The 1949 flying programme was carried out by Lincolns, Lancasters, Valettas, Oxfords, Martinets, Spitfires, Harvards, Seafires and Fireflys. Meteors and Vampires were the most modern aircraft on show. Wartime aircraft were still very much to the fore and the OCU relied heavily on Lancaster IIIs. Apart from anti-sub training these Lancasters could also carry airborne lifeboats for ASR duties. On 27 August 1948 a Lancaster crashed coming in to land, killing all eight of the crew.

Lancaster heavy landing at Kinloss. [Robert Martin]

An aerial view of RAF Kinloss on 26 August 1946.
There are literally hundreds of bombers parked on and around the airfield, almost all destined for scrapping.
[RAF Kinloss]

How the mighty fall.... Halifaxes are scrapped at
Kinloss by 46 MU.
[Gp Capt Dark]

With its fog free equable climate Kinloss was always an important diversion unit with many visiting aircraft. For example on 21 February 1948 six Lancasters of EANS Shawbury landed when they were unable to reach Leuchars after a trans Polar flight.

During the late Forties the work of 45 MU carried on unabated with a peak aircraft holding of 1,059 in October 1946. Most of these aircraft scrapped were Halifaxes, Ansons and Warwicks although in the latter half of the Forties even new Lincolns were being scrapped straight from the makers. The MU also prepared some aircraft for the squadrons - mainly Lincolns.

In October 1950 "Operation Interference" was carried out by two Kinloss Ansons. This was a check on illegal fishing by trawlers. Kinloss became a Master Diversion Airfield officially on 1 January 1951 and almost immediately the airfield was covered with 6" of snow making all grass areas unsuitable for aircraft.

The end of 1950 had seen the arrival of the first operational squadron at Kinloss. 120 had been a very successful anti sub squadron in WW II and now equipped with Lancaster GR3s it came to Kinloss when its former base at Leuchars was taken over by Fighter Command. The squadron completed its move on 17 December 1950 and almost immediately was put on ASR standby for Christmas. On 29 December 1950 the ASR was called out to search for a Halifax missing off the west coast of Scotland. Some debris was sighted but no sign of the crew. 120 had been on a visit to Pakistan before moving to Kinloss and one of their officers had contracted smallpox which had come to light while he was on Christmas leave. As a consequence all personnel at Kinloss were vaccinated as a precaution at the end of December 1950.

During January 1951 the USAAF carried out exercises from the station with a B29, Dakotas and five F84 jets. During bad weather on 12 January 1951 a F84 landed by QGH procedure, the first time a jet aircraft had done so at Kinloss. The early part of 1951 was dominated by construction work as the airfield prepared for 120 Squadron and also the arrival of the new Shackleton aircraft. Work was started on new hard standings and technical buildings. It was noted in the station ORB that due to a population rise to 2000 in the next nine months all out lying buildings would have to be occupied and bed-spaces reduced to 48sq ft per airman.

On 14 March 1951 Lancaster TX264 of 120 Squadron failed to return from a navigation exercise. During the next few days a huge search was carried out by planes, boats and

Aircraft of 6 (C) OTU Kinloss.

Above: Beaufighter of 6(C) OTU coded 'K7' in the summer of 1945

Right: a line up of DH Mosquitoes in 1946.
[R H Gray]

Left: The remains of an engine from a Warwick still in the Culbin Forest in 1991, along with the Author!

Below: Propeller memorial from Lancaster TX264, mounted on a cairn outside Kinloss Mountain Rescue Team HQ.
[Eric Hughes]

mountain rescue but it was not until 17 March 1951 that an Oxford located the crash in the snow on the side of Beinn Eighe. Despite heroic efforts by the Mountain Rescue team the seven bodies of the crew were not recovered until 16 days later, and the eighth body was not found until August 7th. This rescue high-lighted the lack of proper rescue equipment and as a result all MRT would in future have to be properly trained and equipped. The crash site on Beinn Eigh is so inaccessible that most of the Lancaster wreckage is still there. In 1987 the Kinloss MRT brought down one of the propellers which is now mounted in front of their HQ as a memorial to that tragic accident.

1951 saw the arrival at Kinloss of the aircraft which was to become symbolic of Coastal Command over the next two decades. The Shackleton had been designed as an anti-submarine aircraft to replace the Lancaster which had only been an adapted bomber. 120 was the squadron selected for the first Shackletons and the first aircraft arrived at Kinloss on 30 March 1951 with two more a few days later. Intensive training started in April 1951 and by September the squadron had disposed of all its Lancasters and was fully operational with Shackletons. Although the OCU was now to carry out Shackleton training it did not receive its first aircraft until May 1951, though by the end of the year it had twelve on charge. This very busy year of training also saw the re-formation of 220 Squadron on 24 September. It moved to St Eval in November.

The build up of personnel for the new camp caused some accommodation problems. The old wartime huts at Whiteinch and Sea Park were re-opened for NCOs and airmen and 34 officers were billetted in the Carleton and Victoria Hotels in Forres. A big building programme was started in 1951 with 24 officer's married quarters and 96 AMQs getting under way. A new airmen's club was opened in 4 April, 1951 and an old barn in the centre of the camp was converted into a Social Club named Keddie House after the CO of that time, Gp Capt Keddie.

During all this upheaval 45 MU had been busy disposing of its surplus aircraft from a peak of 1,059 in

RAF Kinloss in 1946. The headquarters of 45 MU can be seen in the background. [RAF Kinloss]

Warwick sunset - Kinloss 1946 *[RAF Kinloss]*

Kinloss aircraft line up for AOC's inspection, 1953. *[RAF Kinloss]*

Nose-jobs needed!
Left: Neptune M;G comes to grief at Kinloss and airmen prepare to lower it back down to a more dignified position.
Below: Neptune 217:F after a heavy landing, Kinloss 'sometime in the 'fifties!' [RAF Kinloss]

October 1946. The MUs main job now was accepting, storing and issuing more modern aircraft, first of all Lincolns and later, in December 1951, Canberras. They were also able to work on Hunters when they came into service in 1954. On 26 January 1952 a Shackleton of 236 OCU met with the Queen Mary in mid-Atlantic and passed greetings to the PM Winston Churchill who was on board. A rather embarrassing incident occurred on 13th February when one of 120's Shackletons landed on the disused airfield of Dallachy in mistake for Lossiemouth. As Dallachy had not been operational since 1946 the Shackleton was lucky to get away undamaged.

A tragic crash on 10 October 1952 cost the lives of 14 airmen when Shackleton VP286 appeared to explode in mid-air during an air/sea gunnery exercise in the Moray Firth.

Although the Shackletons were now coming into service throughout Coastal Command there was still a shortage of aircraft to fulfill the Coastal role. To overcome this gap, Neptune aircraft from the USA were obtained under the Mutual Defence Assistance Programme. Four squadrons were to receive this type of aircraft and of these 217 was based at Kinloss from 17 April 1952. 236

OCU also received Neptunes and now trained crews for both types of aircraft. The versatile Neptunes played an important role in Coastal Command until they were returned to America in March 1957.

Kinloss played an important part in Exercise "Beecher's Brook" which was the ferrying of Canadian built F86 Sabres to Britain. These planes were to help boost Fighter Command's strength until the arrival of the Hunters.

Starting in December 1952 a total of 400 Sabres were flown from Montreal via Goose Bay, Blue One in Greenland and Keflavik to Kinloss from where they went to MUs at Aldergrove, Lyneham and Kemble. The last hop from Iceland to Kinloss put the aircraft at the limit of their endurance and radar and radio aids, but despite possible disruption from Russian trawlers they all arrived safely. One did crash near Advie in April 1953 after it had left Kinloss.

120 Squadron had went to Aldergrove in April 1952, and with the disbandment of 217 in March 1957 Kinloss was without an operational squadron until 120 returned with Shackleton MkIIIs in April 1959. In 1956 it was decided to concentrate Coastal training at Kinloss with

First of the new breed - Shackleton Mk.1 VP258 of 120 Squadron 7 June 1951. [Chris Ashworth]

Shackleton VP292 of 236 OCU suffers starboard undercarriage collapse, 22 October 1952. *[RAF Kinloss]*

the amalgamation of the School of Maritime Reconnaissance Training from St Mawgan with 236 OTU to form the Maritime Operational Training Unit (MOTU). This unit was equipped with 17 Mk 4 Shackletons which were 1As minus mid upper turrets and fitted with extra radar positions. These aircraft now in their new livery of grey under wing and sides with white upper surfaces were to fill the Moray skies for the next decade. Their badge signified the area - a seal on a book with the Gaelic' motto :-*"Teagaisg sealgair na fairge"* - *"Teaching the hunters of the oceans'.*

Despite the intensity of flying during these years, only one serious crash occurred. On 10 January 1958 Shackleton VP259 hit the trees on Heldon Hill a few miles south of Kinloss. The two pilots were killed but other members of the crew were dragged clear by one of the Signallers, Sgt Len Birnie, who received the George Medal for his bravery.

The late Fifties and early Sixties saw many changes at Kinloss. 45 MU finally closed in 1956 after sixteen years of dealing with thousands of aircraft ranging from Hawker Hinds in 1940 to Hawker Hunters in 1956. The wartime wooden accommodation was gradually being replaced by permanent buildings although a lot of the old huts remained in use by clubs and other organisations. A new Officer's mess and Sgt's mess were built near the main gate and airmen's living quarters and mess were completed on the south side of the main road through the camp. Kinloss had always been a compact camp, and with the abandonment of out-lying buildings at Sea Park, the majority of living quarters and admin buildings were grouped in a comparatively small area. This area was extended with the building of new married quarters north of the railway line in 1965, but still the need for married quarters had to be met by taking over a new council estate in Forres.

RAF Kinloss was given the Freedom of Forres in 1962 and the same year saw the return of WAAFs to the unit after an absence of 17 years. The last National Serviceman in the RAF, SAC Wallace, departed from the station on 23 January 1963 with much more pomp and ceremony than most of his predecessors. 1963 was marred by a huge explosion in the bomb dump when two airmen were killed.

Operations Beecher's Brook. Sabres and aircrew, Kinloss March 1953. *[RAF Kinloss]*

Above: WB849 'Z' of MOTU.
[Chris Ashworth]

Left: The MOTU crest.
[Chris Ashworth]

Below: Three 120 Sqn Shacks tour the West Indies in August 1963.
[RAF Kinloss]

operated with SAR helicopters. To complete the rescue role there was a fully equipped Mountain Rescue Team which carried out many rescues of climbers in trouble.

Over the years the Shackleton had received many modifications which had increased the all up weight from 86,0001b of the MkI to 100,0001b of the MkIII. To help take off and emergencies with the extra weight two jet Viper engines were rather ingeniously installed behind the two outer Griffons making the first six engined aircraft to fly with the RAF.

The middle Sixties witnessed a series of tragic crashes involving Kinloss based aircraft. On 3 August 1966 a Chipmunk used for ATC familiarisation flights crashed and overturned on a moor near Kinloss. The WRAF passenger escaped but the pilot died before he could be released. On 8 December 1965 Shackleton XF704 of

A change in strategy in 1965 saw the arrival of 201 Squadron from St Mawgan in March and 206 in July. MOTU left for St Mawgan in July leaving Kinloss with three squadrons all operating Shackleton Mk IIIs. As a fully operational station in Coastal Command, Kinloss was tasked with the patrolling of vast areas' of the Atlantic and North Sea checking on Russian submarines and surface vessels. Apart from these arduous tasks the squadrons were also involved in other activities further afield. In 1966 aircraft went on three month detachments to Singapore where they assisted the resident 205 Squadron in the Indonesian confrontation. Later in 1967/1969 there were a series of three months detachments to Shargah for anti-smuggling patrols in the Persian Gulf. There were also 'Westabouts' where solo aircraft carrying their own groundcrew and spares did around the world trips to test the capability of reinforcing distant outposts in times of tension.

Apart from operational duties the station had an important SAR role in conjunction with St Mawgan, and Ballykelly until that station closed. On one of these stations an aircraft was in constant readiness to go to the assistance of aircraft or ships in distress. Many callouts were successful especially when the Shackletons co-

MOTU flypast leaving Kinloss July 1965.*[Chris Ashworth]*

Shackleton Mk 3 XF700 'A' of 120 Squadron.

201/Squadron was doing routine flying from the station when it disappeared in the sea about 8 miles north of Kinloss. The wreckage was later recovered but all 8 crew had perished. On 19 November 1967 WR976, also of 201, hit the sea while exercising off St Mawgan. Two crew were rescued but the other 9 were killed. Just over a month later XF702 of 206 Squadron dived vertically into a mountain in Inverness-shire killing all 11 of its crew.

January 1967 saw centralised servicing being established, a move not universally welcomed as the old squadron loyalties were removed from the ground crew. Final centralisation occurred in December 1969 when Coastal Command was absorbed into Strike Command. The Shackleton was now about to be replaced by a purpose built jet anti submarine aircraft, the Nimrod, which had been developed from the Comet. 201 was the first squadron to receive Nimrods in 1970 and throughout that year all the squadrons gradually replaced their own piston aircraft with the new jets. The last Shackleton departed on 21 December 1970, making a low level flight over the local towns and villages before flying south. The farewell was rather premature as Shackletons were still required for the SAR role until the Nimrods were ready for the job. There were also commitments in the Far East and the Rhodesian blockade from Majunga in Madagascar which were now taken over by 204, the last UK based Shackleton squadron. With the closure of its Ballykelly base in the spring of 1971 this squadron was to come to Kinloss. This would have been a logical choice but it went instead to Honington, a

station which had never had Shackletons or indeed any piston aircraft for many years. Kinloss had been without Shackletons for just a year when 8 Squadron was re formed with Shackleton AEW MkIIs in January 1972. The squadron was housed on a temporary basis on the north side of the airfield until its permanent base at Lossiemouth was ready to accept them in August 1973. Another squadron which had a detachment at Kinloss in the early Seventies was No. 7 which flew Canberras for target towing.

Throughout the Seventies the Nimrods of Kinloss played an important part in the maritime role of Strike Command. They also carried out many detachments throughout the world and always there was the SAR commitment. The excellent safety record of the Nimrod was unfortunately marred by a crash in November 1980 when both pilots were killed as their aircraft was forced down by a bird strike shortly after take off.

As befits a modern RAF station, Kinloss has been constantly up-graded in terms of accommodation and amenities during the Seventies and Eighties. A Major Servicing Unit for all the RAF Nimrods was started in 1971 and in 1974 this moved to refurbished hangars on the north side of the airfield. A Nimrod Simulator was built in

Nimrod - the Mighty Hunter - overflies HMS Eagle.

KINLOSS CRESTS

Nimrod Mk.2 (P) XV255 down low on patrol. *[RAF Kinloss]*

Squadrons and Stations may have badges and crests, but there is also the unofficial art.... The Findhorn Strip Club and the Worlds Biggest Fighter being two Kinloss examples!

1971 and a new Operations Block in 1974. A bulk re-fuelling complex was completed in the Seventies and as this is connected by pipe line to Inverness it obviates the necessity for a continious stream of tankers coming by road. On the domestic side many more married quarters were built and also modern accommodation for the airmen. A swimming pool had been constructed as early as 1968 and a Community Centre was erected in the late Seventies.

In 1982 the Nimrods from Kinloss took on a war time role for the first time during the Falklands conflict. The aircraft were modified for flight re fuelling and also had Sidewinder missiles fitted for self defence. For the next few months detachments from all the Kinloss squadrons operated from Ascension Island and later the Falklands. These operations proved the capability of the Nimrod as a long range maritime aircraft and the many long distance flights included one non-stop from the Falklands to the UK.

To bring the airfield up to Eighties standard a new runway was built parallel with the old main runway and hardened aircraft shelters (HAS's) appeared in the surrounding woods. The latest construction is a security fence erected in 1990. A sign of the uneasy times we live in and at a cost of £1,000,000 a token of present inflation.

The capabilities of the Nimrod were again proven

Kinloss Nimrods range far and wide. Here a 120 Sqn machine is seen over the North Pole in the company of a pair of submarines. The date is May 1991. *[RAF Kinloss]*

Above: Nimrod break! Three Kinloss aircraft run in and break over the airfield. XV228 is closest to the camera. Below: Nimrod down. XW666 ditches into the Moray Firth on 17 May 1995, the tail breaking away and sinking first. *[RAF Kinloss}*

during the Gulf war in the spring of 1991. Aircraft from the three squadrons were active in the war area throughout the whole period, and though their activities were not so publicized as other aircraft, they played an extremely important role in tracking and identifying enemy targets both on sea and land. For the second time in a decade RAF Kinloss proved its operational capabilities to be second to none.

There have been a lot of changes at RAF Kinloss between 1994 and 1998. The end of the 'Cold War' has caused the decline and closure of many RAF stations, but paradoxically Kinloss, and its neighbour Lossiemouth, are actually increasing in size.

With the disbandment of 42 Squadron at St. Mawgan, their aircraft arrived at Kinloss to form the Nimrod OCU (42 Reserve Sqn). To accomodate the

expanded unit, new buildings erected included a new Sgts. Mess, Stores, Operations Block and many new married quarters. Some old quarters were demolished, whilst others were renovated.

Privatisation has crept into into the forces and a lot of duties formerly carried out by the RAF are now performed by civilian firms. The largest of these at Kinloss is Serco which took over the running of the NMSU in June 1995.

On 17 May 1995 Nimrod XW666, on test flight from the NMSU, had a serious engine fire and had to ditch three miles off the coast at Lossiemouth. The crew escaped unharmed and were picked up almost inimediately by the Lossiemouth SAR helicopter. On 2 September 1995 Nimrod XV239 plunged into Lake Ontario with the loss of all the seven crew members while

Two views of RAF Kinloss

Left: Five Nimrods overfly Langcot House on the edge of the airfield. Three other machines await on the hardstandings.

Below. Kinloss also saw involvement in 'Operation Granby' the UK's part of 'Desert Storm'. Here Nimrods, a Victor Tanker and a VC10 are parked on the hardstandings.
[RAF Kinloss]

performing at the Toronto Air Show. A stained glass window has been erected to the memory of these men in Kinloss station church.

In the summer of 1996 it was announced that the replacement for the Nimrod would be an up dated version - the Nimrod 2000. The aircraft is to operate from Kinloss, and possibly as a result of this decision, the airfield was closed for most of 1996 while the runway was resurfaced.

Cut backs in the Maritime patrol force resulted in three Nimrod Mk2s being put into long term storage at Kinloss from mid 1992. Early in 1997 ,the three

(XV234,XV242 and XV247) were stripped of their cocoons and dismantled so that they could travel in the cavernous hold of an Antonov AN124 of Heavy Lift Volga DNEPR to Bournemouth. This aircraft was the largest ever to operate from Kinloss and ironically, came complete with a Russian crew, our former enemies of the Cold War days. Another sign of more open times was the decision to open part of the station so that civilians could view this operation. Many hundreds availed themselves of this opportunity.

Equipped with an entirely new suite of sensors, engines and undercarriages,these three aircraft are

HeavyLift/Volga Dnepr ANT 124 awaits the loading of the fuselage of Nimrod XV242 for the flight to Bournemouth and re-furbishment. [RAF *Kinloss]*

RAF Kinloss in the late 1990s.

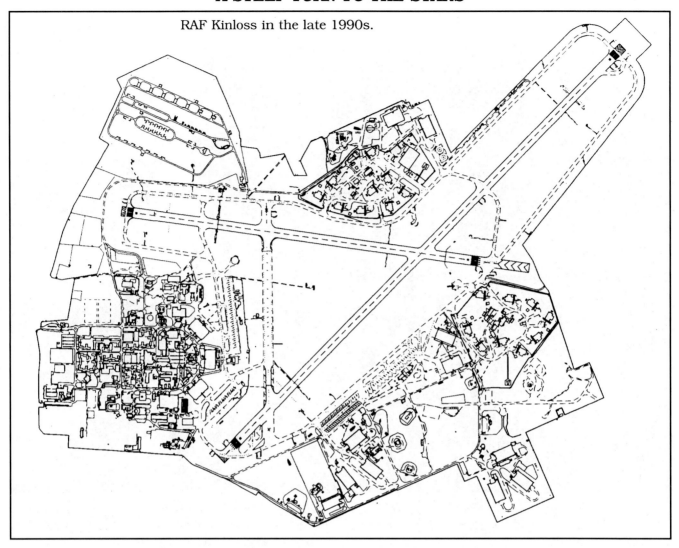

destined to become the first Nimrod Mk 4s and are due to return to Kinloss in an operational role in the year 2000. Another nine Nimrods are scheduled to be upgraded with work being split between Warton and Bourneouth.

In December 1997 RAF Kinloss became the Aeronautical Rescue Co-ordination Centre for the whole of the UK, taking over the duties of Pitreavie and Plymouth. Equipped with a £3 million communications computer, it is linked directly to the Nimrod SAR Squadronrs, the eight military SAR helicopter flights and five RAF mountain rescue teams, The ARCC is expected to handle about. 2,500 rescue incidents a year and will be responsible for co-ordinating mercy missions for an area

of about three million square miles of land and sea stretching from the Faroes in the north to the French and Spanish coasts in the south.

In April 1998 Kinloss was visited by a British Airways Concorde. As part of the *Press and Journal's* 250th anniversary celebrations the paper organised Concorde flights and these had to be flown from Kinloss as the only airfield in the north-east of Scotland capable of handling this aircraft.

With all the recent developments Kinloss is now established as a premier RAF station with a guarenteed future into the 21st century. A far cry indeed from a few wooden huts erected in 1938!

Concorde visits Kinloss as part of the Press and Journals 250th Anniversary celebrations. *[Press & Journal]*

Chapter Seven

ROYAL AIR FORCE LOSSIEMOUTH

Therefore I see , as knit in one society,
Seers, saints and airmen; all who rise
To the pure peace of the clear skies
And read, as in a mirror's face,
The hidden things of time and space.

E. V. Hall

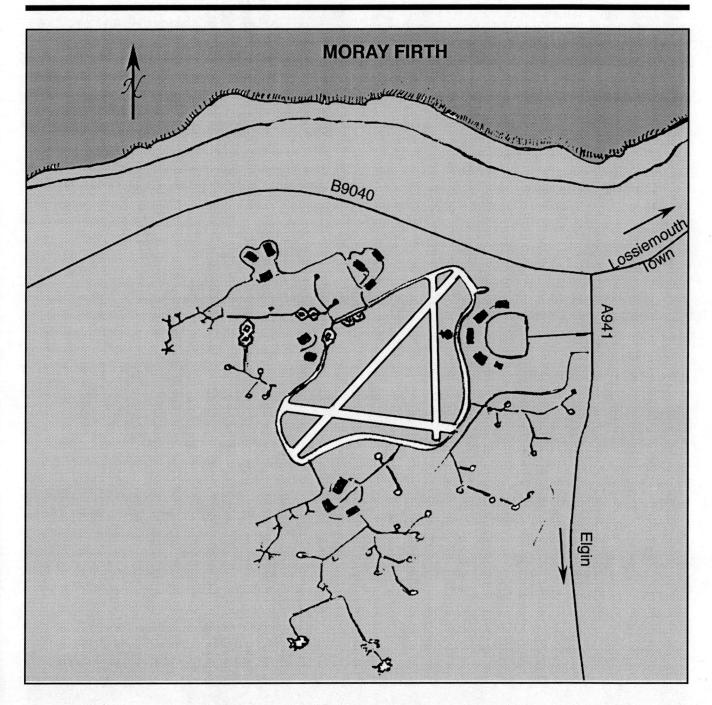

Royal Air Force Lossiemouth 57° 42' 38"N 03° 19' 30" W. 19ft above sea level.

DESPITE its northerly latitude the Moray coast has a well earned reputation for a pleasant climate. Lack of fog, low annual rainfall, and above average hours of sunshine combined with long stretches of sandy beach have helped to make Lossiemouth a pleasant quiet family holiday resort for many years.

The quiet part is now questionable due to the presence of the third largest RAF flying station in the UK. Some would say that this actually attracts visitors but be as it may the flying activities outside Lossiemouth cannot be ignored. Almost any day the casual observer can see and hear a surprising variety of aircraft utilising this huge airfield. Two squadrons and an OCU of Tornados constantly rip the skies apart as they go about their daily training missions. To them can be added the Jaguars from the OCU. There is also the constant clacking of rotor blades as the Sea Kings of 202 Squadron carry out local training or dash off on rescue missions over the sea or in to the hills. Apart from the residents there is a steady stream of visitors both RAF and foreign. It is not unusual to see squadrons of Tornados, Nato AWACS and US transports all competing for airspace above the airfield. When airfields farther south are fogbound, training aircraft often take advantage of the fine Moray weather by utilising Lossiemouth.

The RAF first made their presence felt at Lossiemouth 50 years ago in the spring of 1939 when the station was of officially opened. Flying activities in the

Parachuting from an Avro 504 G-ABLL of Cobham's Circus
[Brian Hansley]

Cobham's Circus - A Moth looping over an Aispeed Ferry. *[Brian Hansley]*

local area were not unknown before 1939 but were sparce enough to warrant some coverage in the local press.

The *Forres Gazette* of 28 October 1914 contained a report of a Hydroplane force landing in the sea off Hopeman. The accident caused considerable excitement among the local inhabitants none of whom had ever seen a flying machine before. This plane, which managed to get away safely after a few quick repairs, probably belonged to the Navy which at that time had a very large base at Invergordon. An early example of air/sea co-operation was noted in the *Forres Gazette* of 5 July 1922 when an aircraft reported the first shoals of herring to the local fishermen.

In 1934 Elgin Town Council discussed the possibility of providing a local aerodrome. Highland Airways were interested in using Elgin as a stop in their Aberdeen/ Inverness flights and had considered a site at Wester Manbeen. Scottish Motor Traction Company actually secured a site at Muirton, Lossiemouth but it is not recorded if this was ever used. This area was also earmarked by the Automobile Association as one of the many landing grounds designated for its members throughout the country during the Thirties. The first sight of large numbers of aircraft in the Moray area occurred in 1934 and again in 1935 when Sir Alan Cobham's Flying Circus displayed various aircraft such as the Handley Page Clive, Airspeed Ferry, Avro Cadet and Tiger Moth. As well as flying displays there was parachute jumping, gliding and opportunities for local people to experience their first flight. A photo in the Courier of 11 May 1934 shows a Miss Joan Meakin with her glider which sports a large swastika

on the fin. She had trained in Germany and was obviously enamoured by the Nazi creed as unfortunately were a lot of her fellow Britons of that era. Cobham's Circus flew from Kinnedar which one presumes was the area now covered by the domestic site of the present base.

Ramsay MacDonald was without doubt Lossiemouth's most famous son, but, even when he became Prime Minister he never forgot his home town which he visited as often as possible. He was obviously very air minded, for, at a time when few politicians took to the air, there are records of him using aircraft for the journey to Lossiemouth on at least thirteen occasions between 1924 and 1934. With no special VIP squadrons at that time the aircraft used were standard RAF types which included a DH9, DH9A, Wapiti and Fairy 111F. These planes landed on various level fields at Coulardbank Farm and Newlands of Drainie. On 10 August 1932 a different type of transport was used when the PM arrived outside Lossiemouth Harbour in a Fairy 111F floatplane, having flown from Lord Londonderry's residence at Newtonards in N Ireland. The last recorded trip of Ramsay MacDonald from Lossiemouth was in a civilian Dragon (Aberdonian) piloted by Capt Nevil Stack on 10 July 1934.

The late Thirties saw a sudden increase in the re-armament programme and this necessitated the building of many new airfields throughout Britain. The wide level plain outside Lossiemouth combined with an excellent climate made it a perfect spot for one of these airfields. In January 1938 five local farmers received notification that their land would be required to establish an air base of

Fairey IIIF Floatplane arriving at Lossiemouth with Prime Minister Ramsay MacDonald aboard, 10 August 1932.
[Lossiemouth Museum via Tony Spring]

The Prime Minister gives a cheery farwell as he leaves for London from Lossiemouth. The date is June 1929.
[Northern Scot].

550 acres made up as follows:

Newlands (Mr W Wildgoose)	180 acres
Coulardbank (Mr H Kellas)	150 acres
Greens (Mr H Mustard)	120 acres
Smithfield (Mr E Philip)	90 acres
Kinnedar (Mr A Adam)	10 acres

Little information was apparently given as to the use of this acquired land and the Northern Scot of March 1938 speculates that it was merely for a landing ground although should an emergency arise it could be converted into a proper airfield.

During the summer of 1938 the land was cleared and levelled, a welcome relief to the local unemployed. There seems to have been a lull in the winter of 1938 due possibly to discussions about water supplies with the local council. But by April 1939 many wooden huts had been erected as also was the steel work for the first hangars.

On 1 May 1939 No 15 FTS was officially formed under the command of Gp Capt P E Maitland AFC CVO, a very experienced RAF officer who had started in the RNAS and had commanded the airship base at Lenabo near Peterhead at the end of the first World War. Gp Capt Maitland recalls arriving at Lossiemouth and meeting a Squadron Leader and three Flying Officers, at a local hotel (thought to be the Steamboat). He thought at the time that it was rather a top heavy command for a Group Captain, but by 14th May eight officers, six Sgt instructors, and 77 other ranks had been posted in. By June 1st this number had increased to 16 officers and 122 other ranks. The first aircraft to arrive were 13 Oxfords from D H Hatfield and Airspeed Portsmouth and five Harts from Netheravon. There appears to be no record of the first aircraft and pilot to actually land on the new airfield but the first course of 30 APOs and 10 airmen pilots started officially on 12 June 1939.

The airfield was still in a rather primitive condition. Aircraft were parked and serviced in the open which necessitated specially long pickets due to the soft nature of the ground. Wind blown sand did not improve the fabric covered aircraft and it was a relief to everyone when the first hangar was completed in August. On 1st August two Oxfords collided over the sea near the Boar's Head with the loss of three lives, Fg Off Yeates, APO Alwood and Cpl Morrell. This was the first of many crashes to affect Lossiemouth and being peacetime it was extensively reported in the local press - the last such reports until 1945.

With the outbreak of war in 1939 the station enforced wartime restrictions such as blackout, obliteration of aircraft markings and the wearing of uniform at all times. A detachment of Seaforth Highlanders arrived for guard duties and A/A defences were erected and manned. No. 1 Course passed out on 16 August 1939 and flying increased with the arrival of Harvards and more Oxfords and Harts from other units. 11 Battles were also received for storage. During the autumn of 1939 enemy aircraft were reported over the local area but these reports were not confirmed and flying training was not interrupted. The first WAAFs (77) were posted in during October and due to shortage of

A furtive camera shot of 'Secret' airfield building at Lossiemouth in 1938.

Airspeed Oxfords of 15 FTS and G-ACCZ, a civilian DH84 Dragon at Lossiemouth in January 1940. *[R.D.Cooling]*

Harvard of 15 FTS, Lossiemouth February 1940.
[R.D.Cooling]

accommodation were billetted in various Lossiemouth hotels (Stotfield, Laverock Bank, and Halliman House).

The winter of 1939/40 was extremely severe throughout Europe. The cold weather combined with poor living quarters accelerated the spread of infectious diseases and in January 1940 the SMO recorded cases of Cerebal Meningitis, German Measles, Measles, Mumps and Whooping Cough. Precautionary measures included fresh air in living quarters, gargling, and limiting social functions so as to stop spread of infections.

On 25 January 1940 twelve Hampdens of 44 and 50 Squadrons arrived from Waddington on detachment. Their purpose was offensive patrols over the North Sea but bad weather forced them to return to their home base on 15 February. Nine Hampdens from 83 Squadron arrived on 23 February, one of their pilots being Guy Gibson, then a junior officer. Wellingtons of 9 Squadron arrived 2 April and they were replaced by Blenheims of 107 and 110 Squadrons under the command of Wg Cdr

Oxfords of 15 FTS 1940. *[R.D.Cooling]*

Basil Embry at the end of the month. With the invasion of Norway the phoney war was now over and the bomber detachments at Lossiemouth started bombing shipping in the Norwegian fiords. It was obvious that the airfields at Lossiemouth and Kinloss had now become strategically important and in consequence it was decided that 15 FTS would move to Middle Wallop. Bomber Command took over the station and 20 Operational Training Unit was formed on 27 April 1940.

Before the OTU was established another unit was formed at Lossiemouth. This was No 46 Maintenance Unit, which, though officially a lodger, occupied a considerable amount of space. Starting off with six Robin and eight Super Robin hangars on the east side of the airfield the MU was soon having to disperse its aircraft in fields and other areas outside. The job of the MU was to accept aircraft from the manufacturers, carry out modifications and fit special equipment before dispatching the planes to the squadrons. As well as a full RAF compliment the MU also had a detachment of civilian ATA pilots for ferry work. The first aircraft to arrive were 16 Hurricanes on 17 April and these were followed by a motley collection of Tiger

Moths, Audaxes and even a Hornet Moth.

20 OTU flew Wellingtons and Ansons but strangely enough there is no record of their arrival in the Station Diary. However this period of May and June 1940 was rather chaotic throughout Britain and its effects were felt as far north as Lossie when the remains of 98 Squadron (Battles and 130 airmen) arrived from Nantes.

This squadron just stayed long enough to reform before going south to Gatwick. 21 and 57 Squadrons with 34 Blenheims arrived from Watton on 20 June and started operational sweeps over the North Sea including a raid on Stavenger on 9 July when four aircraft were lost. The satellite airfield at Bogs of Mayne was now operational and

Oxford of 15 FTS, Lossiemouth 1939/40
[R.D.Cooling]

the Blenheims used this field from August.

The threat of invasion was now very real throughout Britain and Lossiemouth with its long stretches of beach appeared to be extremely vulnerable. It was during the summer of 1940 that the concrete block obstacles and blockhouses were set up along the shore. Most of these are still intact 50 years later. 120 Royal Engineers (Construction Company) arrived in June to build these defences. RAF personnel were given rifle practice and training aircraft were fitted with bomb racks for use in an emergency.

If 20 OTU's diary was rather sparse during this period the 46 MU scribe was more erudite. On 10 July he notes that bombs were dropped by enemy aircraft on waste ground about two miles from the camp. On 15 July the Grand Hotel in Elgin was put "Out of Bounds" to WAAFs - one wonders why. On 16 September a Wellington of 20 OTU and a Blenheim of 21 Squadron collided in mid-air with the loss of three lives. Aircraft parking space was now at a premium. Playing fields were taken over and local farmers were approached for loan of fields, a move strongly opposed by the Ministry of Agriculture.

On 26 October Lossiemouth received its baptism of

Slightly off track - Oxford of 15 FTS, Lossiemouth 1939.
[S.G.Jones]

Bent Blenheim L8784 Lossiemouth, March 1940.
[R. D. Cooling]

Cpl Lovelace admiring the nose art on Blenheim, summer Lossiemouth 1940. *[R. E. Lovelace]*

fire when three Heinkel 111s made a surprise dusk attack on the airfield. Two Heinkels came in low from the north east and bombed a line of Blenheims which were being prepared for night flying. A third Heinkel attacked from the south using machine guns but no bombs. One of the Heinkels crashed, brought down either by the explosion of its own bombs or the station Hispano gun. Like many similar incidents the exact circumstances will never be known. The four man German crew were killed and are buried in Lossiemouth churchyard. The RAF losses were one officer and two airmen killed and others injured. Two Blenheims were destroyed and three damaged, and damage was also incurred by two Magisters, two Moths and a Hurricane. Three hangars were slightly damaged but Lord Haw Haw's claim that the airfield was destroyed in flames was rather exaggerated. Shortly after this attack the Blenheims returned south. 232 Squadron with Hurricanes arrived at Bogs of Mayne but made no contact with the enemy during their stay.

11 October 1940 was the date of an incident little reported at the time but unique in the annals of Lossiemouth. Sgt Geoff Pryor was a U/T air gunner in the rear turret of a 20 OTU Wellington on a training mission from Lossiemouth when he saw a plane appearing at 10 o'clock out of cloud. When this plane opened fire he realized it was a German Ju 88 and at once gave it a quick burst of machine-gun fire which caused it to dive into the sea. Geoff was probably the only air gunner ever to claim a kill when under training and certainly the only one from 20 OTU. Later commissioned, Geoff Pryor was killed over Holland in 1943. The crashing JU 88 had been witnessed by one of Geoff's friends Ron Lyon who was badly injured in a Wellington crash shortly afterwards.

On New Year's Eve 1940 Wellington N2980 was dispatched from Lossiemouth on a training flight. After suffering an engine failure over the Monadhliath Mountains the captain ordered the crew to bale out. This took longer than expected and the Captain and second pilot were left with no alternative than to try and crash land. Seeing a large patch of water the pilot brought his aircraft down and made a perfect landing on Loch Ness. The two crew got out safely before the Wellington slid quietly below the surface of the Loch. One of the crew had been killed when his parachute failed to open but the rest were safe. No attempt was made to salvage the aircraft and it was not until the wreck was found in 1979 that it was decided to try and recover what was a Wellington in

Blenheim Mk.IV of 21 Sqn detatched to Lossiemouth, summer 1940. *[R. E. Lovelace]*

11 October 1940 20 OTU Wellington from which Geoff Pryor (inset) in rear turrent shot down a Ju88 a few minutes after this picture was taken.
[Ron Lyon]

almost perfect condition. Using the latest diving techniques N2980 was finally recovered from its watery bed in September 1985. It now reposes in Brooklands Museum Weybridge being prepared for future exhibition, the second only Wellington to survive and the only aircraft of 20 OTU to be preserved.

There was little flying activity at Lossiemouth during the first months of 1941 due mainly to the state of the airfield which could only be used for emergencies or light aircraft. With the better weather of spring and summer conditions improved and the flying hours of the OTU increased rapidly with a record week of 1022 hrs 40 mins flown between 12 and 18 June. 46 MU continued to increase its activities with more varied aircraft. On the night of 11/12 July an enemy aircraft believed to be a Ju 88 dropped four bombs on the town of Lossiemouth destroying four houses and killing four civilians.

Throughout 1941 detachments from various squadrons continued to visit Lossiemouth from where they carried out raids on Norwegian bases and also mine laying operations. These squadrons included Blenheims from 21, 82, 110 and 114 and Hampdens from 44 and 50. By the end of the year the wet condition of the airfield was making flying virtually impossible and in order to keep up the training programme the Wellingtons were dispatched to Lakenheath in Norfolk, the first aircraft to operate from that newly-built airfield. Living conditions on the camp were not exactly comfortable. Don Bruce, now living at Rye, spent the winter months of 1941/42 shuttling between Lossiemouth and Bogs of Mayne. His memories of Lossiemouth are mostly of mud everywhere, even in the bath houses. At that time the Sgts' Mess was divided

into two sections with the Sgts under training segregated in one section, which could caused some animosity. There was also friction between the RAF and the Argyle and Sutherland Highlanders who were guarding the camp. This could sometimes cause as many casualties as the flying programme. Accommodation on the camp was insufficient for everyone and many local hotels and big houses were commandeered for billets. One of the most unusual of these was the Oakwood Hotel referred to as RAF Station, Oakwood Tea Gardens. This was home for

Group Captain David Marwood -Elton, a survivor from the ditching of Wellington N2980 into Loch Ness, is flown back 'up North' by Dan-Air Services on 12 September 1985 to watch the raising of his aircraft.
[DASA]

Wellington N2980 after salvage from Loch Ness during September 1985. *[Author]*

P/O Hodgson in June 1941 and is mentioned in his book *"Letters from a Bomber Pilot"*.

In January 1942 the German battleship Tirpitz arrived at Trondheim in Norway posing such a threat to the Russian convoys that its destruction or incapacitating became a high priority. At the end of the month a force of 13 Stirlings (including the famous "McRoberts Reply") of 149 and 15 Squadrons plus 13 Halifaxes of 10 and 76 Squadrons arrived at Lossiemouth and from there they made the first bombing raid on the Tirpitz. The raid was a complete failure. A second operation by Lancasters of 44 Squadron and Halifaxes of 10 Squadron on the 10 March was just as unsuccessful as were Halifaxes of 10 Squadron at the end of March. Lancasters of 9 Squadron and Halifaxes of 10 Squadron made another unsuccessful attack on 28 April. It was during this raid that Wg Cdr D C T Bennett was shot down. He escaped back to England in five weeks and later achieved fame as the leader of the Pathfinders.

During 1942 flying by the OTU was intensified and the station diary of that period is a melancholy chapter of crashes. An almost daily occurrence caused by a combination of worn out aircraft, raw crews and severe climatic conditions. Most of these accidents caused death and injuries but some were more bizarre as that witnessed by Don Bruce on 24 May. A Tiger Moth looping at low level lost its passenger. Fortunately he managed to use his parachute but the low altitude bale out caused him severe injuries.

May 1942 saw the first 1000 bomber raids on Germany. In order to complete the magic figure of 1000, aircraft and crews from the OTUs had to be used and these included Wellingtons from 20 OTU. 14 flew to Cologne from Stanton Harcourt on 30 May and on 17 June 13 bombed Essen with the loss of one aircraft. Another 12 Wellingtons went to Bremen from Snaith on 24 and 25 June when one failed to return. On 11 September 9 were detached to Elsham Wolds for a raid on Dusseldorf.

During 1942 46 MU continued to produce many varied types of aircraft, though by the middle of the year Beaufighters were pre dominant. The first of many Lancasters arrived in December. By now the MU had its

'MacRobert's Reply' at Lossiemouth January 1942.
[RAF Museum]

Halifax II W104 of 10 Sqn, piloted by Wg Cdr Bennett, shot down in Norway after a raid on Tirpitz from Lossiemouth 28 April 1942.
[RAF Museum]

own sub pool of ferry pilots.

The last months of 1942 saw what was probably the most important construction project in the airfield's history - the building of runways. The N S runway was completed on 28 November 1942 and on 31 December 1942 it was reported that concreting on all three runways was complete and green camouflage applied. The runways and associated perimeter tracks and hard standings were constructed by a USAAF Engineer battalion. At the same time the AMWD built a new watch tower.

With the opening of the new runways bad weather ceased to be a problem at Lossiemouth from the beginning of 1943. Flying from the OTU became even more intensive with the build up of the bombing offensive against Germany calling for more and more trained aircrews. The increased flying activity inevitably caused more accidents and the station diary catalogues endless crashes with heavy fatalities among the crews. While most crashed aircraft could be located, at least six in 1943 just vanished without trace. In May 1943 it was noted that in future 46 MU would concentrate on Beaufighters and Lancasters with a few Defiants. Spitfires disappeared but not before two of them had been exhibited in the local Wings for Victory Week.

By 1944 Lossiemouth was a large well established station. Living quarters were still wooden huts albeit rather more comfortable than earlier days but a lot of airmen were still billetted in houses in the local area. Because of the excellent weather conditions the station was frequently used for diversions by a wide variety of aircraft ranging from Lancasters and Halifaxes returning from bombing missions to Wildcats and Avengers travelling north to the Shetlands. Although the station received no more air raids a BF 109 was shot down by fighters 40 miles north of Lossiemouth on 20 February 1944 and a JU 88 was reported in the area on 6 May 1944. The last reported enemy air activity near Lossiemouth occurred on the night of 21 June 1944 when a Ju188 of the 1st Staffel Aufklarungs Gruppe from Stavenger in Norway flew into a hill three miles north west of Rothes. All four crew were killed and buried with full military honours at Lossiemouth. Some useful information was apparently gleaned from the wreckage.

Newspaper censorship was obviously not now so strict as shown by the Courant's account of a crash on 22 July 1944. The Starboard wing broke off Wellington HE 212 and fell on the golf course while the remainder of the aircraft crashed in the sea close to the shore. The crash was witnessed by a lot of people who tried desperately to save the crew. A WAAF Cpl Lewis swam out as did a local civilian Harold Woodcock. The six crew however perished and so unfortunately did Harold Woodcock in his gallant rescue attempt.

Wellington of 20 OTU returned from a trip with some bits missing.
[RAF Lossiemouth]

12 September 1944. Eleven hours out from Lossiemouth Flg Off Keeley and his 9 Sqn crew fail to locate Yagodnik. With fuel running low and after five runs and several square searches, a forced landing became inevitable. After jettisoning their bombs in a river the crew put down in open marshland. No one was injured

The end of 1944 saw the last big operation from Lossiemouth. Despite earlier attacks by Bomber Command and the FAA the German battleship *Tirpitz* was still afloat and a possible threat to our shipping. On 11 September, 1944, 42 Lancasters of 9 and 617 Squadrons flew from Bardney and Woodhall Spa to Lossiemouth where they refuelled and set out for Yagodnik in north Russia. 27 of these Lancasters flew from Yagodnik to bomb the *Tirpitz* but although 17 Tallboys were dropped the ship still did not sink. It was then decided to fly direct from Lossiemouth using special overload fuel tanks and uprated engines. An attack on 29 October was aborted due to bad weather as was another one on in early November. Finally on 12 November 38 Lancasters of 9 and 617 Squadrons took off from Lossiemouth, Kinloss and Milltown on what was to be a successful mission. For once the conditions were perfect and 28 Tallboys ripped the *Tirpitz* apart as she rolled over and sank. The last offensive operation from Lossiemouth had been an unqualified success.

In the winter of 1944/45 it was obvious that the war in Europe was drawing to a close. The OTU continued training and still there were crashes and accidents in the

The remains of Wellington LP660 which crashed at the end of the runway at Lossiemouth on 9 November 1944. *[J. Moseley]*

local area. These included a Halifax of 38 Gp which crashed on the beach on 25 November 1944. Four of the Canadian crew are buried in Bellie Churchyard. On 27 February 1945 Wellington LN557 crashed in Seatown, Lossiemouth badly damaging many houses and killing six of the crew. The rear gunner escaped as did all the inhabitants of the houses. There was no further intake of pupils as from 1 May and no doubt there were great celebrations on VE day on 8 May 1945.

One of the sad facts of war was that in the five years of 20 OTU's existance no less than 385 aircrew had been killed or gone missing while flying from the base.

By a strange quirk of fate the worst aircraft disaster to affect Lossiemouth occurred after the war had ended. On Sunday 20 May 1945 a Wellington on test flight had a complete engine failure and despite efforts to turn it out to sea it crashed into a block of houses in the town. In the conflagration that followed the three crew and eight civilians died. Fifty years after the fatal crash in Lossiemouth, the citizens of the town and the RAF contributed to a memorial which was unveiled on VJ Day, 1995.

This was the last fatal Wellington crash and a sad ending for the OTU which finally disbanded in July 1945. With the last OTU course passing out on 3 July 1945 46 MU took over their hard standings and a hangar. The MU was now tropicalising Beaufighters for the Far East and had also added York, Lincoln and Warwick aircraft to their holdings. With the Japanese war ending suddenly in August 1945 the MU had now the mammoth task of disposing of their surplus aircraft, a task made more difficult by the demobilisation of many of their skilled tradesmen.

On 28 July 1945 Lossiemouth and its satellite Milltown were taken over by 17 Group Coastal Command.

"Near this site on 20th May 1945 8 civilians and 3 aircrew lost their lives. This plaque is erected to their memory and to all other civilians and servicemen who lost their lives at Lossiemouth during World War Two".
The words on the memorial unveiled on 20th August 1995.
[Author]

Ignominious end to an old warrior. Lancaster BIII DV302, survivor of 122 bombing raids awaits the axe at 46 MU Lossiemouth 1946.
[R.T.Emeny]

The new units were 1674 HCU and 111 OTU from the Bahamas. By the end of August training had commenced with 41 Liberators, 10 Halifaxes and a Mitchell. There was also a detachment of 280 Squadron Warwicks for ASR duties. About this period the total personnel strength of Lossiemouth was 3,316 RAF and 831 WAAF - a far cry from the eight officers who had started it all in 1939.

The end of World War II was followed by a confused situation caused by a rapid run down of the armed forces. At Lossiemouth the HCU and OTU remained only until the spring of 1946 when it was decided to hand over the station and Milltown to the Royal Navy. This was done officially on 2 July 1946 with a short ceremony when the RAF Ensign was replaced by the White Ensign and Wg Cdr E A Johnston handed over to Capt D MacIntyre. On 7 July, 1946 the station was officially commissioned as HMS Fulmar.

The take over by the Navy probably caused some confusion at first. Frank Simpson now living in east Sussex, had served for some years on 46 MU when he had to go to Inverness hospital just before his demob in 1946. He was extremely surprised to find his old quarters in Navy hands when he returned and had to spend the last few weeks of his service in the less than salubrious huts at Bogs of Mayne. 46 MU did not leave Lossiemouth immediately on the arrival of the Navy. There were vast numbers of aircraft left for disposal now that the RAF was dwindling to a peace time level. A few of these aircraft were refurbished for the RAF and foreign services but the vast majority were broken up and sold for scrap. Sold is perhaps the wrong term as the selling price bore no relation to the original cost of the aircraft and the only people to gain from the deal were the scrap dealers. At one time there were up to 900 aircraft parked on the airfield and the surrounding fields. By November 1946 this number had been reduced to 60 Beaufighters, 38 Lancasters, 38 Oxfords and 39 Warwicks. The final clearance of equipment and personnel was finished on 15th February, 1947.

HMS Fulmar, which was to become the largest Naval

Seafires setting out from 46 MU for France, 1947.
[Mrs A Gerrard]

air station in Scotland, started off its training role in 1946 with 766 Squadron operating Fireflies and Seafires. The excellent weather record was a boon for flying training though ironically the first Air Day on 28 September 1946 was almost spoiled by fog. Milltown was organised as a Deck Landing Training School and was used extensively by all the Naval aircraft. It was now obvious that the old wartime airfield at Lossiemouth had insufficient facilities for a modern air base and extensive building work was started at the end of the Forties. 700 Married Quarters were planned and the first opened in Elgin on 28 September 1949. Unlike the RAF the Navy settled their MQs in the towns of Lossiemouth and Elgin probably helping Naval and civilian families to mix but on the negative side removing the camp as a focal point for social

activities. In 1952 flying was transferred to Milltown while the Lossiemouth runways were extended and improved. These were ready for use again in May 1953. It was during this period that an Aircraft Holding Unit was established for surplus aircraft mostly Ansons and Oxfords. At one time 362 aircraft were held on charge.

Over the next decade practically every aircraft on the FAA inventory operated from Lossiemouth. Seafires and Fireflies were prominent at first and they were followed by Attackers, the first Naval jets in 1953. The next few years saw Vampires, Venoms, Sea Hawks, Scimitars, Sea Furies and Meteors. The AHU became the Naval Air Supply Unit in 1966 and during its time stored such oddities as the Sturgeon, Sea Balliol and Wyvern. There was even a Hellcat KE209 flying as a station hack as late as 1954.

As a training unit Fulmar had more than its share of accidents. The pilot was killed when a Seafire crashed on the 17th fairway of the golf course in May 1949. In June 1949 there was a spectacular mid air collision between two Seafires just off the coast. One crashed in the sea but the other managed to land despite having its props reduced to stumps. It is noted in the local papers (the Courant) that after a Seahawk crash in July 1955 the pilot was picked up by an RN helicopter using the scoop net method. Rescue by helicopter had now been recognised as extremely effective and SAR helicopters became part of the aircraft strength at Fulmar. The SAR Whirlwinds were also used extensively for civilian rescues for example

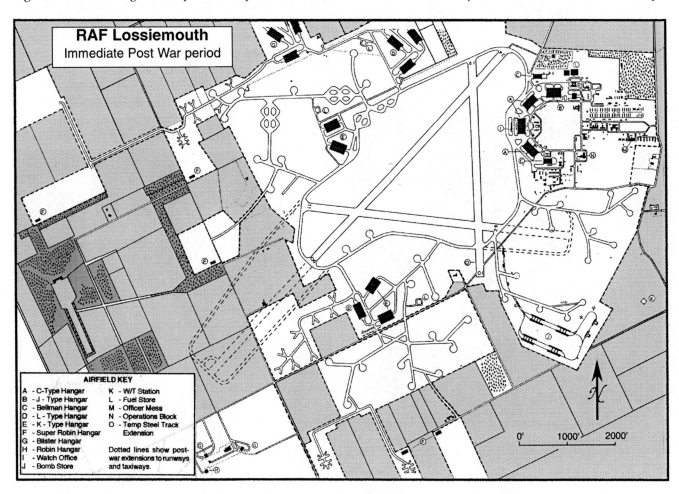

RAF Lossiemouth
Immediate Post War period

AIRFIELD KEY

A - C-Type Hangar
B - J - Type Hangar
C - Bellman Hangar
D - L - Type Hangar
E - K - Type Hangar
F - Super Robin Hangar
G - Blister Hangar
H - Robin Hangar
I - Watch Office
J - Bomb Store

K - W/T Station
L - Fuel Store
M - Officer Mess
N - Operations Block
O - Temp Steel Track
    Extension

Dotted lines show post-war extensions to runways and taxiways.

0'   1000'   2000'

"Operation Snowdrop" when fodder was dropped to starving animals in the Highlands during a blizzard in January 1955.

In 1958 it was announced that £3,000,000 would be spent at Lossiemouth in order to bring up living accommodation to modern standards. The next few years saw the building of new quarters for ratings, Officers and Petty officers as well as a new social club.

March 1962 saw the establishment of 700Z Flight for the proving of the new Buccaneer aircraft. Who would have thought then that over two decades later the Buccaneer would still be a major force at Lossiemouth. Certainly from the early Sixties the Buccaneer in various marks dominated the flying scene at Fulmar. The early aircraft were beset by problems as the number of crashes testify. The crew were killed in August 1962 when one crashed off shore in full view of horrified holidaymakers. In April 1964 the crew ejected safely but their crashing

Above: Hellcat KE209

Below: Fairey Firefly, well known at HMS Fulmar.

Supermarine Attackers of 736 Squadron FAA in November 1953 after their move from Culdrose.

aircraft killed 90 pigs when it landed in Mayne Farm near Elgin. At the end of 1970 after a series of crashes caused questions to be asked in Parliament the Buccaneer Mkls were grounded. The new marks however soon proved their mettle and Lossiemouth continued to be the principal Buccaneer station.

In March 1967 the Buccaneers were able to demonstrate their low level bombing techniques before the world's media. The huge Torry Canyon tanker had run aground off Lands End causing danger of extreme oil pollution in the area. It was decided to destroy the ship by bombing and Buccaneers from 800 and 736 Squadrons were detailed for the operation. 23 direct hits were reported from 36 bombs dropped and the Torry Canyon and its cargo were destroyed in a mass of flames.

By 1967 new ratings accommodation costing £1,000,000 had been completed as well as CPO and POs Messes and WRNs quarters. Lossiemouth was beginning to look like a modern air station but as old hands often point out once a station gets modernised it is on the books for closing.

From the Defence Paper of 1966 the writing was on the wall for the heavy aircraft carriers of the Navy. Despite a "Fly Navy" campaign in 1968 it was obvious that the Navy would soon be losing its Buccaneers. As a prelude to the changeover 736 Squadron started to train RAF aircrew and groundcrew in Buccaneer handling in 1969. By then it was known that the Navy would hand Lossiemouth to the RAF in 1972 and for the next couple of years many well known

De Havilland Sea Hornet

Some of the many types of aircraft used by HMS Fulmar at Lossiemouth between 1946 and 1972

Supermarine Seafire

De Havilland Sea Vixen

Sea Hawks of 806 Sqn FAA

Supermarine Scimitar of 834 Sqn FAA

Sea Vixen FAW21 of 750 Sqn FAA

Westland Whirlwind

Navy Buccaneer over Lossiemouth. *[RAF Lossiemouth]*

FAA squadrons were disbanded or sent to other units. After 12 years of flying from Lossiemouth the last Buccaneers of 809 Squadron flew off to the Ark Royal on 25 September and the same day also saw the departure of the last Sea Princes. The only Naval flying presence now left at Lossiemouth were the Gannets of 849B Flt and the SAR helicopters.

The RAF officially took over Lossiemouth again on 28 September, 1972. A huge programme of runway re surfacing was immediately commenced so the first RAF Squadron, No 8, flying AEW Shackletons, commenced flying from Kinloss although their HQ was at Lossiemouth. The takeover from the Navy had a few problems mainly to do with Naval traditions. Trying to amalgamate the POs and CPOs Messes into one Sgts Mess caused a few headaches and it was some time before the RAF could get used to signs indicating such areas as Heads and Cabins.

The first RAF unit to officially operate from the new Lossiemouth was 202 Squadron "D" flt flying Wessex helicopters in the SAR role. They replaced their Naval counterparts in February 1973. The Wessex were replaced by Sea Kings in 1978. With the new runways and hard standings completed the 12 Shackletons of 8 Squadron returned on 25 August 1973. 8 was then the largest squadron in terms of manpower in the RAF. 226 OCU was re-formed to train crews for the new Jaguars and the first course started in 20 January 1974. In conjunction with this OCU training two Jaguar Squadrons were formed at Lossiemouth before proceeding to their new units. These were 54 Squadron on 29 January, 1974 and 6 on September 1974. The only Naval flying presence was now the Gannets of 849B Flt but these also departed on March 1978. Sadly one of their aircraft crashed on the runway killing both crew in June 1974.

The Navy leaves - a full line-up of aircraft for the flypast. *[RAF Lossiemouth]*

*Badges from some the
Fleet Air Arm Squadrons
based at Lossiemouth
1946 - 1972*

Fairey Gannet - the last surviving naval aircraft at Lossiemouth.

Jaguar over Lossiemouth beach. *[RAF Lossiemouth]*

Line-up of Buccaneers at Lossiemouth ATC. *[RAF Lossiemouth]*

Hunter from 267 OCU over snowy Cairngorms.
[RAF Lossiemouth]

Changes in defence policy meant that an aircraft once familiar to Moray skies now returned. The Buccaneer OCU 237 transferred north from Honington in October 1984 and later on the OCU was joined by 208 and 12 Squadrons, thus concentrating all the RAF Buccaneers at Lossiemouth. The OCU also had Hunters and many other Hunters appeared over the local skies when the Tactical Weapons Training Unit arrived in October 1978.

During the middle Eighties a huge programme of modernisation was started at Lossiemouth. The runways were again re surfaced and new buildings in the shape of Hardened Aircraft Shelters appeared around the perimeter of the airfield. Single room accommodation was built to replace the Naval style cabins.

'Me and my Shadow' - 8 Sqn Shacklton over beach defences. *[RAF Lossiemouth]*

Sea King of 202 Sqn gets airborne on another rescue mission from Lossiemouth. *[RAF Lossiemouth]*

A reason for SAR - a Sea King of 202 Squadron hovers in close, with it's winchman dangling, to a vessel. *[RAF Lossiemouth]*

On 30 April 1990 Shackleton WR965 crashed into a hill in the Western Isles, killing all ten on board.

RAF Lossiemouth played an important role in the Gulf war of 1991. From the start of hostilities many of its personnel were seconded to wartime duties especially those involving Jaguar aircraft. The most outstanding effort however was the operations carried out by the Buccaneers. An aircraft which had never seen action, and was at the end of its career, amazed everyone with its adaptation to desert warfare and was to prove its capabilities as a fighting machine byond all doubt. 1991 saw the demise of the Shackleton after many reprieves, the last five aircraft left Lossiemouth base in June 1991 thus ending 40 year's close association with Morayshire. Auctioned off in July, two were at least obtained by a British consortium. One of these three, WL790, has been flown to the USA, and after servicing flew in the 1997 Oshkosh Airshow. It was then stored at the Polar Aviation Museum and there are plans for it to be returned to Britain for the participation on the air display circuit. WL747 and WL797 were bought by a Cypriot businessman and ferried to Cyprus - latest reports have them looking very neglected at Paphos airfield.

In 1994 the Buccaneers were replaced by Tornados. 12 Sqn took over the aircraft of 27 Sqn when it was disbanded. 208 Sqn was also disbanded and replaced by

flypast! *[RAF Lossiemouth]*

GOODBYE 8 SQUADRON!!

8 Sqn's
Avro Shacklet

The Big End
of the
Last Piston

Assorted 'graffiti' was produced to
commemorate the event!

8 squadron flypast for 8.8.88 Unfortunately
only four aircraft were available!
[RAF Lossiemouth]

617 Sqn 'Dambusters' from Marham. The Tornado Weapons Conversion Unit TWCU - 15 Reserve Squadron - arrived from Honington. The unit's strength was further increased with Tornados from RAF contingent of the Tri-national Tornado Training Establishment at RAF Cottesmore when it closed in March 1999. The Jaguar 226 OCU is now 16 Reserve Squadron. Lossiemouth is also the home of 2622 (Highland) Field Squadron RAuxAF. With the proposed cut-backs in RAF Germany another Tornado squadron will move to Lossiemouth in the late nineties.

Much to the annoyance of the old Coastal hands, the Shackleton Gate Guardian has been scrapped - replaced with a Buccaneer in Gulf War colours in a position by the new camp entrance so that it is almost invisible from the road.

As befitting a modern RAF station, many new buildings have been erected. These include Airmen's Quarters, a Church, a new Guardroom and Main Entrance. The old Guardroom, probably the oldest still in use in the country was quickly bulldozed out of existance before

Buccaneer 'Dirty Harriet' XV332 is seen low over Lossiemouth town in 'Desert Storm' livery
after it's return from the Gulf in 1991. *[RAF Lossiemouth]*

anyone could slap a preservation order on it!

With the Iraqi situation showing no signs of improvment, the Lossiemouth Tornados have taken their turn in policing the troubled area since Operation Desert Storm. In January 1999, 12 Tornados of 12 Sqn based in Kuwait played an important part in the attacks on Iraqi forces during Operation Desert Fox.

The excellent weather and first class modern facilities precludes the station from ever relenquishing its hold as a front line flying unit and it is likely that the coasts of Moray will reverberate to the sound of jet engines for many years to come.

A pair of Jaguar T.Mk.2As of 16 (R)
Squadron from Lossiemouth 1997.
[RAF Lossiemouth]

**Royal Air Force
Lossiemouth
1999**

A pair of 15 (R) Squadron Tornados.
[RAF Lossiemouth]

A Tornado of 12 Squadron in the all-grey colour scheme over the Old Man of Hoy in 1997. *[RAF Lossiemouth]*

'AJJ' a Tornado of 617 Squadron over Stromness in the Orkneys. *[RAF Lossiemouth]*

A pair of 617 Squadron Tornados - AJ-F and AJ-K escort L1011 TriStar ZD950 on its last few miles back from the Gulf in early 1999. The airfield in the bottom right of the picture is Banff . *[RAF Lossiemouth]*

Chapter Eight

STRIKE WING COUNTRY

*"A lonely impulse of delight
Drove to this tumilt in the clouds;
I balanced all, brought all to mind,
A waste of breath the years behind
In balance with this life, this death."*

W B Yeats.

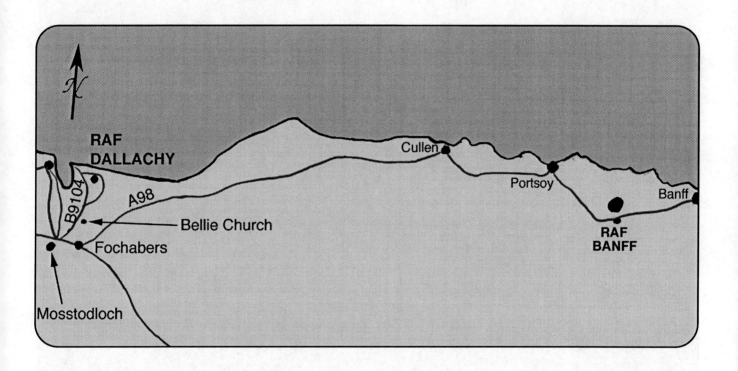

After travelling through the village of Mosstodloch and crossing the Spey bridge, the B9015 is on the left. Two miles down this road on the right side is is a large memorial erected in1992 to the memory of those lost while serving with the Dallachy Strike Wing during World War Two.

The old Dallachy airfield lies to the east of the road and can be viewed from a road which follows the former perimeter track.The control tower and ops block are the only surviving airfield buildings. Returning to the A96, Bellie churchyard on the left side contains some wartime aircrew graves. The A96 now passes through Fochabers where the Pringle museum contains a good display of RAF Dallachy photos and artifacts.

Following the A98 east from Fochabers through Cullen and Portsoy, the old airfield of RAF Banff (Boyndie) lies three miles north east of Portsoy. Little remains of the airfield apart from the runways and perimeter track.

A monument to Banff Strike Wing was erected in a layby on the A98 south of the airfield in 1989.

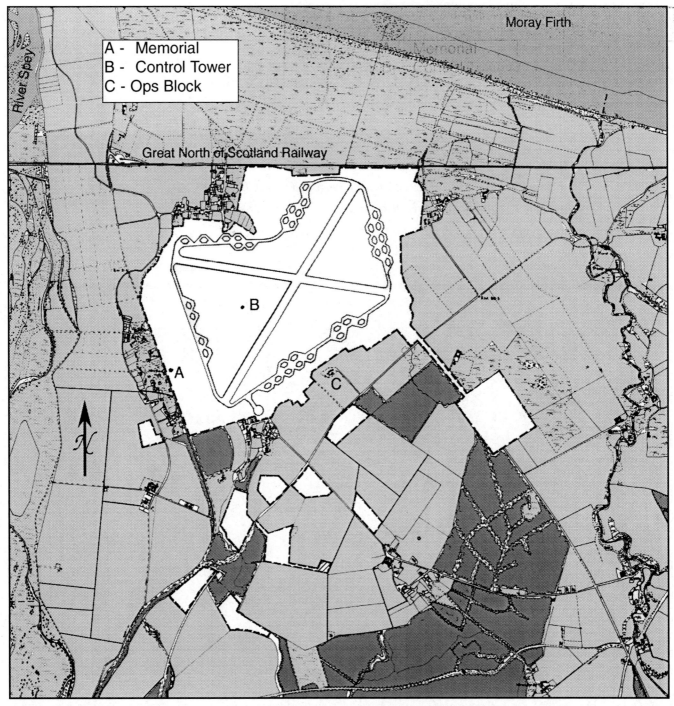

A - Memorial
B - Control Tower
C - Ops Block

Royal Air Force Dallachy. 57° 39' 23"N 03° 09' 09"W

Royal Air Force Dallachy

The B9104 from Fochabers to Spey Bay is a narrow country road meandering between the river Spey and the walled estate of Gordon Castle. To the right of the road a couple of miles from Spey Bay can be seen a building which, though bereft of doors and windows, is very obviously an airfield control tower. This building is the most tangible evidence of the former RAF airfield of Dallachy.

By 1942 this part of the Moray coast appeared to be already overcrowded with airfields at Kinloss, Lossiemouth and Milltown when it was decided to build another one at Dallachy. This was for use by Coastal Command but Bomber Command were also interested in it as a forward base. However, despite the large area of flat land available, a ridge running down the south side of the proposed site impeded a third runway making the airfield unsuitable for heavy bombers. Dallachy was scheduled for completion on 31 March, 1943 and by then the Navy were interested in using it for an Observer School. Despite the desperate war situation of 1942 and 1943 the Navy and RAF appear to have been conducting their own little feuds with little or no co-operation, but the arguments as to who should run Dallachy ceased when the Navy decided it was then not suitable for their operations. The airfield was then earmarked by the RAF for No 3 Coastal Command

OTU but after problems of moving from Cranwell the OTU went to Haverfordwest in Wales.

RAF Dallachy finally started its operational career as a satellite for 14(P) AFU which had arrived at Banff in May 1943. The aircraft used by the AFU were Oxfords which were separated into day and night flights. There was also an affiliated Beam Approach Training Flight. There was now a surplus of fighter pilots and training on multi-engined machines received priority. Dallachy was obviously an ideal airfield for this type of training and a considerable number of flying hours were accumulated in 1943 and 1944. Dallachy was also a happy unit, as recalled by John Clarke, an Australian, now living at Weybridge. His arrival with a group of Australian pilots on 17 April 1943 was greeted by a slap up meal laid on by the WVS at Keith railway station. The abundance of food and local

hospitality was a welcome surprise after the austerities of England. Mr Clarke also recalls practising night flying wearing dark goggles due to the lack of darkness in June. At that time the pilots often noticed a strange R/T "shadow" in the circuit and due, it was thought, to enemy transmissions from Norway as German voices were occasionally heard.

As usual with training units there were crashes at Dallachy though not on the same scale as its neighbours of Kinloss and Lossiemouth. An Oxford piloted by a Sgt Franko crashed on an island in the Orkneys on 18 December 1943 but he was not rescued by the Navy until 27 December 1943. As there was only a lighthouse on the island it cannot have been a very merry Christmas for him.

Before 14(P)AFU was disbanded, one of their Oxfords was involved in a bizarre accident. During low-

Dallachy under construction - photographed by the Luftwaffe in June 1942. *[Ian Keillar]*

404 Squadron Beaufighter unleashing rockets. *[Chaz Bowyer]*

flying on 16 July 1944 it hit a farmer working in his field, killing him outright. The Oxford (believed to be ED151) managed to return to base with a bent propeller. There is no information as to the fate of the pilot, but the dead farmer's mother is supposed to have been given a pension of ten shillings a week.

After the invasion of Europe in June 1944 a lot of the German U-boat fleet started to move from the Bay of Biscay to Norwegian waters. In order to combat this move Coastal Command decided to switch its forces from English bases to the north east of Scotland with Banff and Dallachy as the major units. Flying Training Command was given two weeks to vacate the station, but as there was now a surplus of aircrew, 14(P) AFU and its associated BAT flight were disbanded. During its year's stay at Dallachy the AFU produced 664 pilots with a total flying hours of 65,721.

When Coastal took over on 1 September 1944 it had been intended to operate Wellingtons from Banff and Dallachy but plans were changed and the first aircraft to arrive on 29 September 1944 were five Warwicks of 281 ASR Squadron and Swordfishes of 838 FAA squadron. The first operational flight which was uneventful was flown by two Warwicks on 30 September 1944. The Swordfishes were used for anti-sub searches in the Moray Firth but after 106 uneventful sorties they were withdrawn at the end of October. 281 was equally unsuccessful and left

Flt. Lt. Ilbury and other aircrew of 455 Squadron Dallachy 1945. *[Gp Capt Ilbery]*

Dallachy on 25 October 1944 after 23 operations.

The stage was now set for the arrival of the Coastal Command Strike Wings and the start of Dallachy's major contribution to the war effort. Strike Wings had been formed as the result of bitter lessons learned in the early war years when under-armed and under powered RAF aircraft had been decimated in unsuccessful attacks on enemy shipping. It was not until the advent of the Beaufighter and Mosquito aircraft armed with a formidable array of rockets, cannons, machine guns and bombs, that the RAF was able to form a feasible anti-shipping strike force.

Coastal Command Strike Wings first operated from bases in the south and west of England but with the departure of the U-boats to Norway it was decided to move the Wings to N E Scotland. On 22 October 1944 Dallachy Strike Wing started to form with the arrival of the Beaufighters TFX of 144 RAF and 404 RCAF squadrons. On 24 October 1944 the Wing was completed with the arrival of 455 RAAF and 489 RNZAF Beaufighters. There was also a detachment of 524 Squadron Wellingtons which were to co-ordinate with night flying operations by dropping flares for the attacking Beaufighters.

The first operation of the new Wing started out on 25 October 1944. Twenty two Beaufighters with two fighter Mosquitoes from Banff and an ASR Warwick set out

How not to land a Beaufighter, unless you have no choice! 489 crew examine the damage. Note the 'damage' to the pilot's forehead! *[Author via Fochabers Museum]*

Right: Beaufighter of 404 Squadron.
[Chaz Bowyer]

Below: Briefing in Dallachy's Operations Room.
{Wg Cdr. A.C.Gadd]

Bottom: Operations Block, Dallachy, 1990.
{Author]

German records on 8 November the Beaufighters sank the German merchant vessels Aquila and Helga Ferdinand and damaged the Framnaes at Midtgulen. On 27 November they sank the Italian Fidelitas and damaged the Jersbekat at Sulafiord and on 5 December the Radbord and Albert Janus were sank at Orstenfiord.

1945 started off with heavy snowfalls. This inhibited flying to a certain extent but in the operations which were carried out, a Dutch lighter was sunk off the Norwegian coast on the 6 January and two Norwegian vessels, the Fusa and Trygg were sunk at Korsfiord on the 8th. On the 9th the Sirius and Blaaveis were sunk at Flugsaetfiord and Sognefiord. 524's Wellingtons which had been away having new radar equipment fitted, returned on the 2 February 1945.

9 February 1945 was to be remembered as Black Friday at Dallachy. Enemy shipping had been reported in Forde Fjord and 32 Beaufighters set out to attack in the afternoon. They were accompanied by a fighter escort of ten Mustangs from 65 Squadron based at Peterhead and two ASR Warwicks of 279 Squadron. The original plan of attack from inland had to be abandoned due to the high cliffs in the area and the aircraft had to fly up the fiord into a veritable hail of anti-aircraft fire. FW190s of the Ninth and Twelth Staffeln Jagdeschwader now joined in the fray and a vicious battle ensued.

Spike Holly, now living in Wales, was the navigator of one of the Beaufighters which was attacked from the rear by a FW 190. Returning the fire Spike saw the FW disappear before his own badly damaged aircraft crash landed in the water. Local Norwegians rescued the RAF crew but Spike was so badly injured he had to be handed over to the Germans for treatment. It later transpired that the pilot of the crashed FW was Lt Rudi Linz, an ace with 69 victories to his credit. In all nine Beaufighters and one Mustang were destroyed while the Germans lost five FWs and had some ships damaged.

Most off the 23 Beaufighters which staggered back to base were damaged and two had to belly land at Dallachy. The whole station was shocked by the losses especially 404 which had six Canadian crews missing.

On 11 February 1945 a new type of operation was carried out. Operation "Ashfield" was a co-operative

to attack shipping at Kristiansand in Norway but their trip was aborted due to bad weather. The basic plan for the Norwegian operations was for one "Rover" aircraft to search the fiords and harbours for enemy shipping, and if any was found it would call up the main force to attack with rockets and torpedos.

On 9 December the Norwegian ship Havda was sunk at Flora. Aircraft losses were inevitable and four aircraft and crews were lost before the end of the year. One of these from 404 crashed in the sea after hitting a ship's mast on 9 December. The Warwick ASR aircraft which accompanied major ops were not successful in rescuing any of the crews.

Intensive flying was carried out for the rest of the year and although a lot of ops were aborted because of bad weather some successes were recorded. The Wing ORB gives little details but according to British and

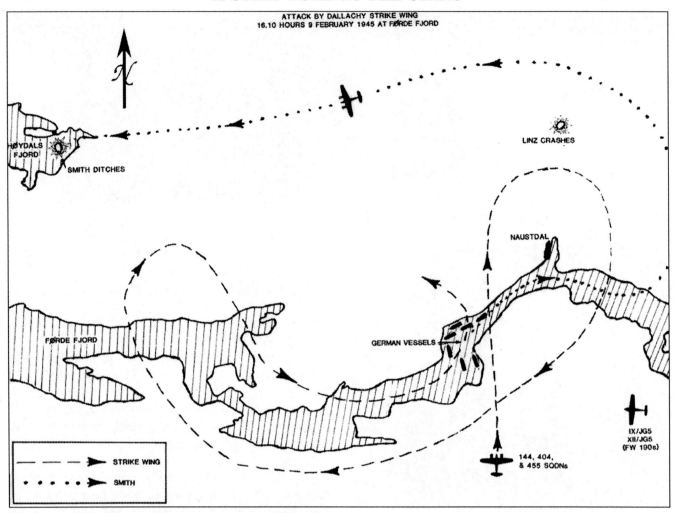

ATTACK BY DALLACHY STRIKE WING
16.10 HOURS 9 FEBRUARY 1945 AT FØRDE FJORD

HØYDALS FJORD

SMITH DITCHES

LINZ CRASHES

NAUSTDAL

FØRDE FJORD

GERMAN VESSELS

IX/JG5
XII/JG5
(FW 190s)

144, 404,
& 455 SQDNs

STRIKE WING

SMITH

Black Friday's Operation. *[Les Taylor]*

Scars of battle, 9th February 1945, Beaufighter NF831, flown by Flt. Sgt
Butler. *[Wg. Cdr. A.C. Gadd]*

action between radar equipped Wellingtons and torpedo Beaufighters. Two Wellingtons went out and one laid a Drem light in the target area. Both Wellingtons now radar searched for enemy shipping while the Beaufighters circled the Drem waiting to be called up on VHF if a target was found. Although this type of operation was a success in the Med this first sortie from Dallachy was a failure. In a second "Ashfield" on 21 February 1945 the Beaufighters failed to find the Drem and had to abandon the trip. On the 16 February, 21 Dallachy Beaufighters plus Mosquitoes from Banff carried out operation 'Chuck' which was to bottle up enemy shipping in Norway in fiords by simulating mining using delayed fused bombs. One aircraft dropped its bombs in Spey Bay after engine trouble. Another two found their compasses seriously affected by the bombs, GEE failure and poor met forecast all added to another failure. A tanker, the Rogn, was damaged in an attack on a convoy at Kristiansand on 26 February 1945. One damaged aircraft tried to make Peterhead but after the navigator baled out safely the aircraft crashed and despite searches the pilot was not found. On 2 March 1945 a Beaufighter had to jettison its torpedo in Spey Bay after a fire. This caused some excitement locally.

Intensive flying was carried out throughout March and April. On the 8 March the German vessel *Phoenicia* was damaged in Kiel Canal and the Danish vessel *Hemidal* at Midgulen. The Lysaker was sunk at Stadlandet on 23 March and on the 24th the *Thetis* and *Sarp* were both sunk at Egersund. In April the *Palmyra* was damaged at Feddefiord on the 4th and a minesweeper sunk on the 11th. The *Elmar* was sunk at Maaloy on 22nd and the

Beaufighter PL-O of 144 Squadron crash-landed at Dallachy, February 1945. *[C B Nicholls]*

Dallachy Strike Wing Beaufighter strike, Norway, May 1945. *[Chaz Bowyer]*

Above: 489 Sqn Torbeau showing off at Dallachy in the autumn of 1944. *[Author via Fochabers Museum]*
Below: Danish freighter Jave under attack from rocket-firing Beaufighters from the Dallachy Strike Wing 3rd May 1945.
[Wg Cdr F.E. Burton]

Ingerseks sunk at Sogniefiord on the 23rd.

In May 1945 the tempo increased as German ships started fleeing north as their homeland was occupied by the Allies. On the 2 May a minesweeper was sunk and a U-boat sunk and another damaged in the Kattegat. The next day two Danish vessels were sunk and another damaged in Kiel Bay. One vessel was sunk and two damaged in what was to be the last operation on 4 May. By VE day Dallachy Strike Wing had flown 2230 sorties, sank 15 ships and damaged 55 others. With hindsight, the amount of operations with the severe loss of life and aircraft, hardly justified the amount of damage done to the enemy, but at the time it was a widely held view that the Germans would continue the struggle in Norway and every effort had to be made to stop them reaching that country.

With the war over, some operations were still carried out. On 11 and 12 May 48 escorting sorties were carried out over *HMS Devonshire* carrying home the Norwegian Crown Prince and other VIPs. On the 16th an

Control Tower, Dallachy, 1990. *[Author]*

Flg. Off. 'Spike' Holly and Flg. Off. P.C. Smith, shot down on 9th February 1945. *[Spike Holly]*

The Dallachy Strike Wing memorial was unveiled in July 1992, when it was overflown by a Nimrod and a pair of Buccaneers. Right: Detail of the Memorial. *[Author]*

attack was made on a U-boat schnorkel off Buchan Ness and on the 21st the final "official" ops were pairs of Beaufighters searching the Norwegian fiords for surrendering U-boats.

404 Squadron moved to Banff in May followed by 489 in June. The other Squadrons 144 and 455 disbanded on 25 May 1945. The war's end saw Dallachy's population rapidly dwindle from a peak of 1530 RAF and 408 WAAF to a mere handful finally posted to Haverfordwest in September. The station was briefly used as 21 Aircrew Holding Unit where many of the thousands of redundant aircrew were prepared 'hopefully' for a civilian career. Dallachy was put on Care and Maintenance on 24 November 1945. The Army used it for Territorial training for a few years and the FAA from Lossiemouth also used the runways for target practice. The many vacated buildings were used for a time by 240 Yugoslavs, former members of the Chetnik guerillas. Despite the many encumbrances a Shackleton from 120 Squadron Kinloss managed to land on Dallachy in mistake for Lossiemouth in February 1952.

Dallachy today still manages to look like an airfield although all buildings are gone apart from the Tower and the Operations Block now used as a chicken shed by a local farmer. The runways are more or less intact and so are the 35 diamond hard standings preserved by new plantations of conifers.

After much effort by local people and squadron associations, a memorial was erected to the memory of those who died while serving with the Dallachy Strike Wing. Positioned at the old entrance to the camp it was unveiled on 30 July 1992. A large crowd of local people and ex members of the Strike Wing squadrons attended with a Nimrod and two Buccaneers carrying out a flypast. On 9 Feb 1995 a service was held at the memorial to commemorate the 50th .anniversary of Black Friday. This was attended by many veterans as well as a detachment af Canadian airmen. An ANZAC service of remembrance was held at the memorial in April 1997. This was attended by Australian Gp. Capt. Ilbery who unveiled the original memorial in 1992.

Royal Air Force Banff
In the autumn of 1987, a team of divers from RAF Lossiemouth Sub Aqua team discovered the scattered wreckage of an aircraft lying under 30 ft of water on the

Short Seaplane re-fuelling off Banff, August 1915.

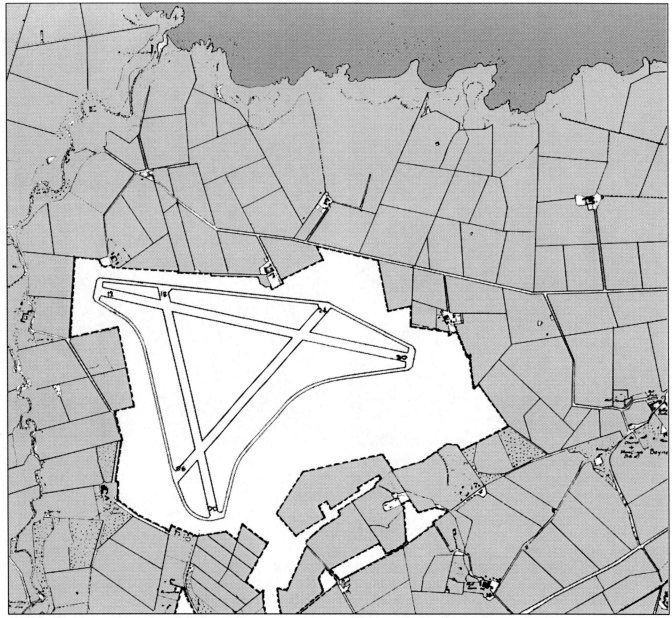

Royal Air Force Banff 57° 40'00"N 02° 38'00"W 250-280ft above sea level.

edge of Lossiemouth Halliman Skerries. Investigation proved that the remains were those of a MkVI Mosquito HR284 which had spun into the sea on 21 December 1944. Both crew members, Plt Off W D Livock, the pilot, and Flt Sgt G L West, the navigator, had been killed. The broken bits of this aircraft are probably all that remain of the many Mosquitoes lost in action when the Banff Strike Wing was involved in the bitter fighting of the last few months of World War II.

Banff is first mentioned in aviation circles in WW I. The caption of a photograph of a Short Seaplane No. 185, states that this aircraft was involved in mine spotting duties at Banff from 18 to 24 August 1915. At that time the seaplane belonged to *HMS Campania* which was a seaplane carrier converted from a Cunard liner. The seaplane may have re-fuelled off Banff but there is no mention of any facilities in the area and Banff was not to feature in aviation circles for the next thirty odd years.

The Banff area came under fire in July 1940 when a 'hit and run' Me111 flew in low over the sea, dropped bombs on Duff House and on houses in the adjoining town of Macduff before speeding out to sea again. The Germans obviously thought Duff House was a military

RAF Banff prior to opening in April 1943.

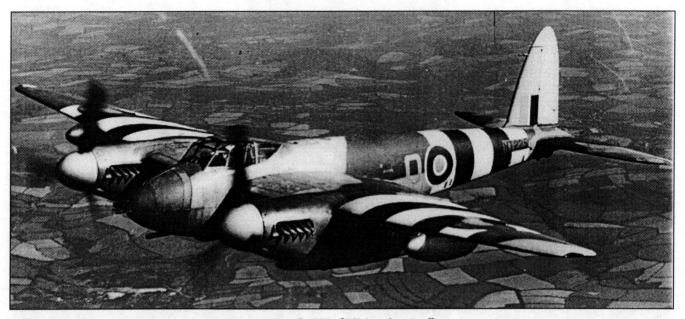

Mosquito Fb XVIII of 248 Squadron Banff.

camp when in fact it was a P.o.W Camp. Six German P.oW.s and two British soldiers were killed and many were wounded.

The plateau called Boyndie, situated above the town of Banff, seemed a good spot for an airfield despite being exposed to the often bitter north winds. Construction started in 1942 and three runways were built, 185° 1400 yds, 236° 1400 yds, and 295° 2000 yds. 25 hard standings of the frying pan type edged the perimeter track. These were distributed along the 185° and 236° runways with a couple at the cannon range in the N.E corner of the airfield. Hangars consisted of three T2 and 13 blister. The watch tower and technical buildings were clustered in sites further south among the woods and fields.

Originally intended as a two squadron Coastal Command station with facilities for bomber squadrons, the station changed masters even before it was opened in 1943. 3 OTU which was to come in April 1943 went instead to Haverfordwest from Cranwell and in April 1943 Banff was transferred to 21 Group FTC and the newly completed airfield opened on 21 April 1943. 14 (P) AFU arrived with Oxfords from Ossington in Notts at the end of May. A very large unit, it had three detached Flights, 1512 at Banff, 1542 at Dallachy, and 1518 at Edzell. Fraserburgh was also used as a satellite. Gp Capt Peck took command of Banff, Dallachy and Fraserburgh.

The next year was an extremely busy one for Banff as the AFU got into its stride and an enormous amount of flying was accomplished. The Oxford was not the most forgiving of aircraft but considering the amount of hours flown the accident rate was not exceptionally huge. The first fatality reported was on 18 July 1943 when Oxford 1284 crashed near Milltown with loss of Sgt Penford. LX265 and LX237 had a mid-air collision with one death on 25 August 1943 and V4158 crashed at Dyce on 29 August, 1943 killing the two crew. A mid-air collision was

reported on 31 August 1943 between LX268 and a Wellington near Elgin while three more Oxfords crashed during night flying in August. Banff did not seem to have many visitors, intentional or otherwise, but it had the mandatory Horsas for Operation Tyndall in August 1943. The intended move of the Coastal Command Strike Wings to the north east of Scotland in the summer of 1944 coincided with a surplus of trained pilots and 14 (P) AFU disbanded on 31 August 1944. During the AFUs stay at Banff it had produced 1,516 pilots and had completed a total of 113,896 flying hours.

Banff and Dallachy were originally intended to house four Wellington squadrons but when 18 Gp Coastal Command took over on 1 September 1944 it was with a Strike Wing of 144 and 404 Squadrons Beaufighters, 235, 248 and 333 (Norwegian) Squadrons flying Mosquitoes. The complete Strike Wing was under the command of Gp Capt Max Aitken, the son of Lord Beaverbrook.

The first operation by the Strike Wing, a Reconnaissance patrol by two aircraft of 333 Squadron, had nothing of interest to report. Because of their local knowledge the Norwegians of 333 Squadron were to do most of the reconnaissance patrols. Also on the 6th a shipping strike by 26 Beaufighters had to be abandoned

Busy armourers, Banff autumn 1944

A busy scene at RAF Banff , spring 1945. *[British Aerospace Hatfield]*

The sun did sometimes shine at Banff!

attacked a U-boat with cannon and machine guns. Many hits were observed and the U-boat was left listing and smoking. Twelve Mosquitoes later searched without success for this U-boat. The normal armament of the Mosquitoes at this time was four .303 MGs in the nose and four 20mm Hispano Suiza cannon in the bomb bay. Some aircraft of 248 Squadron later had the four cannon

because of bad weather. Another patrol by 24 Beaufighters and 13 Mosquitoes on 12 September was equally disappointing, and one Beaufighter had to ditch with the crew being picked up by a fishing vessel. Recce patrols were continuous every day but it was not until 14 September that Banff aircrew drew first blood when 19 Beaufighters and 25 Mosquitoes attacked a convoy of 4 motor vessels and two escorts off the Norwegian coast. Hits were observed and the Sulldorf flak ship was sunk and the merchant vessel 'Iris' damaged. When one Beaufighter was shot down a crew member was seen in a dinghy but the ASR Warwick could not be sent out due to lack of fighter escorts.

Bad weather curtailed ops until 17 September 1944 when 23 Mosquitoes were airborne in three separate anti sub sweeps. They found nothing to report, nor did 23 Beaufighters and 8 Mosquitoes on anti shipping patrol. On 18 September 1944 eight Mosquitoes sighted and

Formidable armament of Mosquito FB XVIII *[Chaz Bowyer]*

Briefing in Banff's Operation Room 1945.

replaced by a version of the six pounder anti tank gun. The combination of MGs, cannon and rockets gave these Mosquitoes Mk XVlll (or Tsetses as they were sometimes called) a strike potential equivalent to a destroyer.

On 19 September 1944 a Rover patrol of 21 Beaufighters and 11 Mosquitoes attacked a convoy of three ships near Askevold, and sank the Lynx and Tyrifiord. One Beaufighter dived into the sea. On 21 September 1944 21 Beaufighters and 17 Mosquitoes attacked and sank the merchant vessels Vangsnes and Hygia at Lister. 24 September was a busy day with 16 Mosquitoes attacking and sinking the Biber and damaging the Storesund off Hjeltefiord. All aircraft returned safely despite heavy flak which had torn off a square foot from the leading edge of one aircraft. Flying for the rest of September followed the same pattern, with a total of 1991.24 operational hours for the month. It was not all work however at Banff and during September the personnel were treated to three ENSA concerts, two station dances and a RAF Gang Show.

There was also a Battle of Britain parade in the town of Banff on 17 September.

During the first week of October, patrols were carried out as normal with some vessels being damaged. On the 2nd two Beaufighters collided near Banff and all four crew were killed. In the early hours of 9 October a Warwick of 281 Squadron took off from Banff loaded with marine markers, flame floats and drift lights. Two hours later these lights were dropped to form a six mile diameter ring about 100 miles west of Stavenger. Eight Mosquitoes and 14 Beaufighters circled these lights waiting for German ships which had formerly travelled unseen in the early morning light. The scheme worked out when a German convoy approached. The freighter Rudolf Oldendorff and the sub hunter UJ1711 were sunk and the Sarp damaged. On the 13 October Banff was visited by correspondents from all the major newspapers who were briefed on the stations' role.

Practically every day now reconnaissance patrols or

'Two-Six!' Removing a bogged down Mosquito at Banff in the autumn of 1944.

Banff Mosquito's destroying JU88's in Kattegat, 21 April 1945. *[Chaz Bowyer]*

Above: Mosquito LR330 crashed landed at Banff after a Norwegian raid on 16 February 1945.
Below: One of winter's nastier jobs, January 1945.

A Banff Mosquito attacks a U-Boat.

armed anti shipping patrols were carried out and many small ships were sunk or damaged. One Mosquito was reported missing on 21 October. With the departure of 144 and 404s Beaufighters to Dallachy on 24 October and the arrival of 143's Mosquitoes from North Coates, Banff had now on all Mosquito Strike Wing.

The remainder of 1944 was spent in constant attacks on enemy shipping and U-boats in Norwegian waters. Many ships were sunk or damaged but there was a steady toll of missing aircraft making the Strike Wing casualties proportionately higher than any other RAF unit during the last six months of the war. On 7 December 1944 a number of German fighters were encountered for the first time by a mixed group of 25 Mosquitoes from Banff, 40 Beaufighters from Dallachy and escorting Mustangs from Peterhead. In the ensuing action four ME109s were claimed shot down and two FW190s collided in mid air. Four Strike Wing aircraft failed to return. Accidents occurred also nearer home. On 18 October a Mosquito on take off crashed into another taxying, killing both crew of the latter. The crew were injured when a Mosquito crashed on return from operations on 26 December.

Despite the pressure of operations Christmas 1944 was celebrated in usual style and by now many local people had befriended the airmen and took part in the festivities. January 1945 started off with very wintry weather but this however did not curtail operations as shown in a photo of that period. On January 15th two

Shipping attack in a Norwegian fiord by the Banff Strike Wing, 1945.

Above: U-Boat 804 under attack by Banff Mosquitos, 6 April 1945. *[ACM Sir C Foxley-Norris]*

Below: A Mosquito of 143 Sqn Banff attacks shipping in Sandeford, 2 April 1945. *[ACM Sir C Foxley-Norris]*

Capturing what the Banff Strike Wing was about - a Mosquito becomes airborne in the autumn of 1944.

large merchant ships were blown up in Leirvik Harbour with however the loss of six Mosquitoes. On 9 January the two crew were killed when their Mosquito crashed on a farmhouse at the edge of the airfield. After a mid air collision on 25 January one Mosquito landed safely but the other crashed with the loss of both crew. On 22 February a Mosquito on a photo training exercise hit a ship's mast and crashed in Buckie harbour injuring the crew. Two days later both crew were killed when their Mosquito crashed near Buckie.

In contrast to most other RAF units the actions of the Strike Wings actually increased during the last few months of the war. As the Germans retreated on mainland Europe there was an increase in shipping to Norway and Denmark and it was feared that Hitler might be intending to make a last ditch stand in those countries. Persistant attacks were carried out by the Strike Wing on this shipping and many vessels were sunk. Also on 9th April, 37 Mosquitoes sank three U-boats in the Skaaggerak. Another Uboat was sunk in the Kattegat on 9 April. 21 April saw an unusual action when 45 Mosquitoes had a chance encounter with 18 Junkers torpedo bombers making a belated attempt to harry allied shipping. Nine Junkers 88s and 188s were shot down. Aircraft from Banff took part in the final shipping strike of the war on convoys in Keil Bay on 4 May. One Mosquito flew so low it came back with part of a mast and German Ensign embedded in the aircraft's nose. Operations did not cease on VE day but continued with convoy escort duties and searches for survivors from ditched aircraft until 21 May. With the end of the European war the Banff squadrons disbanded rapidly. The first to disband on 25 May was 404 which had only come from Dallachy to convert from Beaufighters to Mosquitoes in March. On June 6 143 was re

numbered 14 and stayed on until disbanding in March 1946. 333 went home to Norway in a peaceful role in June 1945 and 235 and 248 disbanded in July. 489 Squadron repositioned from Dallachy on 16th June and disbanded on 1 August. For some reason there was a detachment of Sea Otters at Banff during July and August 1945.

The airfield closed in the middle of 1946 but was afterwards used as target for simulated attacks by FAA aircraft from Lossiemouth. Over the years most of the buildings have disappeared but in 1976 it was re-opened for flying by Banff Flying Club. The re-opening ceremony included one of the few remaining Mosquitoes still flying. The Flying Club no longer exists and Banff now reverberates only to the roar of go carts which utilise the runways for racing.

After much effort by local people and Strike Wing survivors, sufficient money was raised to enable a monument to be erected in memory of those who had lost their lives while serving in the Wing. This was unveiled in a nostalgic ceremony on 28 September 1989.

Many ex members of the Wing came to see the unveiling and the last surviving flying Mosquito in Britain, RR299, did a very impressive fly past. The slim granite memorial at the roadside will now remind passers by of the great sacrifices made by the airmen of Banff Strike Wing during the last few months of WW II.

Recently another Stone commemorating the personnel of 14(P) AFU has been erected beside the Strike Wing Memorial.

The memorial at Banff is dedicated - during which a Nimrod and Mosquito overflew the site.

Left: The memorial stone in it's peaceful, rural setting. [author]

Chapter Nine

THE NORTH EAST CORNER

"Straight on wings I arise and carry
purpose up to the ends of the air"
Robert Bridges.

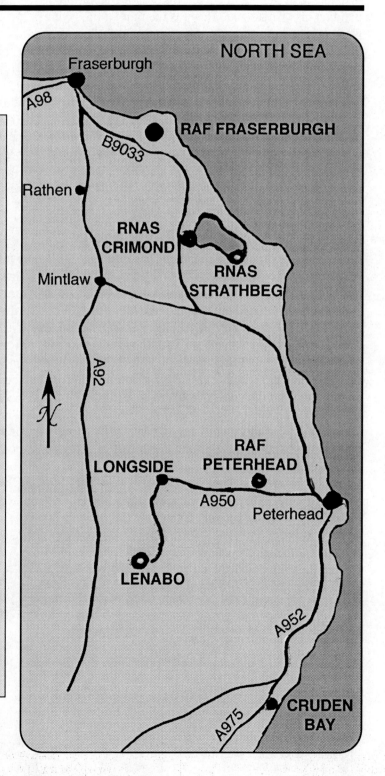

The A98 carries on to Fraserburgh where an easterly road to Inverallochy passes the site of RAF Fraserburgh. A few buildings and part of the runways can still be seen. Going south the A952 passes through the village of Crimond. East of the village and well signposted is the RSPB reserve of Loch Strathbeg. The road to the reserve passes through the old airfield of RNAS Crimond now covered with the aerials of a wireless station. Quite a few of the old airfield buildings still remain. Loch Strathbeg was used as a seaplane base during the latter part of WW1 and some hard standings for a hangar can still be seen near the present boathouse.

Eighteen miles south on the A952 is the port of Peterhead. A WW1 seaplane base has disappeared beneath new harbour buildings though a possible slipway is visible on the shore below the prison.

Nine miles west of Peterhead in the village of Longside, St John's church houses a propeller memorial to the crew of a WW1 airship lost while flying from Lenabo airship station. The site of Lenabo (RNAS Longside) lies about five miles south east of Longside and being completely unmarked is difficult to find . The airship shed bases and wind breaks are still visible as well as parts of some buildings.

The A950 back to Peterhead passes the deserted airfield of RAF Peterhead which still has a lot of old wartime buildings visible.

Ten miles down the coast from Peterhead is the village of Cruden Bay. Near the harbour is a monument to Tryggve Gran who made the first flight to Norway from this spot in 1914.

Most of the airfields in the Moray Firth are situated on the coastal plain as the hilly inland area was not suitable for even landing strips. Nevertheless there is a photo of an aircraft visiting Keith in August 1913. This is the Farman flown by Capt Dawes from Montrose to Nairn stopping at various places en route and giving the local inhabitants their first glimpse of a flying machine.

The only aircraft known to be built in the north east was also constructed at Keith. In the early thirties an Aberdeen aircraft enthusiast invested his Derby winnings in a garage in Keith and started his life long ambition of building his own aircraft. This was the time of the Flying Flea craze and the garage owner, Jimmy Goodall, started building one of these peculiar aircraft in the garage loft. One of his helpers was a Mr Herd, now in his eighties and still living at Keith. His part in the project was the production of the semi circular windscreen from perspex and aluminium channelling. An engineer called Stewart manufactured a beautiful laminated mahogany propeller which was driven by a Douglas motor cycle engine. Jimmy Goodall finished his machine in 1936 and although he had no flying experience he managed a test flight at Dyce the same year. Sadly, shortly afterwards he was killed when the plane crashed. It was one of the many tragedies associated with the Flying Flea which caused it to be eventually banned from flying.

During the Thirties Sir Alan Cobham's Flying Circus travelled all over the country with their various collections of aircraft such as the Handley Page Clive, Avro 504K, Airspeed Ferry and Tiger Moth. They held shows at Macduff, Lossiemouth and Huntly where many north east folk got their glimpse of and some their first flight in what was still an unusual form of transport.

Away from the coast the inland areas of the Moray Firth were comparatively peaceful in both World Wars and yet it was in this quiet farming community that the first enemy bombing raids in the north east of Scotland have been recorded.

The incident happened on the night of 2/3 May 1916 when eight German Zeppelins set off to attack Rosyth and the Forth Bridge. Scattered by gales, only two airships reached Scotland and of these, one, the L14 dropped its bombs harmlessly on fishing boats near Arbroath. The other, the L20 headed inland and turned east at Aviemore. It dropped a bomb at Craig Castle near Rhynie and eight more in the fields around Insch and Old Rayne. The L20 flew on over the North Sea and was wrecked in a forced landing near Stavenger in Norway.

No casualties were caused by the few bombs dropped but the north east was in a ferment of excitement and many old people still living can remember the incident which happened when they were only children. Craig Castle had its own generating plant and was supposed to have been lit up brilliantly for a party, thus creating a target. This was just one of the many rumours and stories that flew thick and fast after the incident but it is likely that it was a case of the Zeppelin being hopelessly lost and dumping its bombs in order to lighten the machine and so gain height.

World War II Bombing Raids

The north east corner of Scotland has not usually been regarded as a danger area during World War II but in proportion to its size and population it received more than its share of German air attacks. In fact Aberdeen was attacked more times than any other city in Scotland. We have already mentioned the attacks on Invergordon, Lossiemouth and Duff House. As we move east along the coast the next incident of importance occurred on Saturday 6 August 1941. On that day a JU 88 bombed and machine gunned the Banff Distillery warehouse. To prevent further fire and explosions a lot of the stored whisky was tipped into the Boyndie Burn causing some disorientation among the cattle and poultry which used it for drinking purposes. Some locals - perhaps over enthusiastic about disposing of the whisky - became rather inebriated and were later charged with theft! When Lord Haw Haw later described the operation as the destruction of an important amunition dump he was probably not too far from the truth. Farther inland a bomb on Huntly destroyed a house and killed a woman about this period.

Jimmy Goodhall in his Flying Flea, 1936.
[James Malcolm]

Huntly house destroyed in air raid 1941.
[Press & Journal]

Above: Craig Castle, view from the north-east.
Below: Zeppelin L20 ditched off the Norwegian coast after Scottish raid on 3 May 1916. *[Smithsonian Institute]*

Peterhead bomb damage, 5 September 1941
[Press & Journal]

Most of the raids were purely hit and run affairs when single German aircraft on reconnaisance or mine laying operations would nip in quickly and drop their bombs on the first buildings in sight. As the raids were of such a brief nature they were rarely intercepted. Peterhead and Fraserburgh situated on a piece of land jutting into the North Sea bore the brunt of these attacks.

Peterhead was the recipient of 78 bombs which killed 38 people and injured 44. 58 houses were destroyed and 138 damaged.

Fraserburgh suffered 23 raids. The worst of these was on 5 November 1940 when a fire at the big store of Benzie and Millars apparently attracted the attention of a German pilot who dropped his bombs killing seven

Fraserburgh houses destroyed in air raid, Frebruary 1943.
[Press & Journal]

people. During the war 87 bombs were dropped, killing 49 and injured 249. 83 buildings were destroyed and 296 damaged.

One of the Fraserburgh raids in February 1943 was the indirect result of a spy plot. Earlier in the War two Norwegians had been dropped in Britain to spy for the Germans and one of these was now a double agent sending false information to the Germans. At the beginning of 1943 he had requested equipment to be dropped by parachute at Fraserburgh. However the German pilot also dropped a bomb causing the death of an 11 year old boy.

Royal Air Force Fraserburgh

The Sea Fury's engine had oversped and was pouring black smoke when the pilot sighted a small coastal airfield and made a safe emergency landing. The Sea Fury, WH617, from HMS Theseus, and piloted by Lt T Barlow, was probably the last powered aircraft to land at Fraserburgh airfield. The date was 9 September 1952.

Fraserburgh, as it was known officially was constructed about five miles east of the town of Fraserburgh, and was also known as Inverallochy or Cairnbulg from the two local villages. Originally built as a satellite for Peterhead, twelve miles farther south, it had three runways, 170° 1100 yds, 236° 1350 yds and 304° 1000 yds and a perimeter track with three loop hard standings and five Hurricane pens each capable of accommodating two aircraft. There were six sites of domestic buildings scattered around the fields to the west of the camp. The WAAFs were billeted farthest from the airfield but being beside the sea no doubt the place had its advantages.

The station opened officially on 6 December 1941 and the first aircraft to arrive two days later were Swordfishes of 823 Squadron. Heavy snow in January

From am earlier era, a Short 187 is seen suspended from a crane in Fraserburgh harbour in May 1917.
[J.M.Bruce/G.S Leslie Collection]

1942 curtailed flying and there appeared to be little activity in the early months of 1942. The Swordfishes were replaced by six Hurricanes from 883 Squadron Crail at the end of January 1942. The next few months saw a few visitors such as a Wellington, Spitfire and Beaufighter. On 26 February the ORB records an Auto Gyro in the area, a most unusual sight. No reason was given for its visit.

In May 1942 it was decided to form a new OTU, No 8, at Fraserburgh. The Photo Reconnaisance Conversion Flight from Squires gate was amalgamated with No 1 PRU advanced training flight Detling to form the new OTU at Fraserburgh on 8 May 1942. The first aircraft for the unit, eight Spitfires and a Master, arrived on 24 May and work was started on building five double blister and one treble blister hangar around the perimeter track.

The job of 8 OTU was to train Spitfire and Mosquito pilots in specialised photo reconnaissance flying. This involved quite long trips of up to six hours duration around the British Isles. It was soon found that

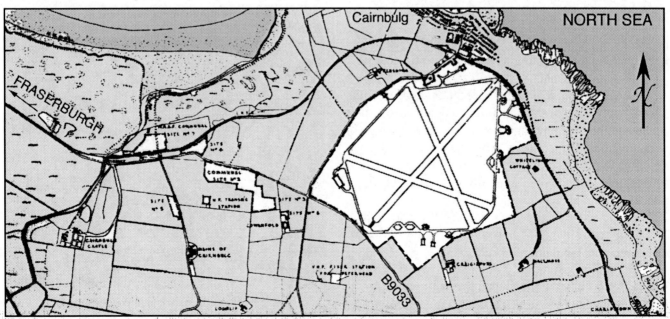

Royal Air Force Fraserburgh. 57° 40' 8"N 01° 50' 00"W. 52 ft above sea level.

Lifeboat lowered by parachutes from a Warwick.
[Saunders Roe]

Squadron Swordfishes operating from 23 October to 8 November. On 26 December 1944 four Warwicks of 279 Squadron arrived from Banff for ASR duties. The squadron's home base was Thornaby with detachments of aircraft at units where ASR cover was considered necessary.

The Warwick had not been as great a success as its companion the Wellington and by 1944, considered unsuitable as a bomber, 350 of them were equipped for Air Sea Rescue duties. For this role the Warwick carried an airborne lifeboat under the fuselage with Lindholme Gear as back up. When a lifeboat was dropped it was supported by parachutes until it hit the water when life lines were shot out by rockets to help survivors scramble aboard. It did not always go according to plan as illustrated by the first attempted rescue from Fraserburgh on 31 December 1944. After escorting four Mosquitos from a Norwegian mission the Warwick was diverted to rescue a crew member from a ditched Mosquito who had managed to get aboard a dinghy. The lifeboat was dropped but the chutes failed to open. Another Warwick from Wick had the same problem when it dropped its boat. Lindholme Gear was then dropped and the airman was seen to reach the equipment. The Warwicks kept watch until darkness fell but, although the ORB states that a search was carried out for the next three days there is no reference to the airman being found.

At that stage of the war the Banff Strike Wing with Mosquitoes from Banff and Beaufighters from Dallachy

Lifeboat being fitted to a Warwick. The bicycle clips on the groundcrew member shows method of transport!
[Bruce Robertson]

Air Sea Rescue Warwick used at Fraserburgh.
[Chaz Bowyer]

Fraserburgh was too small for the OTU's task and, as any extension was ruled out, 8 OTU moved to Dyce on 9 March 1943. Fraserburgh was now offically in Care and Maintenance but the FAA still used it. Such was inter service co-operation at the time. The station was transferred to FTC 21 Group on 6th April, 1943 as it was now required as a satellite for 14(P)AFU which had moved to Banff in May.

For the next eighteen months Fraserburgh was busy with the local flying of the Oxfords of 14 OTU. The station did not appear to suffer from as many crashes as might have been expected from a training unit, although two Oxfords crashed on one day 23 November 1943 with one pilot being killed. There were also two Spitfire crashes on 12 July 1943 and 3 August 1943. On 25 July 1943 a battle damaged B17 crash landed after taking part in the 8th Air Force's first attempt on Norwegian targets. In common with the rest of the north eastern airfields Fraserburgh displayed dummy aircraft (Bostons) in July/August 1943 for Operation Tyndall. The object was to fool the Germans into thinking that forces were being assembled for an invasion of Norway.

With the disbandment of 14 (P) AFU due to a surplus of pilots at the end of 1944, Fraserburgh along with Banff and Dallachy were taken over by Coastal Command. The airfield was quiet at first with only 838

Aerial photograph of Fraserburgh airfield, 1946

was waging a bitter war against German shipping in Norwegian waters. Mustangs from Peterhead protected them and 279 Warwicks accompanied most trips in order to rescue crews from crashed aircraft. Weather permitting 279's aircraft were flying most days in early 1945. On 11 January a Warwick disappeared after it was seen circling a ditched Mosquito. It was reported to have been followed by a ME109 which probably shot it down.

For the last three months of the war the Warwicks of 279 were continiously operating in support of Banff Strike Wing, or searching for ditched aircraft. Apart from Beaufighters and Mosquitos the ASR aircraft also

searched for a Halifax on 4 March, and a Sunderland on 15 March, a Wellington on 5 April and a Liberator on 16 April. Unfortunately few of these operations were successful. The Halifax incident started when a dinghy with three survivors was sighted. Two boats were dropped and then the aircraft was relieved by one from Thornaby. The two empty lifeboats were sighted the next day but there was no sign of any survivors. Hurricanes were also used for ASR duties during this period.

Apart from ASR flying Fraserburgh was used by a maintenance party from Banff in the early months of 1945. They carried out acceptance checks on 21

150

Warwick fitted with airborne lifeboat.

16 May 1945. The remains of 279 Sqn Warwick which crashed during an emergency landing at Dyce. Two crew were killed and a train wrecked in the local station. *[Press and Journal]*

Remains of Parachute Store, Fraserburgh 1988. *[author]*

Mosquitos which had been flown to Fraserburgh by ATA crews for 235 and 248 Squadrons.

Just before the war ended a Ju 188 landed with the crew surrendering on 5 May. On 16 May 1945 a Warwick crashed and caught fire at Dyce killing all the crew. The last operation of 279 was on 31 May 1945 when a Hurricane searched unsuccessfully for a ditched Fortress. The Warwicks left for Keflavik and the Hurricanes departed for Banff when the airfield closed on 10 June 1945.

Although intended as a satellite for Peterhead, Fraserburgh never seems to have been used for that purpose. Never a very busy airfield it was always used in a supporting role for other units, with its heyday as the home of ASR at the end of the war Aberdeen Gliding Club used it in the Fifties but the runways are now blocked by poultry houses of a chicken farm. The majority of the buildings have disappeared with only the Parachute store to remind us of the former occupants.

Loch Strathbeg

The Loch of Strathbeg lies close to the coast at Rattray Head which is the furthest east point of the Scottish mainland. The Loch itself is now an important Royal Society for the Protection of Birds (RSBP) Reserve, famous for its large flocks of wintering wild fowl. Looking at now it is hard to imagine that this stretch of water was a seaplane base over eighty years ago.

Before and during World War I suitable quiet stretches of coastal water were being investigated for use as bases for seaplanes and flying boats which were becoming an important part of the RAF and RNAS. When Lt Cdr Longmore was CO of Cromarty RNAS station in 1913 his surveys of the north east coast included the Loch of Strathbeg. According to his log he thought it suitable for seaplanes but had some reservations about disturbing the local wild fowlers. An Admiralty Committee report of 1918 was satisfied that seaplanes of the large America type could be operated from the Loch but owing to the shape of the Loch and depth of water it might not be able to utilise it at all times. To overcome these problems it was proposed to keep a flight of two machines at Peterhead where the conditions were evidently more favourable. A report in January/March 1918 records six 60 ft x 20 ft huts having been erected. Maps and photographs in the PRO show a small hutted camp including a hangar and jetty built during that period. It was not until the summer of 1918 after the formation of the RAF that it was planned to base six flying boat flights there. 18 Large America*flying boats were to be used. 312 (Flying boat flight) was to form in July 1918, 313 in August and 314, 315, 316 and 317 on 15 October. There is an interesting series of letters in the PRO regarding the possibilities of a seaplane base at Strathbeg. Comments from various high ranking officers were as follows:

Artist's impression of Short 184 over Strathbeg, 1918. *[author]*

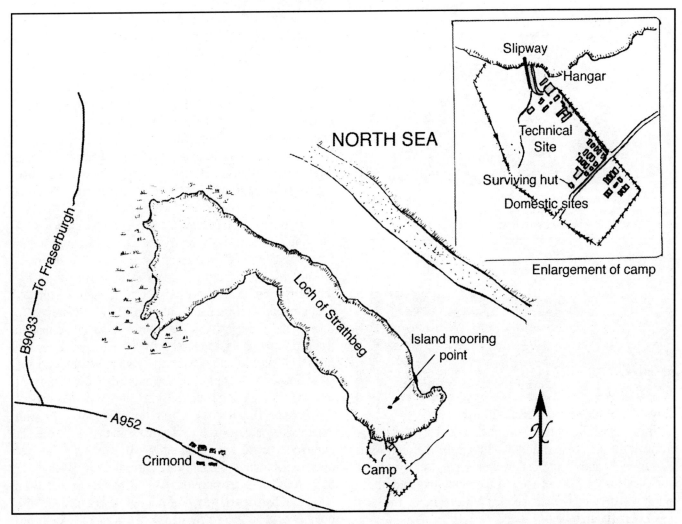

" *Strathbeg is doomed - hopelessly small. Unsuitable for Large Americas. Strathbeg and Peterhead should be abandoned. Don't send Shorts in lieu of Americas for these are useless here. In arranging priorities we put Strathbeg very low on the list.*"

Due to adverse comments like these on the suitability of the Loch and also the ending of the war, the flights never materialised and instead, Short 184s of 400 and 401 flights transferred from Dundee during the Autumn of 1918 for experience on Strathbeg. Another report from the PRO records 26 flights by seven different Short seaplanes between September and November 1918. They were mostly convoy and anti submarine patrols.

There appears to be no record of when flying ceased, but it was probably when 249 Squadron (formerly 400 flight) disbanded in October 1919.

There is still a large concrete base 36 ft x 90 ft at the south side of the Loch. Nearby a modern jetty is built on top of an old slipway. There are also some concrete blocks in the area and on a small island in the Loch. This may have been a mooring area as remains of heavy cables were still visible there until recently. About 300 yds south of the Loch is a corrugated iron hut used as a cattle shed for many years. The red brick chimney partition, wooden door fittings and metal window frames point to it being a military building and probably part of the 1918 flying boat base. This building has now been demolished.

RNAS Loch Strathbeg, 1917. The picture shows the jetty, hangar and various huts. *[PRO]*

Above: Possible remains of RAF building, now demolished at Strathbeg as seen in1990. *[author]*
Below:Possible mooring site on island in loch, 1990. *[author]*

Royal Navy Air Station Crimond/Rattray

With the departure of the flying boats from Loch Strathbeg, flying in the area ceased until World War II. The airfields at Fraserburgh and Peterhead would seem to have been sufficient for this part of the coastline but quite late in the war it was decided to build another at Crimond on the west coast of Loch Strathbeg.

During World War II there appears to have been a constant and often acrimonious battle between the Admiralty and Air Ministry over the ownership of airfields. In September 1942 an Admiralty Planning Officer wrote:- *"It is imperative to the national interests that naval requirements for air stations and facilities should be treated and given equal consideration with RAF requirements, irrespective of the fact that the RAF being first in the field have ear marked all suitable facilities. The present system whereby the Royal Navy has to adapt itself to sites which the RAF with its wider scope of interests has found of no value, can but lead to Naval and national disaster."*

These sarcastic comments could well have been penned about the efforts of the Navy to find a suitable airfield for an Observer School in the north east of Scotland. The Air Ministry were determined to turn Dallachy over to the Navy who were equally determined that this airfield was of no use to them. In the end the Admiralty found its own site at Crimond which being six miles from Fraserburgh and seven miles from Peterhead would seem to create problems with over lapping circuits.

914 acres of land were purchased from the Dowager Countess of Southesk and as this transaction took rather a long time, building work did not commence until March

1943. The airfield was supposed to be open in January 1944 but was still not finished when opened officially in October 1944. Crimond was a well equipped airfield even by 1944 standards. A 40ft wide perimeter track surrounded four tarmac runways, two of 1200 yds. Six aprons were constructed around the perimeter track and there were nine Pentad, six Mains and 22 Fromsen hangars capable of holding up to 130 aircraft. There were also the usual stores, workshops and fuel installations. Living quarters were in three camps dispersed 3/4ml south of the airfield. These had a capacity for housing 363 officers, 1924 CPO and POs and ratings, 18 WRNS officers, 619 WRNS ratings.

Commissioned as HMS Merganser on 3 October, 1944 the unit was designated as a Torpedo/Bomber Reconnaissance aircrew training establishment as the need for an Observer School no longer existed. The job of the school was comparable to RAF OTUs, training batches of young pilots, with probably only 100 hrs air experience, in operational flying tactics. The course included formation flying, dive bombing, low level bombing, naval exercises and night landings. After finishing the course at Crimond the crews moved to Crail for tactical and weapons training. At this stage of the war most of the graduates were destined for the Pacific. The first squadron to arrive was 774 with Swordfishes and (possibly) Walruses and its task was air gunnery training for Telegraphists Air Gunner. The first operational training aircraft were Barracudas of 714 and 717 Squadrons which arrived from RNAS Fearn in October 1944.

The Barracuda, specifically designed as a torpedo dive bomber was an extremely ugly looking aircraft compared with its American contemporaries. Reasonable efficient for its job it was unpopular with its flying crews and could be dangerous when handled by inexperienced pilots. On one occasion at Crimond a Barracuda trying to land in mist, hit the tower aerials and crashed in the aircraft park destroying four aircraft in all.

The first front-line squadron to be stationed at Crimond was 817 which was formed with 18 Barracudas in April 1945. This moved to Fearn on 27 April and was followed by 818 which also moved on 26 June. On 1 July 1945 the

Barracudas were the most widely used aircraft at Crimond.

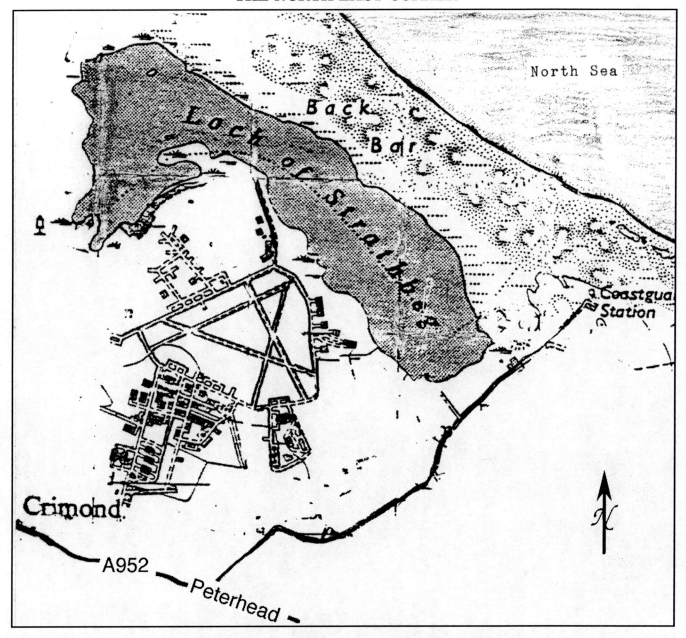

RNAS Crimond/Rattay. 57° 36' 35"N 01° 53' 20"W. 40ft above sea level.

name of the station was changed to Rattray. This was due to postal difficulties and not because the Navy did not like the idea of one of their stations being named after a hymn tune.

TBR training was re-inforced on 30 July 1945 by the arrival of 769 Squadron from RNAS East Haven, but the end of the war on 15 August saw the demise of 818 Squadron. In September 1945 821 Squadron returned from Ceylon and re-equipped with a dozen Barracudas, one remaining at Rattray until disbanding in February 1946. Due to changes in air allocation 774 was disbanded in August 1945 and in November 714 Squadron and 769 Squadron were disbanded due to post war run down. Their place was taken by an Observer Training Unit, 733 Squadron from Arbroath equipped with various types of aircraft. In February 1946 a Naval Operational Training Unit, 766 Squadron, arrived from Inskip with Fireflys and Seafires. The last of the original occupants - 717

Squadron - was disbanded in March 1946 but there were no changes thereafter until the following August when 766 Squadron moved to Lossiemouth and 753 Squadron was disbanded. RNAS Rattray was reduced to Care and Maintenance on 1 September 1946.

The major part of the site was sold privately in May 1963 but ten years later 484 acres were bought back by MOD for use as a wireless station. A forest of huge aerials now cover the site. Although the work of this unit is of a secret nature, access to the RSPB reserve is still allowed through the old airfield and part of the perimeter track is used for motor racing.

Crimond/Rattray was a well built airfield with excellent facilities but with hindsight one wonders at the economy of the project which had less than two year's active life only one of which was in wartime conditions. Legend has it that after closure many surplus aircraft

Crimond from the air, 8 March 1944

Old naval buildings, Crimond, 1990. *[author]*

were broken up and bull dozed into the ground east of the airfield.

That Thing
Remaining anonymous - for obvious reasons - this Fleet Air Arm officer leaves us in no doubt as to his personal feelings about the Barracuda.

Above: Pentad Hangar at Rattray, one of the naval hangars.

> Why should the unoffending sky,
> Be tainted and corrupted by
> This product of a twisted brain,
> That's aeronautically insane,
> This vile and hideous abortion,
> Devoid of beauty and proportion,
> That people call a Barracuda,
> Whose form is infinitely cruder
> Than any other scheme or plan
> As yet conceived by mind of man.
> To see it stagger into space
> Would bring a blush upon the face,
> Of the most hardened Pharisee
> Within the aircraft industry.
> But I suggest we don't decry
> This winged horror of the sky;
> But keep it 'til the War is won,
> And then we'll all join in the fun.
> Festoon the wings with fairy lights
> And wheel it out on gala nights,
> Thus so we'll help dispel the rumour
> That Britons have no sense of humour.

Anon FA.A. Officer

Royal Navy Air Station Longside
The village of Longside lies approximately two miles from Mintlaw on the main road to Peterhead, a further seven miles away. Longside today is a quiet little country village but in the local St Johns church there is a monument which connects the area with a turbulent period during World War I. The monument consists of a wooden propeller removed from an airship which was lost with all hands in the summer of 1918. The airship was one of many which operated from the Royal Naval Airship Station base at Lenabo three miles south of the village.

During World War I the German U-boats threatened to destroy our shipping and so defeat Britain and her Allies. One of the many methods employed to combat this menace was patrolling by airships. Bases had been established in England and southern Scotland but one was needed to cover the area north of Peterhead where the U-boats passed through on their way to the Atlantic. Why the Lenabo area was chosen for this base is puzzling as at the time it was just a vast peat bog.

To transform this bog into an airship station was a tremendous undertaking and in the early months of 1915 the firm of Tawse of Aberdeen started the awesome task.

1916 postcard showing YMCA hut during base construction, [Mrs Mcleod]

Thousands of Irish and Scots navvies laboured night and day digging out the peat which had to be carried out and dumped, though some was used to fuel the steam scoops, bucket cranes and locomotive which were the only mechanical defices used on the site. Transport to and from Longside railway station was still by horse drawn waggons although steam lorries were used for the longer journeys to Peterhead.

With the site prepared, water and drainage installed, roads constructed, and foundations laid the steel erectors and brick layers went into action. Although most wartime camps were of a flimsy temporary nature, RNAS Longside was seemingly built to stand for eternity. A power house, gasworks (for producing hydrogen by mixing ferrous iron with a solution of caustic soda), water works, steam generators, engineering shops, canteens, church, messes and living quarters were all built of solid brick and connected by trim avenues. The camp was surrounded by a steel spiked fence with a main entrance adorned with pseudo classical pillars. The largest buildings on the station were three airship sheds which at 100 foot high must have been prominent

Memorial in St John's Church, Longside. *[author]*
The inscription on propeller boss reads:

Aft propeller 220 hp Renault
From H M A C25 lost at sea
on active service 31-7-18
Capt H R Hopperton. - Pilot
A M 2 E K Adkinson. - Engineer
Corp. L C Faiers - Coxswain
A M 2 A Groves - W/T

landmarks on the Buchan skyline. Although the base was established in an area known as Lenabo it was officially known as RNAS Longside but both names were commonly used locally.

The first RNAS personnel (POs and ratings) set out for Longside in the autumn of 1915. As usual with service postings little information had been given to the men and on arrival at Aberdeen they were surprised to learn that another journey by local train awaited them. This slow journey was the cause of some local curiosity, though remarks like - 'F'a they billies wi' the fite bonnets?' 'I dinna ken, but I heard they are gaun tae flae fae Lenabo', 'That chappie wi' the brass buttons seems taw be the heid laa' - must have been rather unintelligable to the mainly southern Naval ratings. On arrival at Longside railway station they found that their destination was 3½ miles further on with the only means of transport their own two feet. The camp itself was only half built with the semi built huts in a sea of mud not exactly welcoming.

However it was not long before the airship station at Longside assumed the appearance of a permanent camp. More personnel were posted in as the first airship arrived by rail with the deflated gasbag on one huge packing case and the engines and landing gear in

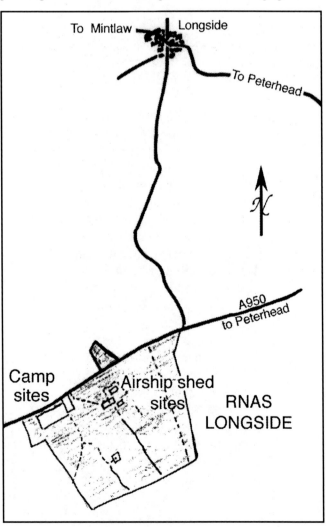

Aerial view of RNAS Longside, 1918. The main sheds and windbreaks are in the centre of the picture, the entrance is middle right. Note the two large gasometers in the centre. *[RAF Museum]*

another. This nonrigid airship, the C (Coastal Type), had a crew of five and a range of 500 miles. Another type used at Longside was the smaller SS Zero with a crew of three and a range of 200 miles. The Longside airships became operational in 1916 with four C class on patrol over the North Sea convoys.

Although very slow the airships could stay aloft for up to 12 hours and their presence above the ships acted as a deterrent to would be U boat attacks. The patrols must have been cold, noisy and extremely uncomfortable for the crews. The only food supplied was chocolate and iron ration biscuits though some enterprising crew men cooked stew over the engine exhausts. Lt Maitland claimed to be the first to cook bacon and eggs by this method although this culinary feat was rather spoiled when the meal was swept through the propeller. Lt Maitland, who later became an Air Vice Marshal in the RAF, was one of only two regular RNAS officers on the station, the other being the Commanding Officer Lt Comm. R.S. Robinson.

By 1917 Longside was well established as an RNAS camp. Social life was not neglected, with a cinema, concerts and band performances and a very popular magazine called the "Battle Bag" produced monthly. A Pierrot Troupe was formed from the many civilian artistes who had been conscripted into the RNAS. These included the Victualling Petty Officer who was a professional singer and the orchestra leader who had been in the orchestra of the Alhambra Theatre in London. With the building of a branch line from Longside railway station the camp ceased to be isolated

and it would appear that the RNAS got along very well with the local people. As well as appearing, in Aberdeen and Peterhead the concert party held shows on the camp for local civilians and some people can still remember visiting the camp as children.

September 1917 saw the arrival of two North Sea airships NS1 and NS3. These airships which could carry a crew of ten had been designed and built at RNAS Kingsnorth, Rochester. The engine installations were unsatisfactory and after taking part in fleet exercises from Longside in September 1917 both ships had serious

Airship NS11 over Lenabo, 1 february 1916. *[W Tice]*

159

defects and could not return to their home base at East Fortune until three months later. The NS airships were now grounded while local modifications were made at East Fortune. The modified airships had a longer range and one flight of 55 hours was recorded during this period. In May 1918 NS3 operating from Longside spotted oil rising from the sea near Montrose and dropped three 230 lb. bombs. Destroyers followed up with depth charges but it was later found that what had been bombed was the wreckage of a sunken British submarine.

On 21st June, 1918 NS3 with Lt Maitland as second pilot was caught in a gale at the mouth of the Firth of Forth. After the envelope was ripped open the airship lost height rapidly and hit the sea tearing off the engine car. Five of the crew escaped and were able to hang on to some wreckage until rescued but the remaining five crew members did not survive.

Landing an airship could be a hazardous business and required a large amount of manpower. When an airship was due to arrive a bugler would cycle around the camp sounding a call for 'Landing Party' and all available men would assemble at the sheds. A 'G' sounded after the call indicated Port Watch and two 'G's Starboard Watch. If more men were required 'Clear lower decks' would be sounded. Despite huge concrete wind breaks, gales could swing around 500 men like nine pins and often the envelopes had to be ripped in order to get the machines down.

Probably the last surviving member of RNAS Longside is Mr William Tice, a sprightly 90yr old now residing at Eastbourne. Mr Tice was a clerk on the camp between November 1917 and May 1919 and has many interesting stories to tell of his stay. Mr Tice sadly died before publication of this book.

He explains that when airships were coming into land 'snatch blocks' (huge concrete blocks with embedded iron rings) were used to anchor the tow ropes. Two lines of men would form up facing the landing airship while the pilot would drop the heavy tow rope which the men would grab and endeavour to twist through the 'snatch block' ring. In this operation they would often be helped by the station dog 'Soona' who burrowed into the pile of tow rope, fetched out the end and carried it to the ' snatch block ' Mr Tice remembers well the entertainments of the camp but is unable to verify the existance of a swimming pool which some local people seemed to think was

The Commanding Officer's residence in what was termed a 'Forward Mooring Area' in the Aberdeenshire woods. The date is 1918.

part of the amenities though this seems extremely unlikely. In the local area Mr Tice remembers Milne's farm selling eggs and milk to the camp and WAAFs arriving at Kinmundy House in the summer of 1918. He also recalls that the captain of N S 11 was a Captain Warneford whose cousin won the V C for shooting down a German Zeppelin.

Airships could also get out of control other than during landing procedures. In 1917 an NS ship experienced engine failure while passing over Peterhead. In attempting to land on Smith Embankment it was slightly damaged by the weathercock on the Town House spire. The landing on the Embankment was accomplished with the aid of spectators who clung on to the tow ropes until RNAS personnel arrived.

During the summer of 1918 the war against the U boats hotted up but few encounters were made by the Longside airships. It was unusual for U boats to fire on airships but the only Longside airship to be lost through enemy action was thought to have been shot down though the Germans never claimed it as a victim. The

Wreckage after gale destroys airship shed, 1918. *[Peterhead Museum]*

Airship NS11 in Lenabo shed, 3 March 1919 *[W Tice]*

airship in question C25 was lost at sea on 31 July 1918 and it is the propeller from this ship which acts as a memorial to the crew in St Johns church.

Interestingly, a pair of BE2Cs are known to have been present at Longside in August 1916, as Ray Sturtivant describes in his Royal Navy Serials and Units'. "No. 8719 and No. 8720 were present for anti-Zepplin Defence. No information as to whether they arrived or where they were supposed to operate from".

In the closing months of the war Longside had five NS, five C and two SS airships. The smaller SS airships could operate from woodland clearings and a photograph shows one of these clearings in Aberdeenshire. No details of these operations are available and it seems strange how an airship could be manoeuvred in and out of a small clearing when so many men were required for the same operation at the home base. How successful the airships were is debatable. Of 27 attacks on submarines around the British Isles only two were credited as being successful. However the presence of these 'Gas bags' over a convoy no doubt had a deterrant effect on would be U-boat attackers. In November 1918 Longside airships NSll and NS12 were the first British airships to patrol as far as Norway, taking 24 hours for the operation.

By the beginning of 1919 most of the airships had been deflated and sold. One ship the NSll which had flown 228 hours during the war was kept by the RAF and won a place in aeronautical history with a world endurance record of 100 hours and 50 minutes in February 1919. Four months later it was lost at sea with all hands.

Manpower was also rapidly reduced and Mr Tice remembers only 60 men on strength when he departed in May 1919. Trucks from the camp were used to carry mail during a coal strike in the early part of 1919. By now the R A F had taken over and Longside was on a Care and Maintenance basis. The government was losing interest in airships and as Longside could not be used for aircraft the Air Ministry withdrew in 1920. The excellent buildings and facilities on the site seemed perfect for development and various proposals were made for meat processing and canning factories. Nothing came of these ventures and the camp was sold to the demolishers for a mere song. No doubt some equipment ended up on local farms and it was reported that a lot of people at that time sported silver grey raincoats made from the balloon material. The site was part of the Aden Estates and after leaving it derelict for a while it was offered to the Forestry Commission who proceeded to plant conifers over the whole area. Longside, or Lenabo, today has a certain ghost like quality. Most of the trees have matured and been cut down thus exposing the remains of the old R N A S buildings, long hidden by the trees. The entrance pillars have disappeared but close to the present entrance are two

Above: Airship C7 cruising over Lenabo area, 1918.
[Peterhead Museum]

Airship C10 at Longside 1918.
[Chaz Bowyer]

Right: An unidentified airship in the shed at Lenabo in 1917. The enclosed nature of the car, unusual for the period is noticable, as is the exposed engines and their radiators behind. It seens that the engineer had his own compartment remote from the main car, closer to his charges! *[Peterhead Museum]*

Below: 'Landing' airship C5 at Lenabo, September 1918. *[Daily Mirror via W. Tice]*

Above: Airship C7 crashes at Lenabo, 21 September 1918 Below: Recreation Hut at RNAS Lenabo, 1918. *[W Tice]*

Above: Airship C10 at Longside, 1918. *[Chaz Bowyer]*
Below: A possible relic of the Officer's Mess Lenabo, 1989. *[author]*

Below: Snatch Block at Lenabo, *1989. [author]*

elaborate fireplaces and chimneys which may have been part of the Officer's mess. The floor of the main shed is largely intact as are the large concrete 'snatch blocks'. Close by are heaps of concrete slabs presumably part of the wind breaks. Throughout the area are various foundations and parts of buildings. The glory of the RNAS station has long since gone but standing among the few relics left one can easily imagine the huge silvery

Crew of NS12. Standing: Cameron, ?, Smith W/T, Orvits, W/T, Reynolds, Bull. Seated: Wagstaff (Cox) Flt. Lt. Chambers, Flt. Lt. Maitland, ?, Betteday. *[W Tice]*

monsters chugging slowly through the Buchan skies in those far-off days over eighty years ago.

Royal Air Force Peterhead

Four miles west of Peterhead an airfield was built in 1941. Part of 14 Gp Fighter Sector, the station was to house fighter squadrons for the protection of the vital east coast convoy routes and also to assist the fighters at Dyce against the hit and run raiders in the north east area.

As often the case with airfields built during this period, operations began before many of the necessary facilities were finished or even started. Station ORBs vary according to the inspiration of their writers and the 1941 section from Peterhead contains many interesting facets of RAF life during that period. The station was officially opened on 7 July, 1941 but most of the personnel arriving had to operate from makeshift accommodation including contractor's huts. This must have caused some friction as according to the ORB the civilian workmen could not be persuaded to work during inclement weather. Wg Cdr Parker was the CO with a strength of 15 officers and 156 other ranks. Two thirds of the perimeter track was completed and two of the three runways were operational provided the winds were not blowing with too much strength. The ground surface had been graded but was still so soft that any aircraft leaving the perimeter track was liable to be bogged down.

Despite the problems, 132 Squadron was formed with Spitfire Is on 7 July, 1941 and became fully operational on 14 August. Unfortunately the next day they had their first casualty when a Spitfire crashed near Crimongarth killing the pilot Sgt McAdam. On the 19 September 1941 a mid air collision caused the deaths of Plt Off de la P Disney and W/O Wallace.

The living quarters were not yet completed and most personnel were billeted in Peterhead town. In July a search of the local area failed to find anywhere suitable for emergency landing grounds but in September the airfield at Fordoun was allocated as a satellite. On 26 and

27 July personnel were brought in from civilian billets to camp accommodation. It was probably just a coincidence that the Fighter Command CinC Air Marshal Sholto Douglas arrived for an inspection the same day. The ORB contains constant references to routine work being carried out. For the benefit of interested readers the writer summarises this as cleaning and preparation of huts and messes, sanitary duties, guards and just about every unpleasant job imaginable. A posting to Peterhead at that time cannot have been too exciting.

Uneventful flying patrols continued with the Spitfire Is of 132 being replaced by IIBs in September. By 31 July, 1941 the strength of the station had increased to 28 officers, 492 airmen and 21 aircraft. Building work was still not complete and further problems arose in August when the water system broke down. A temporary Beresford pump was fitted but water rationing had to be introduced.

Enemy aircraft attacked the town of Peterhead on 9 August, 1941 causing damage and casualties. Apparently offers of aid from the RAF were turned down by the local ARP. On 18 August the CinC Home Forces, Sir Alan Brooke arrived in connection with army exercises.

The threat of a German invasion was still very much in the minds of the authorities. Apart from normal duties all personnel had to be trained for a back up role in anticipation of this event and most of this training had to be carried out after normal working hours. Four Bofors guns complete with A/A crews arrived on 20 August causing some chaos as their stores and equipment had gone astray on the journey north. Airmen were being trained in the intricacies of bayonet fighting while the officers practised with Tommy guns.

By the end of August the station strength had risen to 35 officers, 672 airmen and 18 aircraft. At the beginning of September building work was again interrupted when workmen were taken away for other jobs. Despite this, pillar boxes and private phone facilities were constructed.

An entry in the ORB for 6 September, 1941 makes curious reading. :- *"The manufacture of pikes, a weapon adopted in order that all personnel should be in possession of some sort of arms, is slowly proceeding"*

Aerial photograph of RAF Peterhead, April 1943.

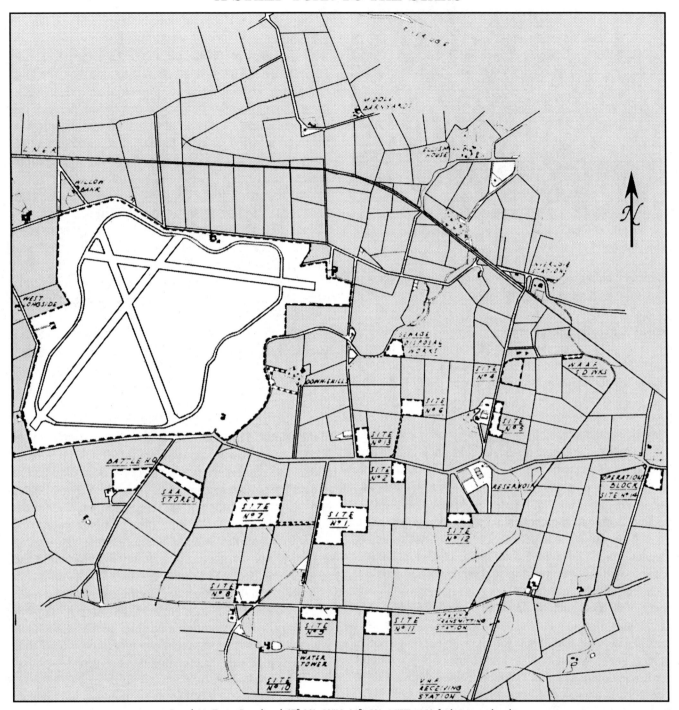

Royal Air Force Peterhead 57° 30' 53"N 01° 52' 15"W. 150 ft above sea level.

Apparently pikes were issued to the LDV in 1940, but to be still using them in 1941 seems to indicate a poor state of defence readiness. On 17 October it is noted that 270 pikes had been manufactured. As these weapons were never used one wonders what became of them eventually. On September 13th the Station Commander and other officers visited Fort George for a demonstration of a Smith gun. It had been proposed to issue these guns to the RAF for self defence - in place of pikes perhaps.

In September it was decided that the newly built watch tower was unsatisfactory but this decision was later over ruled. On 24 September the airfield A/A guns

fired on an aircraft which disappeared without being identified.

On 29 October 1941 a Spitfire crashed at Killymond Farm Longhaven killing the pilot. The next day a hit and run JU 88 attacked the airfield damaging two aircraft and buildings and killing Flt Lt Jackman.

The fighter strength of the station was increased on 18 November, 1941 by the arrival of the Spitfire l ls of 416 Squadron. The first WAAFs came in December 1941 although a couple of their officers had arrived earlier in the year. A new airfield was now opened as a satellite at Fraserburgh 14 miles away.

1942 opened with heavy snow. However the

164

airfield must have been in reasonable condition when twelve Stirlings were diverted in on February 6th. When these Stirlings took off on the 7th one crashed into a Spitfire causing damage but no casualties. This was the famous 'MacRoberts Reply' which with other Stirlings of 15 Sqn had been diverted to Peterhead after the *Tirpitz* raids when their forward base at Lossiemouth became snowbound.

From 1942 onwards Peterhead saw constant movement of squadrons. Looking back at wartime records this seems to be a regular pattern on many stations and one wonders how these constant upheavals affected squadron efficiency. The FAA also used Peterhead with nine Swordfishes of 823 Squadron arriving in December 1941. B Flt of 132 squadron departed for Tain in February 1942 with ground crews travelling by Harrow.

A different type of flying started on 19 February 1942 when 8S FTS arrived from Montrose with Hurricanes and Masters. They blotted their copy book straight away by crashing three Hurricanes and one Master on landing. About this time an Auto Gyro was in the area but no official reason was given for its presence. On 1 March, 1942 416s Spitfires were replaced by Vbs but three of these new aircraft were damaged on landing. 416 was replaced by 603 Squadron on 14 March 1942. The pilot was killed when a Spitfire crashed on 26 March 1942. Throughout 1942 Spitfire squadrons 164 and 602 stayed for short periods and FAA Sea Hurricanes also used Fraserburgh. On 28 May 1942 a Spitfire of 416 crashed in the sea and although the pilot Sgt D Allan was rescued by the ASR he died later. August saw the arrival of Fulmars of 886 Squadron although it is difficult to imagine these obsolescent aircraft being of much use in a defensive role.

Enemy aircraft were reported to have dropped bombs in the area on 25 April. Despite constant patrolling few contacts were reported and in fact the first blood was on 27 May 1942 when a Spitfire of 416 damaged a HE 111, a persistent visitor referred to as 'Weather Willie'. Beaufighters of 125 Squadron eventually shot it down but later in the war, after codes had been cracked, the 'Weather Willies' were allowed to carry out their work so that their results could be used by the RAF. Peterhead was also used by 1479 AAC with Defiants, Martinets and Oxfords for target towing. Other aircraft on the station in 1942 were a detachment of Beaufighters of 125 Squadron Fairwood Common, and a Walrus of 282 Squadron for ASR duties came in 1943.

1943 opened with a new squadron and new aircraft at Peterhead. This was the Polish squadron 309 operating Mustang ls. On 24 May 1943 there was a mid air collision near Fraserburgh between a Beaufighter and a Hampden. Apart from the resident aircraft Peterhead had 111 visiting aircraft in July 1943. During Operation Tyndall in the autumn of 1943 Peterhead had a dummy camp built with 20 dummy Bostons and two real ones to heighten the effect of a prospective invasion of Norway. On 28th August, 1943 a Mosquito of 618 Squadron crashed in a nearby field. On 1 December 1943 1479 AAC was formed into 598 Squadron under a reorganisation of all A/A flights.

Early 1944 saw the departure of 129 Squadron Spitfires and the arrival of 350 Squadron. One of 350's Pilots, Sgt Morel, had a remarkable escape on 21 March 1944. After an engine failure over the sea his plane ditched before he could parachute to safety. With his cockpit jammed shut and parachute opened and dragging, his future seemed bleak but suddenly breaking free he was picked up almost immediately by a fishing boat. On 18 March 1944 Flt Sgt Gorman was killed when his Spitfire of 453 Squadron crashed near the airfield.

Two views of Mustang IV's of 65 Squadron tdeparting from Peterhead, 20 April 1945.
[Press and Journal]

The FAA 899 Squadron operated Seafires from the airfield between May and June 1944. On 10 July 1944 an Albermarle in transit to Kinloss crashed nearby at Newton of Bruxie killing all nine of the crew. On 8 November 1944 a Halifax of 1666 HCU crashed on take off.

Like all north east airfields Peterhead had its quota of diverted aircraft from the big bombing raids of 1944. Two Lancasters from the last successful Tirpitz raid landed on 12 November 1944 and six Lancasters from a Trondheim raid landed on 23 November. The night of 21 November 1944 saw the arrival of an unusual visitor in the shape of Stirling LK272 of 161 Squadron. This squadron along with 138 were the famous 'Moon' Squadrons operating from Tempsford in the role of dropping arms, equipment and agents in occupied Europe. On that particular night the aircraft had made a successful drop in Denmark but returned home to find all southern airfields fog bound. Failing to get a diversion message the aircraft flew farther and farther north, until, just as the red fuel warning lights were flickering, Peterhead pundit lights were seen flashing. A perfect landing was made but the engines died through lack of fuel as the aircraft taxied to dispersal. The Stirling's troubles were not over however as the next day on its way home to Tempsford it was fired on by Navy gunners over the Humber.

The end of 1944 saw a considerable stepping up of action from Peterhead. The Strike Wing from Banff which was now constantly attacking shipping off Norway required fighter protection and this role was filled by Peterhead Mustangs. 315 and 65 Squadrons arrived in October 1944 and these were followed by the return of 309 in November. 19, 122, 234 and 601 came in the early part of 1945. 603s Beaufighters also used the airfield.

With the increase of operations (or maybe a new scribbler) little mention is made of non flying activities in the ORB of 1944. A station magazine 'Windward Ho' was started in May and there are a few mentions of leatherwork classes. During 1944 the station farm produced 27 tons of potatoes, 17 tons of greens and five tons of oats.

Heavy snow and high winds followed by floods isolated the station for a few days in January 1945. Escort duties for Banff Strike Wing continued unabated until VE Day. By this time the station had three runways 1500, 1460 and 1272 yds respectively. There were now five Teeside and eight Blister hangars. The final personnel strength was 1576 RAF and 389 WAAF. With Peterhead no longer required by the RAF the squadrons all disbanded or left for other stations in the summer of 1945.

Nothing much seemed to have happened with Peterhead after 1945 until it was auctioned off in 1959. Most of the hangars and other buildings soon disappeared but in 1975 the airfield got a new lease of life when North Scottish Helicopters started using it for North Sea oil transportation.

A new hangar and other buildings have been built and this wartime airfield seems set on a prosperous future. It is now officially called Longside which is rather confusing as the W W 1 airship base at Lenabo was also called Longside although neither seems close enough to the village of Longside to warrant adopting that name.

Peterhead Harbour

Peterhead Harbour is now recognised as the premier white fishing port in Europe and always presents a very busy scene with dozens of fishing boats leaving or departing or being unloaded. Because of the increased use of the port many new jettys have been built over the years and in consequence some of the older constructions have been covered over and lost. These would seem to include the seaplane base used by the RNAS and RAF at the end of WW I. In 1913 Lt Cdr Longmore, the Commanding Officer of the Cromarty Air Station travelled to Peterhead in HMS Hermes in order to investigate the possibility of using the harbour as a seaplane base. He appears to have been satisfied with the site but there seems to be no record of flying during the war apart from vague references to Curtiss Large Americas in 1918. An Admiralty letter of August 1918 noted that the present shed at Peterhead to be used as operations base for six large America flying boats. Major repairs being carried out at Dundee. During 1918 there was to be a build up of flying boats in the north east but with the end of hostilities the proposed bases at Loch of Strathbeg and Peterhead were abandoned. Below Peterhead prison there is a small sandy beach and from that beach two obviously man made stone piers stretch out just above the surface of the water. This could conceivably have been a seaplane slipway but until further evidence is forthcoming this is pure supposition.

In April 1940 a seaplane did land in Peterhead Harbour. This was one of the Norwegian planes escaping from the German occupation.

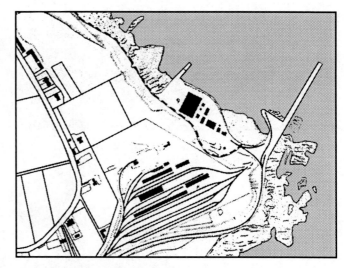

Peterhead Bay - 1918

A bit of a mystery this - Southampton III S1059 beached after landing at South Bay, Peterhead in August 1930. Unusual is the enclosed cockpit, a modification that, according to some souces, was only aplicable for Southampton's going to Iraq and 203 Squadron!
[D.G.Mackie]

FINALE

We end this story with an account of a flight, which, although strictly outside the Moray Firth area, was probably the only aviation record to be recorded in the north east of Scotland.

A small plaque erected at Cruden Bay south of Peterhead, records the fact that it was from here in 1914 that the first aeroplane flight to Norway started out. The pilot was Tryggve Gran, a Norwegian explorer who had accompanied Capt Scott to the Antarctic in 1912. Back home he became an enthusiastic flyer and in an age of aerial firsts he decided to be the first to fly from Scotland to Norway. In July 1914 he arrived at Cruden Bay with his plane, a Bleriot named Ca Flotte. Bad weather and insurance problems delayed the flight and the final blow

came with an announcement on 27 July that because of the worsening situation between Germany and Britain no flights out of the country would be allowed after 30 July. On the morning of July 30 good weather conditions were reported and Gran managed to take off. Within an hour he was back having ran into a bank of fog. This fog had lifted by lunch time when Gran decided to try again. By now a large crowd of spectators had gathered to watch. These included Dame Clara Butt who was holidaying at nearby Slanes Castle. Before departing a local girl added a Scots thistle to the little red devil on the Bleriot. At 1.09 Gran took off for the 500 mile flight.

When one considers that the Bleriot was much the same type of aircraft that had crossed the 20 mile English

Tryggve Gran ready for take-off from Cruden Bay, August 1914.

Channel with some difficulty only five years earlier it says a lot for the courage and skill of Gran that he should even consider the far riskier trip to Norway. A reserve tank of fuel in the passenger's seat squashed Gran into his seat but that was the least of his problems. Thick fog, strong contrary winds, momentary engine failure and airsickness were just some of the hazards the pilot had to face before he finally touched down on the beach at Orrevatnet near Stavenger at 5.19 pm, four hours and ten minutes after take off. Gran was immediately a national hero in Norway but the outbreak of WW I a few days later swept his exploit from the world's press. During WW I Gran served with distinction in the RFC (one of the few foreign nationals, to be granted permission). Between the wars he made many flights in the Scandinavian area but during WW II he slipped from the hero's pedestal when he was honoured by the Quisling government. In 1971 he re-visited Scotland to unveil a memorial at Cruden Bay.

Although the flight of Tryggve Gran was largely unrecognised at the time it is worth recording as the pioneer of the thousand of flights both civil and military which in the Nineties daily criss cross the skies above the Moray Firth.

Memorial at Cruden Bay commemorating Tryggve Gran's flight

GLOSSARY OF COMMON ABBREVATIONS

AFU	Advanced Flying Unit		MU	Maintenance Unit
	(P) Pilot		MCU	Marine Craft Unit
	(O) Observer		MOTU	Maritime Operational Training Unit
AGS	Air Gunnery School		ORB	Operations Record Book
AMQ	Airmen's Married Quarters		OTU	Operational Training Unit
ASR	Air Sea Rescue		OCU	Operational Conversion Unit
ATC	Air Traffic Control		PSP	Pierced Steel Planking
AACU	Anti-aircraft Co-operation Unit		PRU	Photographic Reconnaissance Unit
ADDLs	Aerodrome Dummy Deck Landings		RAAF	Royal Australian Air Force
AEW	Airborne Early Warning		RCAF	Royal Canadian Air Force
ATA	Air Transport Auxiliary		RNAF	Royal Norwegian Air Force
BAT	Blind Approach Training		RNZAF	Royal New Zealand Air Force
BHP	Brake Horse Power		RNAS	Royal Naval Air Service
C&M	Care and Maintenance		RNAS	Royal Naval Airship Station (World War I)
CO	Commanding Officer		RFC	Royal Flying Corps
ELG	Emergency Landing Ground		RLG	Relief Landing Grounds
FAA	Fleet Air Arm		SLG	Satellite Landing Ground
FTS	Flying Training School		SAR	Search and Rescue
HSL	High Speed Launch		UAS	University Air Squadron
I/C	In Charge			

BIBLIOGRAPHY

During the course of my researches I have consulted various books and publications. The following list is a selection of these publications not in any particular order:-

Sunderland at War *by Chaz Bowyer* .... Ian Allen Ltd

Coastal Command *at War by Chaz Bowyer* .... Ian Allen Ltd

Mosquito at War *by Chaz Bowyer* .... Ian Allen Ltd

Beaufighter by Chaz Bowyer .... William Kimber

Britain's First Warplanes *by JM. Bruce* .... Arms & Armour Press

Aberdeen at War .... Aberdeen Press and Journal

Search Find and Kill *by Norman L.R. Franks* .... Aston Publications

Flying Cats *by Andrew Hendrie* .... Airlife Publishing Ltd

Aircraft of the RAF 1918-1978 *by J.W.R. Taylor* .... Macdonald and Janes

Aviation Landmarks *by Jean Gardner* .... Battle of Britain Prints

Avro Shackleton *by John Chartres* .... Guild Publishers

The Lancaster at War *by M.Garbett and B.Goulding* ..... PBS

Lancaster at War 2 *by M.Garbett and B.Goulding* .... PBS

British Aircraft of World War II *by John Frayn Turner* .... Sidgewick & Jackson Ltd

The Strike Wings *by Roy C.Nesbit* .... William Kimber

Illustrated History of the RAF *by Roy C. Nesbit* .... CLB

British Military Airfields 1939-1945 *by David Smith* .... Patrick Stevens Ltd

Action Stations 7 *by David Smith* .... Patrick Stevens Ltd

Coastal, Support and Supply Squadrons of the RAF
by John R. Rawlings .... Janes Publishing Co Ltd

British Naval Aircraft since 1914 *by Owen Thetford* ...... Putnam

The Avro Shackleton .... British Aerospace

The Shackleton *by Chris Ashworth* .... Aston Publications

From Sea to Sky *by Sir Arthur Longmore* .... Geoffrey Bles

Aircraft of the RAF since 1918 *by Owen Thetford* .... Putnam

The British Bomber since 1914 *by Peter Lewis* .... PBS

Sir Keith Park *by Vincent Orange* .... Methuen

Zeppelin *by Manfred Griehl and Hoachim Dressel* .... Arms and Armour Press

Military Airfields in the British Isles
by Steve Willis and Barry Holliss .... Enthusiasts Publications

Squadrons of the Fleet Air Arm *by Ray Sturtivant* .... Air Britain

Sky Spy *by Ray Holmes* .... Airlife

The British Airman *by Roger Freeman* .... Arms and Armour Press

A STEEP TURN TO THE STARS

A STEEP TURN TO THE STARS